BECOMING A BAT MITZVAH

BECOMING A BAT MITZVAH

A Treasury of Stories

Arnine Cumsky Weiss

With a Foreword by
Cheryl Magen

Scranton: The University of Scranton Press

The author expresses her gratitude to those whose names and photographs appear for permission to use their material. Every effort has been made to ascertain the owner of copyrights for the selections used in this volume and to obtain permission to reprint copyrighted material and passages. The author will be pleased in subsequent editions to correct any inadvertent error or omission that may be pointed out.

Library of Congress Cataloging-in-Publication Data

Weiss, Arnine Cumsky.
Bat mitzvah / by Arnine Cumsky Weiss ; with an introduction by Cheryl Magen.
p. cm.
ISBN 1-58966-065-X
1. Bat mitzvah—Anecdotes. 2. Jewish teenagers—United States—Biography—Anecdotes. 3. Jewish teenagers—Religious life—Anecdotes. 4. Jewish women—Biography—Anecdotes. 5. Jewish women—Religious life—Anecdotes. I. Title.

BM707.W46 2002
296.4'434--dc21 2002018405

Distribution:

The University of Scranton Press
445 Madison Avenue
Scranton PA 18510
Phone: 570-941-3081
Fax: 570-941-8804

PRINTED IN THE UNITED STATES OF AMERICA

This book is dedicated to the very strong women in my life:

My mother - Helen Cumsky
Who provided the structure

My sisters - Yolana Stern and Francine Grossman
Who gave their support

And my daughter - Allie Weiss
Who added the color

CONTENTS

ACKNOWLEDGMENTS xiii
Arnine Cumsky Weiss

FOREWORD xv
Cheryl Magen

INTRODUCTION xix
Arnine Cumsky Weiss

1: THE FIRST BAT MITZVAH 1
Judith Kaplan Eisenstein, Ph.D.—May 6, 1922

2: RECIPES FOR LIFE 4
Rachel Abrams—April 1, 2000

3: THE BAT MITZVAH DILEMMA: ONE ORTHODOX FAMILY'S SOLUTION 9
Felissa Rubin–January 15, 2000

4: EXCEPTIONAL 14
Rebeka Scheiss—March 6, 1999

5: I SHINED WITH SHIRA 18
Shira Rockowitz—November 6, 1993

6: *NAVI* 21
Nava Gold—March 6, 1994

7: B'NOT MITZVAH NEW ZEALAND STYLE 24
Mandy Copeland, Diana Hoskyn, Naomi Johnson,
Margaret Laurenson, Helen Levin—January 16, 1993

8: SENIOR PROJECT 32
Kate Stambler—May 31, 1999

9: ONE STEP ALONG MY WAY 35
Eva Metzger Brown, Ph.D.—September 28, 1991

10: *ALEINU* 43
Daniella Ioannides—May 1, 1999

11: SUNSHINE 49
Carrie Linden—November 30, 1991

12: EIM B'ISRAEL 52
Mothers in Israel—April 16, 1999

13: SUCH A LOT OF FLOWERS 58
Stephanie Scibilia—May 24, 1997

14: THE BAMBOO CRADLE 61
Devorah Schwartzbaum Goldstein—May 1984

15: THE ROAD NOT TAKEN 69
Dr. Laura Selub von Schmidt—June 2, 2000

16: HONORING THE EVERYDAY: 74
MY DAUGHTER'S YIDISHE BAS MITSVE
Meg Cassedy-Blum—April 1998

17: FOR THE LOVE OF IRIT 83
Yoni and Suzi—July 1998

18: WOMEN OF VALOR 88
Sarah Danzig—January 25, 1998

19: A GREAT MIRACLE HAPPENED HERE 94
Lucy Goldhair—December 11, 1999

20: FROM RUSSIA WITH LOVE 100
Natasha and Anna Oziraner—May 25, 1992

21: THE QUEEN'S EQUAL 106
Rebecca Miller—May 22, 1999

22: MOTHERS AND SONS 110
Emily Trunzo and Craig Trunzo—May 27, 1988

23: THE HOUSE THAT DAD BUILT 114
Elizabeth Secor Skolnick—October 30, 1999

24: EVERYTHING COMES TO HE WHO WAITS 119
Adelyne Rubinstein—March 20, 1999

25: WITH A LITTLE BIT OF SOAP 123
Elana Erdstein—May 21, 1992

26: MOTHERS AND DAUGHTERS 128
Merle Pranikoff and Kara Pranikoff—March 11, 1988

27: CODA 132
Fayth L. Balsam—February 14, 1998

28: *SHEHECHIYAUNU* 137
Rabbi Amy Eilberg—November 1967

29: THERE CAN BE MIRACLES 142
Selena and Elianna Starr—December 5, 1999

30: SOMETHING BORROWED, SOMETHING BLUE 147
Katie, Eli, and Tali Perret-Jeanneret—May 1995

31: GOD BLESS AMERICA 150
Alexandra Nessa Berg—May 28, 2000

32: CLOSING A CIRCLE 154
Asnat Groutz, M.D.—October 9, 2000

33: MURDER SHE WROTE 158
Leora Rockowitz—November 16, 1996

34: THE CHINESE BAT MITZVAH 162
Sarah Mittledorf—January 31, 1999

35: THE PARTNER 168
Penina Gold—March 14, 1999

36: A CUP OF TEA 172
Janet Ruth Falon—March 1984

37: A PRIVILEGE 176
Barbara Birshtein, Ph.D.—December 1980

38: COCOON 180
Karen Binney—December 13, 1997

39: B'NAI MITZVAH 185
Jennifer Woda, Daniel Charlick, M.D.,
Zia Fuentes, et al.—June 16, 1984

40: TRIPLE BAT MITZVAH 192
Jacqui Gordon, Adrienne Gordon, Marion Gordon
Moskovitz—November 25, 2000

41: NO LIMITS 197
Desiree, Serenie, and Yeshiva Cohen—April 30, 1995

42: UP ON THE ROOF 201
Juliana Wurzburger—May 20, 2000

43: SPRING 205
Aviva Kempner—April 15, 1989

44: ON THE WINGS OF EAGLES 213
Samantha Mandeles—July 15, 2000

45: SET THE NIGHT TO MUSIC 219
Amy Poran—June 25, 1983

46: THE GARDEN OF EDEN: PLANTING NEW SEEDS 222
Eliza Halle Ruder—October 9, 1999

47: MY ROCK 236
Alexandra Weiss—October 24, 1998

Glossary 242

Authors Note 244

About the Author 246

ACKNOWLEDGMENTS

During the course of writing this book, I had the pleasure of meeting and interviewing the contributors and their families, either by phone, by e-mail, or in person. I want to thank all of those gracious people who agreed to share their stories and allowed me to include them in this book. The range of stories is far and wide, yet the depth of emotion for this rite of passage, which is uniquely ours, is shared throughout. What I learned from the women (and the men) I met is that regardless of the conventionality of their ceremony and no matter where their practices fit into the gamut of Judaism, each service was equally spiritual and meaningful. We have much to gain by reveling in our diversity.

I'd like to thank Cheryl Magen for her generosity in sharing her expertise in writing the foreword for this book. She is the epitome of a Jewish educator. She has a rare talent for infusing Judaism into any setting, making it wonderfully fun, and not compromising any of its integrity. Cheryl is also a leader and a visionary being, instrumental in providing one of the first accessible camping program for Jewish deaf children and their families.

I want to thank Harriet Cabelly not only for allowing me to write about two of her daughters, but for being an unlimited source of referrals. Carol Yunker was kind enough to act as a sounding board, while at the same time sharing stories that she knew of up and down the East Coast. And I would like to thank Dr. Eva Metzger Brown, Ellen Cassedy, Carrie Linden, Nancy Wolfson-Moche, Katie Perret, Abby Ruder, and Naomi Johnson for sharing their talents and allowing me to include the stories that they wrote. Very special thanks to Rabbi Ira Eisenstein, of blessed memory, the founder of the Reconstructionist Rabbinical College and the husband of Dr. Judith Kaplan Eisenstein, for allowing me to include the story that his wife wrote about her own Bat Mitzvah, the very first one in the United States. Tremendous thanks to Naomi Johnson for her willingness to organize and mobilize the B'Not Mitzvah group in New Zealand and to Bobbie Cohen, who provided all of the information from Toronto, Canada, about the Mothers in Israel group Bat Mitzvah.

From the very first phone call when I asked him what he thought about the idea for these books and throughout the process of writing, Rabbi David Geffen has been a terrific source of information, support, and encouragement. I thank him for his willingness to help, his enthusiasm, and his guidance. And I want to thank the University of Scranton Press for taking a chance and allowing a dream to come true.

Many other people were a source of referrals, information, support, and encouragement. Many thanks to Ruth Freistat, Jane Rosen from the Jewish Theological Seminary, Betsy Moylan from the University of Scranton Library, Janet Holland, Joanne Jackowski, Paula David, Dolores Gruber, Jack Rabin, Cora Schenberg, Susan Gottesman, Lisa Richards, Dr. Judy Davis, Ruth Seligman, Naomi Eisenberger from the Zvi Tzedekah Fund, Lani Moss from the Jewish Reconstructionist Federation, Miriam Weissman from the North American Conference on Ethiopian Jewry (NACOEJ), Dr. Yale and Marilyn Bobrin. Special thanks to Monica and Ira Stern, who not only shared the story of Irit Portugues and Yoni and Suzi, but who are a wonderful inspiration for all of their behind-the-scenes work.

On a more personal note, thanks again to Dr. Hector Diaz, Mike O'Malley, and Ruth Gerrity, who offered wonderful support and kept up with my weekly progress. My mother, Helen Cumsky, gets another big hug, just for being my mother. My friend Barbara Graham always manages to be more than a friend and more like my family. And to my brother-in-law Roy and especially my sister Yolana, who were my reality checks, my anchors, and my lifeline; everything was more fun because I had them to share it with.

A big thank you to my children, Matt, Allie, and Ben, for recognizing that I needed to write this book and for good-naturedly forgiving my distractedness. And finally, thank you to my husband, Jeff, who has been my biggest supporter, my partner, and my best friend.

FOREWORD

by Cheryl Magen

Judaism sees the emergence of a young woman as cause for celebration and ceremony and calls it the Bat Mitzvah. This transition to womanhood should be marked with specially crafted rituals that will create lasting memories for the Bat Mitzvah girl and her family. Although some people view Judaism as a stagnant set of traditions, the advent of Bat Mitzvah is one area that allows for creativity and innovation. Because Bat Mitzvah is a relatively modern addition to Jewish ritual and observance, it has no specific religious guidelines, and each family can create something new and different to mark acceptance into Jewish adulthood.

Historically, Bat Mitzvah was referenced in Jewish texts before actual ceremonies took place. Just as rabbinic law holds that a boy matures at age 13, a girl matures at age 12, when physical puberty and social maturation begin, also according to rabbinic law. The earliest Bat Mitzvah ceremonies took place in France and Italy and then became more widespread in Israel and other countries; the first Bat Mitzvah in the United States was in the early 1900s.

The Bat Mitzvah ceremony can consist of different components, depending on the culture and religious norms of the particular community. My own Bat Mitzvah was on a Friday night in a Conservative synagogue. I was given the opportunity to read Haftorah and lead a few prayers. Looking back on that event, I thought it was a first step toward equality, but it now seems antiquated and religiously inappropriate by any current religious standards; if it were a *Shabbat* morning, then reading Haftorah and leading some of the prayers would have made more sense because that is where those parts of the service are normally placed. I wish I had been given the opportunity to have an *aliyah* to the Torah or to read from the Torah, but in my synagogue, women's participation in the prayer service was limited. Other girls in my generation were given the chance to deliver a short speech about a section of the *Mishnah* (rabbinic law) and then celebrated with a traditional *seudat mitzvah*, a feast marking the end of a particular book that was studied. And because those girls could not be called to the Torah, the girls' fathers or brothers would be called to the Torah instead. Yet another alternative for Bat Mitzvah girls could be a Bat Mitzvah in the context of a women's *minyan* (gathering of a ten-person quorum for public prayer), allowing the young women options usually reserved for males.

Because Jewish law does not provide strict guidelines for Bat Mitzvah ceremonies, many venues can be chosen. Some girls choose to have their Bat Mitzvah ceremonies in the synagogue, some in school, others at home. Some synagogues offer a collective service for groups of Bat Mitzvah girls. And because Bat Mitzvah is a modern addition to Jewish practice, many women who missed their opportunity at age 12 or 13 enter a course of study later in life and have adult ceremonies in their twenties or sixties or eighties.

Bat Mitzvah is a time for each family to dedicate itself to continued Jewish education and involvement, and when a family realizes that a Bat Mitzvah isn't the end of a course of study, but rather a beginning, its daughter will begin to see herself as others do: as an adult in the Jewish community. She will be ready to embark on a lifelong journey of Judaism that is rich in tradition, by learning and participating in social action projects in her synagogue and local community.

Because the ceremony and celebration leave room for personalization of this rite of passage, the Bat Mitzvah girl, her parents, and her teachers should give careful thought to the process so that their choices reflect the values of the Bat Mitzvah, as well as of the family and local community. Emphasis should be placed on the ceremony and ongoing commitments to social action, community projects, or acts of *tzedakah*, rather than on designing a bigger, better party than the "Jane next door."

Becoming a Bat Mitzvah is a bold statement of a young woman's individual commitment to God and to the Jewish community in which she lives. Bat Mitzvah is a religious transition that will hopefully inspire her to pursue a life filled with Jewish learning, observance of rituals, and commitment to the Jewish values of positive leadership, preserving the earth, and taking care of people in need.

Although our ancestors, Sarah, Rebecca, Rachel, and Leah, never had Bat Mitzvah ceremonies, they did leave us with a tradition of leadership and dedication to family and to community that can-and should-be expressed in every Bat Mitzvah service. Each emerging woman can make her mark on the world, beginning with how she designs her entry into Jewish adulthood through the Bat Mitzvah ceremony. Bat Mitzvah is a time for families to share the possibilities of the future when the Bat Mitzvah girl, on her special day, publicly declares acceptance of Judaism and individual commitment to the values cherished by Jews all over the world.

Cheryl Magen became a Bat Mitzvah on a Friday night in the 1960s and has taught many Bat Mitzvah courses to adult women who wanted to connect to God and the Jewish community.

1

THE FIRST BAT MITZVAH

Judith Kaplan Eisenstein, Ph.D.—May 6, 1922
(written by Dr. Judith Kaplan Eisenstein)

Photo courtesy of Jewish Reconstructionist Federation

This story has been adapted from an article in Keeping Posted *by Judith Kaplan Eisenstein, supplied by the Jewish Reconstructionist Federation, reprinted with permission by Rabbi Ira Eisenstein. Judith Kaplan Eisenstein was the oldest daughter of Rabbi Mordechai Kaplan. In 1934, she married one of her father's closest disciples, Rabbi Ira Eisenstein. The mother of two daughters, she was a noted musicologist, composer, author, and lecturer. In 1992, at the age of 82, Dr. Kaplan Eisenstein was honored on the occasion of the seventieth anniversary of her Bat Mitzvah. In 1996, Dr. Judith Kaplan Eisenstein died at the age of 86.*

It was a sunny day in early May of 1922. My two grandmothers, rocking gently in chairs provided for their special comfort, communed in Yiddish. Their conversation was not intended for my ears, but since Grandma Rubin was slightly hard of hearing, and since both were moved by intense emotion, I could eavesdrop without any difficulty.

"Talk to your son," said my mother's mother. "Tell him not to do this thing!"

What was this terrible thing my father was about to perform, and which they both sought uselessly to prevent? He was planning to present me in public ceremony in the synagogue as a Bat Mitzvah.

The synagogue was the newly established Society for the Advancement of Judaism, which had been holding meetings for only a few months. I was midway between my 12th and 13th birthdays. At the time of my 12th birthday, the time at which Jewish law recognizes a girl as a woman, subject to the *mitzvot*, there had been no synagogue where such a ceremony could be conducted. This was my father's first opportunity to put into practice one of the basic tenets of his yet unnamed philosophy of Reconstructionism, namely, the equality of women in all aspects of Jewish life.

It would be less than the truth to say that I was as full of ardor about the subject of this ceremony as my father was. Let's say I was ambivalent, being perfectly willing to defy the standards of my grandmothers, pleased to have a somewhat flattering attention paid me, and yet perturbed about the possible effect this might have on the attitude of my own peers. In addition, there was the slightly unnerving fact that Father hadn't, by May 5, decided exactly what form this ceremony was to take—and it was Friday, *erev Shabbat!*

Everything else was in readiness. Invitations had been sent to family and friends for a party in our home on the evening following *Shabbat* I had asked only one or two close friends, in addition to my fellow members in the Yarmuk Club (a Hebrew-speaking club for girls that met weekly at the Central Jewish Institute).

Everything was in readiness except the procedure itself. On Friday night, after *Shabbat* dinner, Father took me into his study and had me read aloud the Torah blessings. How severely he corrected my diction! He then selected a passage from the weekly portion, the magnificent Holiness Code from the *parsha Kedoshim*, which I practiced reading in both Hebrew and English.

The following morning, we all went together—father, mother, disapproving grandmothers, my three little sisters, and I—to the brownstone building on 86th Street where the Society carried on its functions. Services were held in a long narrow room that led into a wider and more spacious one. In the wider room was the *bimah* with the Ark. The men of the congregation sat in that room and also used up one-half of the narrow room. Women's rights or no women's rights, the old habit of separating the sexes at worship died hard. The first part of my ordeal was to sit in that front room among the men, away from the cozy protection of my mother and sisters.

The service proceeded as usual, through *Shacharit*, and through the Torah reading. Father was called up for the honor of reading *Maftir*. When he finished the Haftorah, I was signaled to step forward to a place below the *bimah*, at a very respectable distance from the scroll of the Torah, which had already been rolled up and garbed in its mantle. I pronounced the first blessing and from my own *chumash* read the selection that Father had chosen for me, continued with the reading of the English translation, and concluded with the closing *brachah*. That was it. The scroll was returned to the Ark with song and procession, and the service resumed. No thunder sounded, no lightening struck. The institution of the Bat Mitzvah had been born without incident, and the rest of the day was all rejoicing. It was many years before the full privilege of being called to the Torah was granted to a girl, even at the Society for the Advancement of Judaism. By the time my own daughters reached the age of Bat Mitzvah, however, it was taken for granted. They learned to chant the cantillation of both the Torah and the Haftorah, and each, in turn, read on *Shabbat Kedoshim* not only the highly ethical code of behavior in the Torah, but the poetic words of the final chapter of the Book of Amos.

2

RECIPES FOR LIFE

Rachel Abrams—April 1, 2000

Rachel is a junior at Kushner Yeshiva High School in New Jersey. She loves to bake, and is an active participant with NCSY, and volunteers at a local nursing home.

On the stage is a lavish set of a modern-day kitchen. Not one detail has been left to chance. The colors are Rachel's favorites and every detail, intricately painted, is symbolic of her history. The purple iris on the wall is her grandmother's favorite flower. The bowl of fruit represents the produce business that was the livelihood of her other grandparents. The china pattern painted into the set's breakfront was the same one that her mother grew up with. And on the refrigerator, affixed with magnets, is a photograph of Rachel and her sister Ariel, along with their cousin Stephanie's Bat Mitzvah invitation.

The narrator, a woman with long red curls, enters the stage carrying an "aged" box of Passover dishes. She looks lovingly down at them, places them on the floor, and begins:

> Every year I open this box for Pesach. And what do you think I am unpacking? Dishes? Pots and pans? (She smiles and shakes her head.) No. I am unpacking my family. They are all in here, the women of my past. Some of them are still with us, others only live in blessed memory. But they are all here, in a pot for chicken soup, a glass for raisin wine, a recipe for gefilte fish. So every year I unpack my Pesach dishes and remember who I am and where I came from. (She unpacks the recipe book and looks up at the audience.) You children are always asking me to tell you stories-come, here, sit nearby and I'll tell you a story; the story of the first year I was old enough to help with the holiday cooking. . . . I had just turned 12 and Bat Mitzvah, and was helping my Grandma Jackie get ready for Pesach.

The narrator in the play represents the Bat Mitzvah girl, Rachel, as a grandmother looking back at her life. Playing the narrator is Rachel's mother, Jamie Podhurst. It is easy to see the resemblance between mother and daughter, especially in their coppery red hair. With this introduction, the story quickly comes back to the present with a young Rachel, playing herself, learning the lessons of keeping a kosher home. There on the stage, in that mythical kitchen, Rachel receives valuable lessons imparted by the women in her family, both past and present. With joy and humor, they take turns passing on their favorite recipes and rituals, all the while weaving tales of the colorful characters who indulged in these delicacies.

She learned that Great-Grandma Basha's gefilte fish was made from only the freshest fish. The fish were so fresh, they were carried home live in a pail from Pitkin Avenue and swam around in the family bathtub until Grandma Basha was ready to gefilte them! She found out that Great-Grandma Minnie was a hard-working woman. She raised three children, took care of her aging mother, and worked all day in the fruit store, side by side with her husband, Sam. When she allowed herself the luxury of a small repast, her favorite pastry with coffee was the Sour Cream Coffee Cake she made from her own recipe.

As the audience watched with rapt attention while the story unfolded, they were treated to lessons in Torah, history, and love. Some had tears in their eyes because this history was also theirs. If not actually related to the Bat Mitzvah girl, they, too, remembered grandmothers and great aunts who, sometimes despite great odds, were responsible for the perpetuity of the traditions. In their minds they pictured the warmth and the aroma permeating their own childhood hearths.

As members of an Orthodox synagogue, Rachel, her mother, and her father, Lewis, decided that the Bat Mitzvah had to be more than just a party. It had to be a spiritual and intellectual pursuit connected to the *parsha* and a personal expression of Rachel. The Torah portion for that week, *parsha Shemini* from the Book of Leviticus, contains the laws related to keeping kosher. Taken literally from the text, they are "dry" at best. Delivering a *D'var Torah* from the social hall on the "do's and don'ts" of *kashrut* laws would be tedious, so they brainstormed the best way to incorporate Rachel's *parsha* into something meaningful. The catalyst for creativity was the limited parameters of what would be acceptable in the synagogue.

Rachel likes many things, but she loves to act and loves to cook. From there, the idea slowly took shape. Because, as women, they were not permitted to do many things to celebrate this occasion, they wanted the Bat Mitzvah to be an expression of women, a multigenerational expression. They thought about a play, a cookbook, or a family memoir about food. Before going further, they decided to enlist the cooperation of the women in their family. Jamie sent a form to every female relative and asked her not only to return it with her favorite recipe, but to please add a memory of that recipe. This started a lot of reflection in the family, as daughters remembered their mothers' and grandmothers' recipes and when, where, and with whom they were eaten.

At the same time, Rachel and Jamie sat down with Phoebe Sharp, Rachel's acting teacher. Rachel and Jamie tossed out scattered ideas of what they would like to incorporate, and, as a visionary, Phoebe molded them into shape. Between the three of them, they wrote the play that would be presented on the morning of Rachel's Bat Mitzvah.

Beth Shalom is a traditional Orthodox *shul.* The men sit in the middle, and the women's sections are raised on both sides, with a *mechitzah* (partition) of green ferns. Lewis, Rachel's father, chanted the Haftorah and delivered a speech paying tribute to the women in his family, especially the Bat Mitzvah girl. When the ceremony was over, the overflowing crowd was treated to a delicious *Kiddush* in the social hall. After the meal, while the room was being rearranged so that guests could see the stage, copies of *Recipes for Life: A Bat Mitzvah*

Memoir and Cookbook were being distributed. This lovely spiral-bound book is the compilation of the treasured recipes of the Podhurst/Abrams families, incorporating short vignettes about each recipe's originator and early consumers. Both Grandma Basha's gefilte fish and Grandma Minnie's Sour Cream Coffee Cake recipes are included in the cookbook. For the audience, the book also offered some insights about the women who were about to be portrayed on the stage.

Jamie, a talented artist, painted the set and Phoebe provided the costumes. Rachel played herself; Jamie played Rachel as a grandmother; and the rest of the cast was played by Rachel's aunts and cousins. As the play unfolds, Rachel learns more than just the laws of keeping kosher. She learns that her Grandmother Jackie (played by Jackie's daughter, Mindy) maintains a kosher home because it is a way of life, not just a way of eating. She tells her granddaughter, "I don't keep a kosher home because I am forced to; it's my way of having my faith be a part of everything I do in my kitchen. When I cook, I am part of a community—my friends, my family, and my mother before me."

Granny Pearl (played by Pearl's daughter Beth) joins them on the stage and adds her insight about the *kashrut* laws: "[Keeping Kosher] is not so much remembering [your ancestors] as honoring, and keeping something alive. Maybe it's a way of connecting to our past, but it's also a way to bring traditions into the future. It's not just that Jewish people keep kosher, it's also that being kosher has kept the Jews. . . . If you have something that you can be part of every day in the simple things you do, then the harder things you face will be a little easier."

The play continues, with Rachel's ancestors making appearances in the kitchen and sharing sage bits of advice related to tradition, Torah, family, and home. It closes with the narrator, reflective and grateful for the knowledge learned in that kitchen and filled with a sense of continuity as she now shares some of her insights with the audience. When the curtain closed, the cast was greeted with raucous applause.

At the play's conclusion, one surprise presentation was made to Rachel by her Aunt Beth (Lewis's sister). In spite of the large crowd, she spoke directly to Rachel:

> As you so beautifully expressed in your Bat Mitzvah play, THE WOMEN have always strengthened the fabric of our family by nurturing, caretaking, providing, cooking, clean-

ing, doing, making, and even decorating our homes. This is our way.

And these same women have always strengthened the fabric of their communities as well. Our women touch the lives of people. Whether by literally nourishing and fortifying other people's bodies through hard work all day at a fruit store or hard work all night at a hospital or by nourishing other people's minds as teachers, educators, mentors, and leaders. Or by nourishing other people's spirits as artists and creators, adding beauty to the world around us, or as healers and helpers easing some of the pain. This is the legacy which I know you will carry on in your life.

As a symbol of this—I want to give you a piece of your Great-Grandma Basha's embroidered lace. Despite its delicate artistic design, it has survived through the years. Thin, tiny threads, woven, stitched, and tied with care, create a fabric of great beauty, richness, and complexity.

As you weave a life for yourself, may you also strengthen the fabric of your family, enrich the fabric of your community, and beautify the fabric of the world. Always following in the path of the women of our family, may you continue to make the world a better place by being and becoming the wonderful person you are meant to be. AMEN!

GREAT GRANDMA MINNIE'S SOUR CREAM COFFEE CAKE

1 c. sugar
½ c. butter
3 eggs
½ pint sour cream
2 c. sifted flour
1 tsp baking powder
1 tsp vanilla

Topping:
¼ c. sugar
½ tsp cinnamon
½ cup chopped nuts

Cream butter and sugar. Add eggs and sour cream; beat until smooth. Sift together dry ingredients and add to the egg mixture. Add vanilla, blend thoroughly. Pour half the batter into a small greased pan. Sprinkle with half the topping mixture. Add remaining batter and sprinkle remainder of topping on top. Bake at 350 degrees for 50 minutes. ENJOY!

3

THE BAT MITZVAH DILEMMA: ONE ORTHODOX FAMILY'S SOLUTION

Felissa Rubin—January 15, 2000
(by Nancy Wolfson-Moche*)

Felissa Rubin is an honors student at the Hillel High School in Miami, Florida, where she is an active participant in the Women's Tefila Service. She is interested in arts, theater, music, writing, dance, politics, and theology. In the summer of 2002, she traveled to Lithuania and Latvia where she participated in a project that is bringing the last of the Nazi war criminals to justice.

Photo credit Maurice Weiss

---

* Nancy Wolfson-Moche is an internationally published journalist, specializing in lifestyle. She lives in New York City.

It is nine o'clock on a windy January *Shabbat* morning. About 100 women and 20 men are gathered in a second floor meeting room at the Majestic Towers, a condo in northern Miami's Bal Harbour. All have come to celebrate Felissa's Bat Mitzvah.

They are gathered here because it is right across the street from the Shul of Bal Harbour, where Felissa and her parents *daven* almost every *Shabbat*. But what is about to happen could not happen at the *shul* across the street, run by a Chabad rabbi.

The room faces the ocean, which is in an unusually rough and agitated state this particular Saturday morning. Inside, the women sit in chairs arranged in a horseshoe around a makeshift *bimah* (borrowed from a local Orthodox day school) and an Ark (from a local Conservative day school). Inside the Ark is a Torah, on loan from a local Orthodox man, a "Carlebach" feminist, who wishes to remain anonymous. This generous man bought the Torah with the intention of lending it to Orthodox Bat Mitzvah girls like Felissa, who otherwise might not have the opportunity to read from the Torah.

Among the women are Colombians (Felissa's mother is originally from Colombia), Costa Ricans, Panamanians, Israelis, Brazilians, Swiss, New Yorkers, and Floridians. Their clothes reflect their far-flung origins: suits ranging from hot pink to subdued gray, silk dresses in prints and solids, and a few long, boxy *frum* skirts topped with long-sleeved boxy jackets. Hemlines run the gamut. Shoes range from sexy stilettos to clunky oxfords. There are straw hats in many different shapes and sizes.

Off to one side, close to the entrance to the room, the men sit behind a trellis covered with rented greenery. This serves as a makeshift *mechitzah*. Some of the men are fidgeting. looking this way and that, as they might do in a foreign city when experiencing something for the first time. This is not surprising, because, for many, Miami is a foreign city, and for most, it is their first time sitting behind a *mechitzah*.

Felissa is wearing a light blue silk shantung suit. Her shiny shoulder-length brown hair, which had been topped with a stylish velvet hair band the night before, is pulled back and clamped in a big butterfly clip, the way she might wear it while studying or taking a test. This is one sign that Felissa is serious about what she is about to do. She stands up at the *bimah* next to her teacher Miriam Rube, who motions for her to begin. With her back to the guests, Felissa faces the Ark and the ocean, as she sings. "*Shochen ad marom ye kadosh shemo*."

She gains speed and strength as she continues, reciting the psalms. Felissa focuses her attention on each word of the *Shacharit* service. The room is hushed, while everyone present concentrates on the act of

praying. Noticeably absent is the usual movement in *shul*—the perpetual going out and coming back in and whispering that is commonplace in many Orthodox synagogues. During the *Amidah*. or Silent Prayer, Felissa turns to the crowd like an experienced leader, gauging who has finished praying and who has not and when it is time to get on with the service.

When it is time for the Torah service, Felissa looks around at her mother and grandmother, as if to remind them that they are up next. Ronnie Becher, a leader in the Orthodox feminist movement who has traveled from Riverdale, New York, comes up to the *bimah* to be the *gabbay*. Becher prepares everyone for what will follow, explaining how the service will proceed as women come up for *aliyot* as Felissa reads *parshat Bo* from the Torah.

Still, no one is quite prepared for what actually happens. The first person called up is Joann, a native of Miami, who is a *Levi* (chosen because of *Bimkhom Kohen*, the practice of calling up a *Levi* for the first *aliyah*. in the absence of a *Kohen*). This is the second time she has come up to the Torah (the first was at her own daughter's Bat Mitzvah, almost two years ago in Israel). Joann compares the experience to the magic of her wedding day: "Standing next to Felissa and watching her pray to God, with the words of the Torah falling off her lips, was really an indescribable moment," she says. "I felt closer to the Torah, closer to God, and spiritually uplifted. I felt my soul, and I found that happening throughout the service, not only when I went up for my *aliyah*."

Felissa's grandmother, Matilda, and her mother, Raquel, come up to the Torah for the third and fifth *aliyot*. Jaya, a family friend who was raised in Costa Rica, is called up for the sixth *aliyah*. Dressed in a chic navy blue chalk-stripe suit, she is a tall, stylish woman who approaches the *bimah* with confidence. She begins in a loud voice. "*Barkhu et Adonai ha-m'vorakh*." The congregation responds, "*Barukh Adonai ha-m'vorakh l'olam va-ed*." This is her cue to repeat those words. But her voice cracks, and tears rush to her eyes. For a moment, she is unable to speak

"I had heard hundreds of boys go up to the Torah and say this prayer, so I knew it very well," Jaya says afterward. "It was the same Orthodox setting that I'd grown up in, and that was dear to me, but I had never been allowed to be a part of it. So when I actually uttered the words, I felt for the first time that my presence mattered, that they were counting on me to say this prayer, and I felt a spiritual connection with God that I had never felt before. I was overcome with emotion. This experience was very, very powerful." In fact, Jaya's experience had an effect on everyone: there was an almost palpable electric energy and hardly a dry eye in the room.

Several weeks later, Jaya, who has since joined a monthly women's *tefillah* group, says, 'From this experience I learned that Judaism is a religion of action. The meaning comes from the action. *Na'aseh v'nishma* is the Hebrew way of expressing this concept: No matter how you try to apply meaning to things, they won't have a meaning until you do them."

Felissa reads the entire Torah portion without hesitating or making an error. Laura, Felissa's aunt from Colombia, does *hagbah* (lifting the Torah scroll), and Debby, a family friend, *gelila* (redressing the scroll before it is returned to the Ark). Felissa reads the Haftorah easily, as she had read the Torah. The women then dance through the makeshift *shul*, carrying the Torah. They take it across the *mechitzah* into the men's section, too.

At about eleven o'clock, after the Torah reading but before *Musaf*, the women's *tefillah* service is over. The wind howls as the crowd crosses Collins Avenue and files into the main sanctuary of the Shul of Bal Harbour, in time for the Torah reading and Musaf service there. Felissa's father, Aryeh, gets the *Maftir aliyah* and reads the Haftorah, the same words that his daughter had read minutes before, across the street.

Afterward, Felissa is called up to the *bimah* to give a *D'var Torah*. She begins by explaining that the first part of her Bat Mitzvah took place across the street. 'While I know that to some this may be somewhat unorthodox, I appreciate having been a part of it and am equally appreciative to be able to share this part of my Bat Mitzvah with all of you in the shul," Felissa smiles, having just outlined her family's solution to one of the biggest dilemmas facing the modem Orthodox world.

Felissa not only made her family and friends proud, but her performance served as a catalyst for the whole community. Several of the women present formed a Women's *Tefillah* Group. They meet monthly, on weekday evenings. Although they come from different backgrounds and have different levels of proficiency in Hebrew, they gather to study prayers, rituals, and Torah and to discuss the meaning and

relevance of these. Some of the women in the group have begun to study Hebrew, privately or in larger classes.

Felissa's parents also helped to foster learning throughout the community. In honor of Felissa's Bat Mitzvah, they sponsored a lecture series at their *shul* They invited three prominent scholars to discuss topics ranging from "Feminism in the Orthodox World" to "Hunting for Nazis of the Holocaust" to "A Rabbi's Millennium Message."

Jaya's daughter Michal had a Bat Mitzvah five months after Felissa's. She led a *Kabbalat Shabbat* service and put together a booklet that included poetry by her grandmother, her father, and herself. She studied about the history of ushering in *Shabbat*, the prayers, the songs, and the candle-lighting ritual. The process has changed the meaning of *Shabbat* in her life, and in her mother's life. "Before Felissa's Bat Mitzvah, I never really thought about the prayers that my daughter Michal would say at her Bat Mitzvah—I was more concerned about logistics, like where we would have it. Felissa's Bat Mitzvah enriched my perception of what a Bat Mitzvah could be," Jaya says. "So I spent several months exploring the options. And on the evening of Michal's Bat Mitzvah, I stood up and thanked her for all that we'd learned from this experience together."

4

EXCEPTIONAL

Rebeka Schiess—March 6, 1999

In the story of the Golden Calf, it was the women who maintained their faith in God and refused to relinquish their jewelry in order to build the idol. Empowered, cerebral, and introspective, Rebeka takes her place among the ranks of strong Jewish women. Although living now with constant pain from the failed surgery, she chooses instead to ask, "What is the next mitzvah I must do?" and "How can I become a better Jew?" She does not consider herself to be that unusual—just like our ancestors, she remains steadfast in her faith, despite adversity, and refuses to relinquish her strong sense of purpose, feelings of hope, and plans for the future.

It was snowing. Not that light, white powder that you think of when you overturn the cityscape in a glass paperweight, but heavy, thick, wet stuff that just kept falling. On Thursday of that week, more snow had fallen in one day than on any other single day anyone could remember. This historical distinction was one that the Scheiss family could have lived without, but, like everything else, the Scheisses took it in their stride. The seventeen extra inches that fell on that Saturday morning certainly made them more cautious, but they proceeded, just as they had with every other roadblock they'd faced in the last fourteen years, to do what needed to be done.

Rebeka was supposed to be born on March 7, 1985. It is common for babies, especially first babies, to over- or undershoot their due dates, but Rebeka arrived a full four months early and weighed not much more than four sticks of butter. In her eagerness to arrive, not all of her physical systems were completely formed. In spite of undergoing six surgeries, Rebeka uses a wheelchair, due to cerebral palsy, and is blind.

Her Bat Mitzvah could have taken place in November 1998, thirteen years after her birth month, but the family chose to commemorate her original due date with the celebration. Integrated into regular classes, Bat Mitzvah lessons were added to an already full schedule that included occupational and physical therapy, vision services, orientation and mobility, and accelerated Spanish. Due to the creative efforts of Rabbi Donald Gerber and her talented teacher, Mr. Elliot Fix, the lessons were presented both tactilely and auditorily, so Rebeka could learn the *trup* (tune). Rebeka's father, John, with the help of a family friend, downloaded the *parsha* and Haftorah from the Internet, transliterated it, and printed it in Braille.

The forty-two inches of snow that had fallen made the morning's preparations that much more hectic. Rebeka's personal care attendant trudged through the snow to assist with her morning hygiene routine. In spite of the weather, the hairdresser still showed up to do her hair. And since Thursday's state of emergency ban had been lifted, they could drive to the temple.

Attired in a black velvet and silver suit, Rebeka looked elegant. Clothes are unimportant to her, with her main concern being to look appropriate rather than trendy. However, her mother and grandmother searched for an outfit that was not only "appropriate," but that would fit a tall, thin woman-child and would cover her back brace and leg braces.

Congregation Etz Chaim meets in a church. The table that serves as the *bimah* was too high for Rebeka to reach from her wheelchair, so an alternative had been brought in. Rabbi Gerber performed the first part of the service, but Rebeka sat up in the front with him through the entire service. The rabbi considered every exceptional aspect of this Bat Mitzvah and made the traditional very special. Because many non-Jewish family and friends were in attendance, the rabbi offered explanations for the significance of and rationale for much of the service.

Several family members got involved with the "physical" part of the ceremony. When it came time to take out the Torah for the reading of the *parsha*, cousin Zack, who had just become a Bar Mitzvah himself, carried it, so that Rebeka could wheel herself around the temple for the traditional procession. Her brother Jordan carried a smaller ceremonial Torah in the procession.

The Torah, the Five Books of Moses, hand-lettered on parchment, is considered so holy that we are not permitted to touch it with our hands. It is handled solely by the wooden spindles on which it is wound. Normally, the Torah scroll is unrolled to the correct section and the Bar or Bat Mitzvah reads from it with the aid of a *yad*, a hand-shaped pointer often fashioned from silver or wood. When the Torah was placed on the *bimah*, and opened to the appropriate place, Rebeka was given special permission to lay her Braille sheets over the parchment. As her fingers flew across the pages, she was, indeed reading from the Torah. Although not normally shy, when she was first called to the Torah, she was nervous about getting up in front of the congregation. After a very "fast" first paragraph, however, she slowed down and did just fine.

For many Jewish girls, becoming a Bat Mitzvah is a matter of course—the next step—an expected rite. The decision to become a Bat Mitzvah for Rebeka was a very conscious choice. The child of a Jewish mother and non-Jewish father, Rebeka was allowed to decide which religion to follow. That decision evolved over time, and from the day she decided to practice Judaism, she knew she wanted to become a Bat Mitzvah. Being a very spiritual young woman, Rebeka feels connected to her religion and wanted to be closer to God.

When Rebeka completed both the Torah and the Haftorah reading, she addressed the congregation. In her speech Rebeka discussed several ideas that were found in the morning's *parsha*. Her favorite part highlighted the lessons learned from the "Golden Calf." She explained. "We can learn that we must always have faith in God even when there are difficult moments in life and God may seem far away from us."

John, Rebeka's father, was next called to make a few remarks. He shared the following thoughts:

> In the case of our firstborn, He strove mightily. Through the good works of doctors, nurses, therapists, relatives, and

friends, He continues to do so. From your rather fragile and tenuous grip on life at your birth, Rebeka. you have blossomed into the accomplished young lady we see before us today. God reaffirms for us, through your repeated accomplishments, like the one we witness today, the awesome power of what faith and love for Him and each other enables us, enabled you, Rebeka, to achieve.

To say that we are proud of you understates by tenfold what we feel. You have achieved so much by this accomplishment and the countless others you enabled us to bear witness to over your fourteen remarkable years.

Thank you for strengthening our faith and love. Thank you for sharing God's miracle with us today and every day. Though your sight is diminished, your vision is exceptional! Thank you for helping us see what matters most.

Rebeka considers her Bat Mitzvah celebration to be the most special day of her life and the most significant thing that ever happened to her. Afterward, she felt different in that she has been filled with a deep sense of peace and closeness to God. These feelings have served her well, for three months after the Bat Mitzvah, Rebeka underwent yet another necessary surgery, this time to straighten her spine. In the operating room, moments before the anesthesia was administered, she quietly uttered, "Just a minute . . . I need to say something." Almost inaudibly, she started to say the *Shema* in Hebrew. The medical staff stared at her in confusion and prepared to proceed. The anesthesiologist, Dr. Feldman, halted their actions with a simple, "Let her do this."

In the story of the Golden Calf, it was the women who maintained their faith in God and refused to relinquish their jewelry in order to build the idol. Empowered, cerebral, and introspective, Rebeka takes her place among the ranks of strong Jewish women. Although living now with constant pain from the failed surgery, she chooses instead to ask, "What is the next mitzvah I must do?" and "How can I become a better Jew?" She does not consider herself to be that unusual—just like our ancestors, she remains steadfast in her faith, despite adversity, and refuses to relinquish her strong sense of purpose, feelings of hope, and plans for the future.

5

I SHINED WITH SHIRA

Shira Rockowitz—November 6, 1993

"Save me!" groaned a frustrated Shira Rockowitz, as she and her parents sat down to plan her Bat Mitzvah. Shira was an eighth-grade student at the Solomon Shechter School of White Plains. Over forty students were in her class and she was one of the youngest. Every weekend of their Bar and Bat Mitzvah year, there was another party. Another dress, another theme, more catered food, and Shira wanted no part of it. . . . She had had enough! She wanted to celebrate becoming a "daughter of the commandments" with something Jewish—not with a luau, a simulated ball park, or a remake of the Garden of Eden.

Shira's mother, Julie, had seen an advertisement that an old New York landmark, the Eldridge Street Synagogue on the Lower East Side, was looking for volunteers to help clean it up. At the turn of the century, as many as 1,000 people had attended holiday services in its magnificent sanctuary. Built in 1887, the building was now deteriorating and its former splendor was hidden under years of dust and neglect. The sanctuary had been closed in the 1950s. In spite of the physical decline, the Eldridge Street Congregation has survived, not missing a Sabbath or holiday service (which are now held in the *beth hamedrash* [house of study] on the ground floor) in over 110 years. A local effort has been initiated to restore the historic structure and convert it into a heritage center. Julie, a Jewish educator, thought that this project might be a great idea for one of her classes, but when she told her family about it, they realized that this was the perfect place to celebrate Shira's coming of age.

Shira had a lovely and very traditional Bat Mitzvah in Temple Beth El of New Rochelle on the day before her party. At the end of the services, the rabbi wanted to announce where the group was going the next day, but the family had given him a "gag order." The invitations were deliberately vague and only indicated what to wear (very casual), where to meet, and the assigned time. This large group of kids, who virtually grew up together and in some ways seemed like siblings as well as classmates, boarded special school buses equipped with seat belts for the trip into the city.

When the kids arrived in the *shul*, they were given their first "taste" of the Lower East Side. The appreciative staff members of the Eldridge Street Synagogue brought out traditional food. They passed around pickles with black bread and locally baked rugallah. While the kids munched, they were treated to a history lesson of this once glorious building in an area that previously bustled with Jewish life. And then, they were ready to work.

Buckets, mops, rubber gloves, dust masks, and cans of brass polish—all the "fixings" for a successful party! No Bat Mitzvah would be complete without a complimentary T-shirt, and this fete was no different. Shira's family passed out the oversized shirts that boasted, "I SHINED WITH SHIRA," and the guests willingly donned these over their already casual attire. Many of the youngsters, who had housekeepers at home, rolled up their sleeves and dusted, waxed, and polished. If the forty-nine kids (with adult supervision) did not exactly "whistle while they worked," they did spontaneously break into song as they compared techniques for buffing and shining. Even though the job seemed somewhat daunting and overwhelming, the students were able to see the fruits of their labor. When they first arrived, one group started on a very black railing. With cans of NOXON and lots of elbow grease, the hidden grandeur of the brass started to shine through.

Tired, hungry, but feeling very satisfied, the Bat Mitzvah continued its theme of "back to our roots," and the kids went to Ratner's for its famous dairy meals that include blintzes, potato pancakes, and soup you can eat with a fork.

Instead of the traditional sign-in board for guests to write brief comments, Shira had a sign-in book. The book provided immediate feedback. Her friends wrote comments like, "This is a great idea!" and "What a great way to celebrate!" But then again, this is a special group of kids. Since so many students were in the class, the kids, teachers, and parents got together to discuss how to handle their last year at the school. It just seemed silly to all give gifts to child A, and then the same thing to Child B the next week, and so on. They devised a better plan for how to celebrate this special B'Nai Mitzvah year together. Instead of giving gifts to each other, they decided to take that money to send the whole class, plus their teachers, to Israel together. It was the first time the school had come up with this kind of a plan, and it was so successful that subsequent classes have followed in their footsteps. The kids had a great time, learned a lot, were well-behaved, and, rather than a drawerful of duplicate Bat Mitzvah gifts, they came back with two weeks' worth of memories that will last a lot longer.

For Shira, her Bat Mitzvah was not an isolated experience. Her family has always been involved in community service, and her parents serve as strong role models. Two years after the Bat Mitzvah, she heard about a community project in Reno run by the American Jewish Society for Service. She jumped at the chance to get involved and spent the summer with fifteen other volunteers, tarring a roof, refurbishing a deck, and building a community playground. With both the Bat Mitzvah and her summer of service, Shira could have sent a check and let someone else do the work, but she wanted her mitzvah to be an active one. She's had "hands-on" experiences for *gemilut hasadim* (acts of kindness). When she first asked her parents to "save her" from the drudgery of one more stereotypical Bat Mitzvah, little did she know that she and her friends would have a hand in "saving," preserving, and restoring an old giant to its former glory. There were no limbo contests, group karaoke, sunglasses, or Hawaiian leis. Rather than disposable "give-aways" that ultimately end up in the trash, Shira and her friends took away a lesson that was meant to be kept.

P.S. If you would like to help, or if you have questions for the organization, please write to the Eldridge Street Project, 12 Eldridge Street, New York, NY 10002, or email at: contact@eldridgestreet.org

6

NAVI

Nava Gold—March 6, 1994

As a junior at Rockville Center High School, Nava was honored for 100 hours of volunteer time at South Nassau Communities Hospital. Her special course of study enabled her to work with a job coach in the hospital, at the Recreational Center, and in her school office. Upon graduation, she hopes to work full time in a hospital, with duties ranging from administrative work to food service.

Although the Bat Mitzvahs of Orthodox Jewish girls are treated differently from their counterparts in other movements in Judaism, nonetheless, they are greeted with the same enthusiasm and joy. Because of separate seating in the synagogue and the prohibitions against females leading the service in a mixed-gender congregation, Orthodox young ladies have had to devise some creative ways to celebrate their entrance into adulthood.

Nava Gold came of age by delivering a D'var Torah (literally translated as a speech about the Torah) at a party on a Sunday afternoon in the presence of the rabbis from the *shul*, members of the congregation, and her family. This was no easy feat.

The nine-month gestation period is more than just a time for a baby to develop. It's a time for the parents-to-be to arrange for physical necessities, as well as to prepare themselves mentally for their new status. It's also a time to formulate hopes and dreams about what life will be like upon the birth of their newborn. They anticipate how they will nurture, interact, thrive, and grow with their children. A mental picture is formulated, much like the visual musings in the Sunday comics. And as in the funny papers, when the balloon breaks, its owner is left with shattered dreams.

When a child is born disabled, the mental picture of their healthy child is destroyed, leaving the unsuspecting parents with broken pieces. It is a difficult process, but it is incumbent upon the grieving mom and dad to pick up the fragments and create a new picture—a different picture, but one incorporating a different set of lines and a palette of different colors.

When Nava, her second child, was born with neurological deficits, Harriet Gold grieved, grew from that process, and then moved on. She embarked on a personal emotional journey of picking up the pieces and creating a new picture—a picture that features the strengths, not the weaknesses, and the abilities, not the disabilities, of her daughter.

Nava is enrolled in a course of study for mentally disabled students that focuses on developing important job skills. She has a lovely disposition and an outgoing, friendly personality. Sometime early in school, she was nicknamed the "Mayor" because she walked through the halls smiling and saying "Hi" to everyone. Gifted with an amazing memory and thoughtful enough to care, she remembers the aches and pains of those close to her and always asks how they are feeling. Fiercely independent, she is sometimes frustrated by limitations she doesn't know she has.

There was never a question that Nava—like her older sister Esther and, later, her younger sister Penina—would celebrate becoming a Bat Mitzvah. Despite her stuttering, she would still read a *D'var Torah* in the presence of her community. Months before her 12th birthday, another complication arose. Nava became very ill. After comprehensive testing, she was diagnosed with ulcerative colitis. Despite her losing twenty-five pounds, her face was bloated from the steroid used to treat her illness. Regardless of this additional hindrance, the preparations for the Bat Mitzvah continued.

Nava met weekly with Rabbi Kelemer of West Hempstead, and they discussed the topic and content of her speech. The holiday of Passover was approaching, and of the many lessons one can learn from this celebration of freedom, they decided to explore the

afikomen. Of the three special matzos that are set on the seder table, the middle one is broken in two and one half is hidden. Depending on family tradition, the finder of this segment is rewarded with an already purchased prize or the promise of one. The triumph of finding the *aflkomen* is not in unearthing a crumbling piece of matzoh, but, rather, what it represents. There is meaning beyond the surface, potential, and joy; you just have to look for it.

March 6 arrived and Nava looked lovely in her black velvet dress. Notwithstanding her puffy cheeks, her hair was styled and shiny and her eyes soft and twinkling. The cause of the swelling, prednisone, also produced an interesting but unexplained phenomenon. Previous to the illness, Nava had stuttered severely. However, while she was on the steroid, in addition to her mood swings and bloating, her stuttering had noticeably decreased. Medical experts were loath to declare any connection or cause-and-effect relationship. Whether medicine or miracle, on the day that it counted most for Nava to speak clearly, she delivered her *D'var Torah* without any impediment. She spoke without pause, only to giggle when she mentioned that sometimes she wished her sisters were like the *afikomen*—hidden and out of sight.

Finishing up to a din of applause, she then raptly listened while others took the microphone and addressed her. A consistent theme pervaded the messages—Nava's unique strengths. Her mother talked about how brave she was during her illness, stoically tolerating the symptoms, as well as the treatment. Her grandmother explained the derivation of her name. From the "Song of Songs," translated from the Hebrew, *Nava* means "lovely" or "beautiful." Coupled with her last name, Gold, she is indeed a precious gift. The party was complete with singing, dancing, and a delicious meal.

As parents, we are "works-in-progress." Our newborns come without directions. Just as they grow and thrive, we, too, develop and mature. In the process of nurturing, we learn to dig deep and find the strength needed to face situations for which we have no training or preparation. We learn to take that long-anticipated bundle of joy and respond to him or her, rather than force our offspring into matching our preconceived expectations. Like the *afikomen*, there is delight, celebration, and even victory in looking past the dry, brittle, flat board and discovering the bounty that lies beyond.

7

B'NOT MITZVAH NEW ZEALAND STYLE

Mandy Copeland, Diana Hoskyn,
Naomi Johnson, Margaret Laurenson,
and Helen Levin—January 16, 1993
(by Naomi Johnson)

Since this important occasion, the five of us have all, to varying degrees, participated in synagogue life, with a number being regular lay leaders. New Zealanders—or "Kiwis" as we like to call ourselves—are known for our "do-it-yourself" skills, and a visiting rabbi from Malta once commented that we were a "do-it-yourself" congregation.

Photo credit Peter Hoskyn

On January 16, 1993, five very nervous women followed Rabbi David Goldberg to the *bimah* at Beth Shalom, Auckland, New Zealand, for this congregation's first group B'Not Mitzvah for five adult women. Beth Shalom is a Progressive Jewish congregation (Reform, in the language of the States), which has a strong tradition of involving women in all aspects of synagogue life. Beth Shalom has been in existence for almost forty-five years,

and we are fortunately growing with an influx of immigrants, particularly from South Africa.

For various reasons, the five women—Mandy Copeland, Diana Hoskyn, Naomi Johnson, Margaret Laurenson, and Helen Levin—had not celebrated a Bat Mitzvah at the usual age. (I had really wanted a Bat Mitzvah at age 13, but for many reasons, one of which was my father's state of health at the time, this was not possible.) As Rabbi David Goldberg explained to us, there need not be any age limit on one of Judaism's most important customs. The five of us felt the strong need to achieve this milestone in our religious lives before we were too much older. Our ages ranged from 22 to 55 years. We all bought new clothes for the occasion, and we all wore *tallit.* This combined ceremony for adult women was certainly a first for Beth Shalom, and we believe it was a first for New Zealand.

Two of us in the group undertook Hebrew studies in the first quarter of 1992 to improve our Hebrew reading in the services; we both felt the need to brush up our skills from Hebrew School days many years ago. These classes provided us with the inspiration to embark on a further course of study and to enlist others to join us. We studied weekly with Rabbi Goldberg from July to December 1992, covering a wide range of Jewish topics, then prepared ourselves to take the *Shabbat* morning service and read our Torah portion. It is Beth Shalom's tradition that the service is led by the Bar or Bat Mitzvah, and our B'Not Mitzvah was no exception. Perhaps the nickname "David's Harem" for our study group may not have helped Rabbi Goldberg's rabbinical reputation; however, our performance on that day would have provided him with good vindication!

To steady our nerves, Rabbi Goldberg produced a bottle of brandy just before the service started. We are sure the poor 13-year-olds do not receive this welcome assistance! The *shul* was filled to capacity with family, friends, and congregants to share in this milestone. One of the most moving moments was passing the Torah from one to another and knowing that Jewish women in the Progressive Movement can enjoy full religious equality. As our invitation card said, "and the Lord remembered Sarah" we felt truly remembered.

Despite our butterfly stomachs and worries about whether we would remember all the tunes, get tongue-tied in our Hebrew, or slip up in our *parsha*, the service went without a hitch. I delivered the *drash* (the speech about the Torah portion)—the *parsha* was *Shemot*,

Exodus 3, verse 1:20, which is a very well-known story of the Lord appearing to Moses in a thorn bush blazing with fire, yet not being consumed.

After the service, the congregation and guests joined the five of us for a celebratory *Kiddush.* At this point, we did feel like the proverbial 13-year-olds as we were showered with gifts—something none of us expected because we were not of the usual Bat Mitzvah age.

A photo and an article appeared in the following day's national Sunday newspaper, which meant that for weeks afterward friends and work colleagues asked us all about it. For me, it even put me back in touch with a Japanese friend I had lost contact with, who saw the article on a flight from Auckland to Japan.

When Beth Shalom celebrated the fortieth anniversary of the synagogue in 1996, a montage of photos was put together to record the history of the *shul.* Our B'Not Mitzvah was well represented in the photos as being one of the milestone events in Beth Shalom's history.

Since this important occasion, the five of us have all, to varying degrees, participated in synagogue life, with a number being regular lay readers. One of the distinctive things about Beth Shalom is that we have had to make do without rabbis in the past, thus have a well-skilled team of lay readers who can provide *Shabbat* and High Holy Day services. New Zealanders—or "kiwis," as we like to call ourselves—are known for our "do-it-yourself" skills, and a visiting rabbi from Malta once commented that we were a "do-it-yourself" congregation.

We would like to record our deep appreciation to Rabbi David Goldberg for his supervision and leadership in helping us reach this important milestone. We hope that we can inspire other women to achieve Bat Mitzvah later in life—as we have demonstrated, it is never too late.

POSTSCRIPT
by Naomi Johnson

I have been involved with Beth Shalom now for forty years, starting from when I joined Hebrew School as a child. I think I am the "youngest oldest" congregant!

I have served on the board as the honorary secretary and have been on the Ritual Committee. Currently, I am on the Rabbinic Liaison Committee and a lay-reader.

I am also an active member of the Second Generation of Holocaust Survivors Group in Auckland, having joined this group from its inception about seven years ago. I take responsibility for communicating by e-mail with the members of our group, advising of meetings and sending out articles of interest, most of which these days come via the Internet. My father came to New Zealand as a refugee from Berlin in November 1938. He lost both his parents in Auschwitz toward the end of the war. I am currently helping German author Freya Klier to prepare material for her book, which will document the stories of a number of refugees from Europe who settled in New Zealand. Of course, my father's story is included.

How does Judaism fit into my life? Judaism is central to my life, providing a focus and a good way of living. The basic tenets of Judaism lead to a good set of values, which are very relevant to modern life. Being Jewish also provides a good sense of community. Beth Shalom is a very caring community, always willing to cheer with you when things go well and to be supportive when life is not so good. The community certainly cheered with us on the day of our B'Not Mitzvah!

ADDITIONAL MUSINGS

by Helen Levin

As the oldest of the participants and not considering myself terribly academic, I had no thoughts of doing this until Naomi put the idea to me. I agreed, thinking that if it did not work for me, then I could just drop out and no harm would be done. However, once we got started, I got hooked on learning more and, of course, carried through with the idea.

I was born in London on the 23rd of August, 1938, and came to New Zealand on an emigration scheme that was offered back in 1960. The emigration scheme consisted of paying 10 pounds Sterling to the New Zealand, Australian, or Canadian governments and promising to stay for two years, after which time there was no obligation to stay. Anyone wanting to return earlier had to refund the fare money to the New Zealand government. I chose New Zealand, as I remembered listening to a man from New Zealand House coming to our school and telling us how good it was in that country.

My parents, of course, did not want me to go, but at 21 years of age I liked the idea of the adventures that I would experience. We traveled by ship, the *Southern Cross*, a Shaw Savill liner, and had six weeks on the water, stopping at exotic places such as Curacao, Tahiti, and Fiji.

A job had been arranged for me with a company in Christchurch, South Island of New Zealand, as a shorthand typist—no computers in those days. While in Christchurch, I went along to the local synagogue and met the rabbi and his wife. They really took me under their wing and introduced me to their congregants. I was invited to dinner with a great many people.

After about twelve months, I decided to try my luck in Auckland in the North Island. I stayed initially with a doctor and his wife, Harold and Joyce Baker, who were introduced to me by the rabbi in Christchurch. The Bakers took me to a Jewish club that has been defunct now for many years, and there I met my husband, David. David twice attempted to ask me for a date, which I refused because I was baby-sitting and which David thought was a polite brush off. We did eventually get together, though, and after about three months, we decided to marry. It meant, of course, that I would settle in New Zealand, and my parents were none too happy about that situation. My husband is descended from pioneer Jews and is a fifth-generation New Zealander. Things turned out very well for us. We brought up two children, a son and a daughter, and we have a lovely granddaughter. I have been a member of Beth Shalom for a considerable time and served as a board member for the *shul*. I am also the voluntary secretary for our Burial and Benevolent Society (Chevra Kadisha) and have held this position since 1996.

As a side business, David and I run "Shalom Tours," taking Jewish tourists, mostly Americans, on a five-hour tour that includes lunch in our home. We advertise on a web page of the website "Out and About." We love meeting people, and we greet our guests as strangers and they depart like family members.

The Bat Mitzvah was a very happy and fulfilling occasion. We took the Saturday morning service and split up the prayers between the five of us, but the singing was done in unison, as we were all a bit nervous to sing on our own. The Torah portion was also split between the five of us. It worked out well and Rabbi David was a tower of strength to us.

I felt a sense of achievement and pride at the culmination of the service, and since then I now participate regularly as a lay leader with the rabbi. In our congregation, because we are an isolated country, we always have lay readers, as many times we have been without a rabbi and our congregation has many talented people who can keep the services running.

ANOTHER PERSPECTIVE
by Margaret Laurenson

My forebears came from England, Ireland, Austria, and Australia, beginning in 1841. They came to New Zealand, believing they would find a better life. They were pioneers, and life was far from a bed of roses. It was tough, and some of them knew what it was like to be hungry. We honor them today for their spirit, strength of character, and their faith. We, their children, live in such a beautiful country. I am a Jewess by choice. My mother's grandfather was Jewish and married in 1879 in New Zealand. For many years, I wished to know and to return to my roots.

I now live in a rural farming community three hours away from the city of Auckland. I am a county member of Beth Shalom, and as no synagogue is close by, for special events I travel to Beth Shalom. I am semiretired, but work part-time in a security job and a mental health halfway house. My background has been in the nursing field, child residential work, and working with the sick and underprivileged children.

As with everything in life, there is a right time for things to happen. I doubt if I would have done a Bat Mitzvah on my own. I was 52 years old at the time. The opportunity to do it as a group with friends was reassuring and prompted a historical event that might not have happened—plus, we had a rabbi, at that time, who encouraged us and made me feel, "Yes, this is what I want to do."

My mother, relatives, school friends, work colleagues, and clerical friends were all there to support me on this special day. All of my friends were moved by the service: for many of them, it was their first time in a synagogue. We had a *Kiddush* after the service, and the five of us contributed to a very nice luncheon.

The B'Not Mitzvah was part of my spiritual journey, giving me a sense of achievement. I'm glad I had the opportunity to share this precious time in my life with four of my women friends. "I am becoming who I have always been." I'm proud to be Jewish; it is part of my living. "Just as the Lord remembered Sarah," I believe on January 16, 1993, as we stood on holy ground in the sanctuary at Beth Shalom, we, too, were surrounded by the Divine Presence and honored as women.

SOME LAST THOUGHTS
by Diana Hoskyn

I was brought up in a very caring, loving environment, in a family that was and still is very community-minded, but not affiliated to any particular religion. I was always interested in Judaism, even as a youngster. I tried to convert to Judaism in my late teens, but met with closed doors from the Orthodox synagogue. I met my Jewish partner in my late twenties who told me about the Progressive Synagogue in Auckland. One day we found it while jogging. (I belong to the jogging club. We are told that the Auckland Joggers was the first jogging club in the world.)

Julian (my partner) at that point was not affiliated with either Jewish community in Auckland. As a result of my interest and insistence, we started going to Beth Shalom, which was much more welcoming. I started the conversion program about a year later and studied for a good twelve to eighteen months under the guidance of a young American rabbi, Rabbi Edward Rosenthal, who now lives in the United States, and with tutors from the Conversion Committee. That was about 1985.

I have been very active in Beth Shalom over the years. For a long time, I was responsible for the kitchen and used to prepare a light lunch to be eaten after the Saturday service. I served on the board for a few years, and I am still on the board of the burial and benevolent society.

I have attended a number of adult education programs run by Beth Shalom. Once I started my Bat Mitzvah studies, a South African woman, Arlene Weinberg, helped me with my Hebrew. Arlene had lived in Israel and was a great support person for me. I was 39 at the time, and the fact that a group of others wanted to do it presented an opportunity to me. I wouldn't have had the courage to do it by myself.

My family wasn't surprised by my decision to do the B'Not Mitzvah. My father was impressed. My son was so impressed that he

volunteered to videotape the ceremony. My family came on that day and was very proud of me afterward, as I was the first person from my family to become a Bat Mitzvah.

I was so nervous before the ceremony—in fact, I didn't dare have a swig of the brandy that Rabbi David Goldberg offered us prior to the service, for fear that I would forget everything that I knew!

Afterward, I felt a huge sense of relief and a sense of complete belonging to the synagogue because I was now in every way part of Judaism, having completed this major life-cycle event. I felt that I could hold my head up with any other Jew. I have continued my association with Beth Shalom, which is where I belong. I have always felt very, very comfortable with Judaism, which is right for me. My goal in life now is to travel a lot more and to spend time in Israel.

8

SENIOR PROJECT

Kate Stambler—May 31, 1999

While other seniors glide through their fourth quarter, Kate worked harder than ever. No matter how hard she worked during those three months, and no matter how many times she wanted to give up, the tears and the frustration were well worth it. She no longer had to say, "I wish I had . . ." She did it. And she did a good job. She's got the "A" to prove it.

A connection to roots, affirmation of faith, re-dedication to heritage, or just because that's what is expected. There are many reasons for a young woman to become a Bat Mitzvah. But Kate Stambler's impetus was a little different. She became a Bat Mitzvah as her senior AP English Project.

Becoming a Bat Mitzvah was something she had talked about, but never acted upon. She didn't go to Hebrew school when she was younger because she was struggling through school already, and her parents thought that it would add too much stress. It wasn't until junior high school that she started attending BCHSJS, the Bergen County High School of Jewish Studies, which was virtually a Sunday school for high school students. During these classes, she was really turned

on to Judaism. The classes focused on different factors of Jewish culture. There were no tests, outside reading, or homework. It was pure learning for learning's sake and Kate was excited. They learned about Jewish medical ethics, the Holocaust, Yiddish literature, and Jewish history. Over the years, there was some attrition in the number of students; regardless, Kate stayed through high school.

In her senior year, her adviser, Mrs. Susan Dunn, told her about a new program being instituted. Seniors were given the option of doing a senior project in lieu of their last quarter in AP English. The project could be whatever you designed, as long as you put in the designated number of hours and wrote a paper detailing the experience. Kate, always a self-motivated person, jumped at the opportunity.

The original draft of her proposal to the Senior Project Board started out dealing with Jewish medical ethics. But by the time she had talked it all through in her head, she had switched the topic to becoming a Bat Mitzvah. In reality, becoming a Bat Mitzvah was a by-product of the project, because the official proposal was that she would learn to read Hebrew, as well as write a paper on "Light, the Menorah, and Judaism."

The first hitch to this project was proposing it to the board. The board was a very secular group that was unfamiliar with the rite of Bat Mitzvah in general. Kate had to painstakingly describe every detail. Although the board members didn't quite get it, her exuberance came across and they realized that if she thought this much of the project, they'd give her the green light.

The second hitch was that she proposed the idea in February. The project began officially in March and had to be completed by June 1st. Kate had never read Hebrew in her life, and she had three months to learn it all: the Hebrew, the blessings, and the Torah portion.

Kate began with a crash course in learning Hebrew that started with the very basics of the alphabet. It was a self-teaching program that required at least two hours of study each night. Her mom had already taken the course and was able to lend a hand. Next, Kate enlisted the help of the rabbi in her synagogue. Just as the secular board was confused about a project that involved a religious rite, the rabbi was dumfounded by the proposal of a religious rite that was attached to a senior project. However, Kate's enthusiasm was catchy, and he warmed up to the idea. The rabbi taught the *trup* (tune) of the Torah portion and helped with the research for her paper.

With time again being so short, no Saturday mornings were available for her Bat Mitzvah, so they set the date for Monday morning, May 31st—Memorial Day. At 9:00 A.M. that morning, the invited guests, about seventy-five friends and family members, came to celebrate. Kate's one disappointment was that because it was a long holiday weekend, her adviser, who had gone the distance with her, was unable to attend. Wearing her new Bat Mitzvah suit, Kate led all of the prayers and even added a few. Her mom, a music teacher at a nearby Jewish school, sang a song with a friend. Since there is no Haftorah on Monday mornings, Kate read the full *parsha*. She could have just memorized it and recited it. No one would have known. But that's not her way—Kate would have known, so she read every word of it!

Then it was time for her speech. She wanted to combine her love of art history with what she'd learned in the *parsha*. She talked about the menorah and offered an analysis of how light is used and what light represents in Judaism. She also researched menorahs of different eras and locations and emphasized how they took on features of the culture of the country of origin.

Even though this was her senior project, Kate's mom and dad, who had been supportive through the whole thing, got up to say a few words. As of 11:30 A.M. that morning. Kate became a Bat Mitzvah and her senior project was completed just under the wire. Well, almost. Back at school the next day, while turning in her paper, the board asked for an impromptu presentation. Feeling spiritual from the day before, she quoted from Ecclesiastes and told them, "to everything there is a season." And her "time" came during her senior year in high school.

While other seniors glide through their fourth quarter, Kate worked harder than ever. No matter how hard she worked during those three months, and no matter how many times she wanted to give up, the tears and the frustration were well worth it. She no longer had to say, "I wish I had . . ." She did it. And she did a good job. She's got the "A" to prove it.

9

ONE STEP ALONG MY WAY

Eva Metzger Brown, Ph.D.—September 28, 1991
(written by Eva Metzger Brown, Ph.D.)

Ten years later, I can see more clearly than I could when I began my studies where my Bat Mitzvah fits into the progression of my life. More than an end point, it was a beginning that started me on a journey of Jewish study, which continues; it furthered my dream to become a full-fledged writer, communicating thoughts on my experiences, and perhaps teaching along the way; it helped me reconnect with my four grandparents, in four cemeteries, where I laid stones for them from their next generations. It helped turn my professional attention to the study of the impact of war on the next generations; it helped lead me to create, in my living room, a "Holocaust table," where my visa and that of my parents, a photo album of Nuremburg—before and after the war—and more recent articles are displayed. At holiday times, this table is filled with an array of books from which I studied. And when my grandchildren have a question, we go to these books and search together for answers and new questions. I count my blessings.

And when my father died, I said Kaddish for him for he had survived:
He and my mother had survived the Holocaust with one child, a daughter;
And I asked myself, if he had survived with one child, a daughter
It must mean that girl children can say Kaddish;
And so I said Kaddish for him—"in transliteration."
And I wondered what I was saying.
My grandmother had often said to me of German writings, "Read them in the original." That is what she would say to me.
And so one day. a year ago, I listened to her voice and started learning Hebrew and studying texts and studying prayers and studying for my Bat Mitzvah.

I said these words ten years ago on the occasion of my Bat Mitzvah. I was 53 years old. I was a wife, mother of three, new grandmother, daughter, and practicing psychologist. Why had I decided to celebrate my Bat Mitzvah as an adult? Why had I decided to celebrate at this time? There were no expectations from parents, friends, or my community that I do this. There were no guidelines that said, "Now." There had to be additional motivations to the inner voice of my grandmother that told me, 'You are ready to take this on." Today, I offer you, the reader, some thoughts on the questions "Why?" and "Why now?"

As with all people who celebrate their Bar or Bat Mitzvah as adults, mine was based on events that had and had not occurred earlier in my life. In 1950, when I was 12, most young girls did not celebrate their Bat Mitzvah, even though Judith Kaplan, daughter of Rabbi Mordecai Kaplan, had broken the ice by celebrating her Bat Mitzvah in 1922. Instead, young girls got confirmed; I did not get confirmed. Though we felt strongly identified as Jews, my parents were not affiliated with a synagogue, I did not attend Sunday school, and I did not learn Hebrew. There was no practice of Judaism in my home. Instead, the focus was on recovery from the Holocaust. All of my father's energies were directed toward recreating a life that felt financially secure, again; my mother's efforts were directed toward regaining her strength and spirit; I was guided to "fit in," become Americanized. Our time in Europe appeared to have been forgotten.

Only decades later would I put together my Holocaust story. I was born in Nuremberg, Germany, on July 13, 1938: Hitler was in power. On November 9, 1938, *Kristallnacht*, Nazi thugs broke into our apartment and with clubs in hand, smashed everything in sight. Two days later we left for Paris. With the outbreak of war in 1939, the French rounded up all male "foreign aliens," including my father, and sent them to detention camps. My mother and I left Paris for Angers, a smaller—we hoped, safer—town. This did not prove to be the case. In 1940, the Germans bombed Angers while my mother and I were walking in the street; we were both wounded; my mother's left leg was shattered and later amputated. I was stitched up and sent to a Catholic orphanage, while shrapnel in my brain remained undetected. For four months, I was separated from both my parents; I was not yet 2 years old. As France began to fall into the hands of the Nazis, the ever-expanding web of detention camps collapsed. Once freed, my father contacted the French Red Cross and requested that they find my mother and me. Miraculously, we were reunited. The family then made its way toward the Pyrenees, for the ports of Portugal, only to learn that no ships were taking refugees. Retracing their steps, my parents headed back to France and the port of Marseille. There, visas awaited us. Our luck had turned; we had made the American quota. My parents secured passage on one of the last boats to leave France and, finally, we escaped the chaos in Europe for good. On August 6, 1941, we arrived in the United States.

Six million Jews were to die in this war, 1.5 million of these being children. My parents and I had to live with this knowledge; we had to live with the death of my paternal grandmother and my maternal great-grandmother in Theresienstat, we had to live with the loss of generations of family life as my parents had known it; we had to live with a family dispersed on three continents. I had to live with the loss of a childhood, the loss of my first language, and the loss of a Jewish education. Panic had marked the first three years of my life; silence would define the next fifty.

When I was growing up, no one spoke about what I had lived through in Europe—no one in my family, no one in my school, no one on television, no one in the movies, no one in the newspapers. Holocaust museums did not exist; there were no pilgrimages back to Europe to visit the scorched earth of the past and no days commemorating the *Shoah*. I grew up in a world of silence about why things were the way they were and what had happened to my family and to my grandparents. As I remember it—for ten years, at least—there was no talk of things Jewish. Parts of our lives were shut down, in hibernation; parts of myself were shut down, too. I had no words, no feelings that I let surface about "those times"; there was only denial. The denial in my childhood years helped me to adapt to a new world, a new life, but in the long run it hindered me from healing from the psychic wounds of the war.

During my high school years, my parents re-awoke to things Jewish. They learned Hebrew, traveled to Israel often, and joined a Conservative synagogue. But in some ways, it was too late for me; my most formative years for Jewish education were over and Holocaust silences still haunted the family. For many years, my past remained disconnected from my present everyday life. I was busy. I got married, had three children, and completed my doctorate and postgraduate training in psychology—a sign, perhaps, that I was preparing myself for the day when I would investigate my past.

When my children came of nursery-school age, my husband and I joined a synagogue and enrolled them in Sunday school. We shared a wish that they begin their Jewish education early, and with theirs, I began my own. I was not conscious of this at the time, and yet I was aware that as I read Jewish storybooks to my children, I read them also to myself. As my children began preparations for their Bar and Bat Mitzvahs, I read the Torah and the commentaries. As my children learned to chant the traditional melodies, I started to hum the tunes. As I put together Bar and Bat Mitzvah booklets, sequentially, for David, Carolyn, and Michael, I learned the order of the Sabbath service. Yet it never occurred to me that I might study for my own Bat Mitzvah. Looking back, I can see now that certain other things had to happen before I would feel ready to take this step.

When my father died in 1984, I was devastated. He had talked about himself very little; I did not really know him well. Yet I decided to meet with a psychiatrist to try and find the words to make sense of the impact of my father's death on me, my sense of loss, my sense of the many traumatic losses in my life. It took me a long time to share my Holocaust story with him, and when I started to open up, it was not words I found . . . but tears. I thought I would never stop crying; he reassured me that I did not have to. He understood something that I had not allowed myself to feel. He let me know, in not so many words,

that Holocaust losses are worth remembering, worth grieving, and worth working through even decades later. As I began to talk with him about the war and about the years after the war, the walls of silence began to crumble. I began to speak with him from the core of my innermost self, and I began to talk with others, too.

In 1988, I was asked to speak to my Jewish congregation on the occasion of Rosh ha-Shanah. I retold the story of the *Akeda* and I shared how I understood the meaning of the survival of Isaac. Then, I talked publicly for the first time about my own Holocaust survival. The response to my talk was overwhelming. Friends, acquaintances, people I did not even know came into the aisle, as I returned to my seat, to press my hand or give me a hug. I felt overwhelmed; I could have cried, but I did not. However, the experience changed something for me; I saw, I learned, I felt that some people out there were not as afraid of my past as I was and they had the kindness to show me. I had taken the critical step in coming out as a Jew, as a survivor, and as a writer. I had given words to my story and had shared it with others. A year and a half later I began to study for my Bat Mitzvah.

The news that I was to become a grandmother was an additional force pushing me in this direction. I had broken my silence, and I had become aware of what I did not know of Jewish ritual and tradition. Now, with the anticipation of a new life, a new generation, I had an immediate calling: Jewish continuity, the antidote, as I saw it, to the murder of millions of Jews and their next generations. I thought that if I should live long enough for my grandchild to ask me questions about Judaism, I would like to be in the position of having studied and reflected upon the wisdom of the Sages so as to give him, and the ones that might follow, meaningful answers. The steps of Bat Mitzvah preparation struck me as providing a structure and a goal upon which I could do these things and, simultaneously, build up my Jewish education. I became committed; I learned many, many things on my journey, but the most important one was that Judaism is not a religion that directs us to find answers (for our grandchildren) but a religion that transforms us to look for the right questions to ask ourselves about our feelings of faith, the reasons for our existence, and the choices between good and evil in our everyday lives.

My teacher was my rabbi, a woman who had come, the year before, as the first rabbi of our congregation. Her presence was a gift to me at this time in my life. She was a resource who became a friend.

She proved more than willing to share what she knew and loaned me materials to research and understand the deeper meanings of my Torah, *Maftir*, and Haftorah portions. Sukkot is a festival based on the harvest, the ingathering of the peoples from exile, *tzedakah,* peace, joy, and the hope of a better world to come, through actions taken today. What better *parsha* for a Holocaust child survivor than one that celebrates life, faith in an invisible God, and *tikkun olam*.

Generally a late riser, I began to set my alarm for 6:00 A.M., every morning, seven days a week, for a year and a half—during Jewish holidays, on vacations with my husband, and on weekends when family or friends came to visit. Incrementally, I learned to read Hebrew and graduated from humming the tunes to reading the words of the melodies: I made my own Bat Mitzvah booklet and wrote introductory statements for each portion of the service for the benefit of those who were as unfamiliar with the service as I had been; I debated the design of my *tallit*, until I settled on its theme—"life," weaves of eighteen bands of alternating sand-colored threads. My library of Jewish texts and Holocaust memoirs began to grow, with the *Encyclopedia Judaica* becoming a staple of everyday life, as did Holtz's *Finding Our Way* and Greenberg's *The Jewish Way.*

My Bat Mitzvah would be a mix of a traditional service interspersed with memories of the Holocaust. To the *Hallel*, I added personal statements from four women: Anne Frank and Ruth Westheimer, children during the war, who recognized the good in the world despite their own suffering; and Hannah Senesch and Henrietta Szold, who devoted themselves to saving lives, at great expense to themselves. I expanded the *Kaddish* with remembrances of my grandparents, each one buried far away from their partners due to the war's dispersion; and I asked the entire congregation to rise and recite *Kaddish* for their loved ones and for those who no longer had loved ones to say *Kaddish* for them. Despite the threads of mourning and remembrance, my Bat Mitzvah and Bat Mitzvah preparation was a time of great joy for me: joy in learning, joy in connecting with my Jewish historical roots, and joy in solidifying my Jewish sense of self. I had never lost my faith, but now it was better grounded in a foundation of Jewish knowledge.

Before my big day arrived, my rabbi said to me, "You don't want the gifts we give to the children—a *Kiddush* cup, a certificate, do you?" "Oh," I said, "I absolutely do," and we both burst out laughing. She told this story to the congregation as she handed me my *Kiddush*

cup on the *bimah*, and I have had it told many times to me again, with a smile and with an understanding that it does not matter how old you are when you celebrate your Bat Mitzvah, a part of you is still a kid at heart. Next to these, one of my greatest gifts was a letter written to me by one of my children. He said, "I will never forget the first time I sat next to my mother in a synagogue and heard her reading Hebrew and singing the *shirot* with words. . . . I am very proud of you, Mom. It is not because of what you are doing . . . but how you have done it. The ability to hear one's inner voice and then to honor it is a remarkable gift."

As I neared the end of my Bat Mitzvah studies, I asked my Jewish community if I could establish, with my husband, The Children's Fund. In lieu of gifts, I asked that donations be made to fund scholarships for Sunday school tuition, underwrite child care for parents attending services, and subsidize payments for the community's day camp. I had learned the hard way that it is a great loss if you are denied early exposure to things Jewish. I hoped that the fund would change this for some children.

Ten years later, I can see more clearly than I could when I began my studies where my Bat Mitzvah fits into the progression of my life. More than an end point, it was a beginning that started me on a journey of Jewish study, which continues; it furthered my dream to become a full-fledged writer, communicating thoughts on my experiences and perhaps teaching along the way; it helped me reconnect with my four grandparents, in four cemeteries, where I laid stones for them from their next generations. It helped turn my professional attention to the study of the impact of war on the next generations; it helped lead me to create, in my living room, a "Holocaust table," where my visa and that of my parents, a photo album of Nuremburg—before and after the war—and more recent articles are displayed. At holiday times, this table is filled with an array of books from which I studied. And when my grandchildren have a question, we go to these books and search together for answers and new questions. I count my blessings.

I have lived sixty years beyond the Holocaust. I have had the time to redress and repair some of my losses. And I have found that each time I do, the rewards are greater than I ever imagined. For all the reasons I have given for wanting to study for my Bat Mitzvah and all the inhibitions I have had to overcome, I never foresaw the gifts that I would be given: the gift of being heard and feeling embraced, and the gift of a wandering Jew come home—"gathered-in."

Adapted from an unpublished memoir on healing.
Bat Mitzvah on the Intermediate Sabbath of Sukkot-Tishrei 20, 5752.

10

ALEINU

Daniela Ioannides—May 1, 1999

Daniela teaches American Sign Language at Pioneer Valley Performing Arts Charter High School in Hadley, Massachusetts.

When you see Daniela Ioannides surrounded by a group of high school kids, it's hard to distinguish teacher from student. Not only does her pixie appearance belie her age, but she also exudes a warmth and an openness that engages even the most reluctant of students. Daniela teaches American Sign Language in a high school for the performing arts in Hadley, Massachusetts.

It's hard to imagine that this captivating young woman was a scared, sad little girl. Her blue-collar New England Catholic parents had no idea how to raise their only daughter, born deaf (they also have a hearing son), so they settled on a version of benign neglect—heavy on the neglect, not always benign. There was no warmth, no nurturing, no communication. There was, however, lots of criticism. Daniela was always afraid—afraid she would do something wrong to displease them. Afraid that if she did something wrong, they would throw her out of their home. Having no clear set of their expectations, she would incur their wrath repeatedly without understanding her infraction.

Daniela's savior was school. Her parents enrolled her in a residential oral school where deaf students work on their speech, lip reading, and residual hearing skills, in addition to academic subjects. Sign language is forbidden. Daniela arrived in school on Sundays and stayed until Friday afternoons, when she took the dreaded trip back home. During the week, surrounded by her peers and a supportive staff, Daniela thrived. She not only succeeded academically, but also developed a very mischievous side. At school she became famous for her pranks and devilish behavior. And yet on Fridays, she returned home and immediately reverted back to timidity and uncertainty.

Another savior for Daniela was her grandmother, who found it easy to see her granddaughter as she was—a talented young girl, rather than a helpless deaf waif. Daniela looked forward to the times that she would sleep over at her grandparent's house. However, on one of these sleepovers, an event happened that was the beginning of a major life change. Daniela went into the guest bedroom and prepared to go to sleep. Her grandparents, devout Catholics, had hung crucifixes in several rooms. A crucifix hung over the bed where she normally slept. She had slept under it many times, but something was different this time. The figure seemed to be watching her and made her very uncomfortable. She felt very eerie, removed it, and set it on her grandmother's prized possession, the Singer sewing machine.

When Daniela was in middle school, a Jewish classmate brought in a menorah and explained about the holiday of Chanukah. Something was triggered in Daniela. Some deep-down, uncovered, dormant connection was nudged awake. Judaism. A spark was ignited that could not be extinguished. Daniela started to search for information on Judaism, but did so privately. She did not want to set herself up for ridicule or leave herself open for interfering staff and students to try to dissuade her. She learned everything she could about Judaism, and the more she learned, the more she realized that she had finally found the elusive piece to fill that empty space. Not only a place for her to belong, but this was the core of who she was.

When she was 18 years old, before she had even graduated from high school, she set several goals for herself. Even though in her heart she already felt Jewish, she vowed that she would have an official conversion. She would choose a Hebrew name, visit Israel, learn Hebrew, and become a Bat Mitzvah. Although she had set some lofty spiritual goals, her professional goals were somewhat lacking. Without any guidance, this bright young lady was allowed to graduate from high school without any career plans. When the cap and gown were put away, Daniela found herself in the meat department of the local supermarket after several years of doing odd jobs. She managed to slice, wrap, and bag away two more years of her life without any hope of getting out. As it happened, one of her classmates came to visit and brought news of the outside world. He told her about a college in Washington, D.C., that was specifically for deaf people. Daniela had heard of Gallaudet University, but she knew that they used sign language there and she had grown up hearing about the inferiority of communicating with sign language. Her friend told her to be openminded and put her in touch with a counselor from the Office of Vocational Rehabilitation, who helped to get the college application process going. Once again, Daniela did all of this on her own, without any parental support or cooperation. Several years after high school graduation. Daniela enrolled herself at Gallaudet University and got out of the meat department, out of Massachusetts, and out of her grandparents' house. (She had moved out of her parents' house after graduation.)

Gallaudet was a shock. Growing up as an oral deaf person who was bombarded with myths about sign language, she found herself in the middle of her own cultural and linguistic revolution. At first the signs, fingerspelling, and facial expressions were just a blur of activity. Eventually, not only did she understand their meaning, but she was struck by the beauty of the language. It had its own grammar and syntactical structure. Abstractions and shades of meaning could be expressed, sometimes with only a subtle motion. At Gallaudet, she was surrounded by bright young deaf men and women, who—especially in the aftermath of the "Deaf President Now" campaign. when the first deaf president of the university was chosen only after a weeklong student protest—found themselves filled with pride about who they were. Daniela had come "home."

A perk of Gallaudet is its geographic location, Washington, D.C. While pursuing her academic studies, Daniela could pursue her spiritual dreams as well. She found the nearby congregation, Tifereth Israel, and began formal study for her conversion. She studied with the temple's rabbi, and when he felt she was ready, Daniela, with an interpreter, faced the *Bet Din* (Jewish court of law). There, in front of a panel of three rabbis, Daniela successfully answered all of their questions. She next went to the *mikveh* where she immersed to complete the process. Now, one of the downsides of deafness is needing an interpreter to facilitate communication. In most situations, there is no problem, and often the sight of the interpreter is a welcome one. However, a dip in the *mikveh* is an act of ritual purification. It is a time for the individual, in his or her own most natural state, to offer a blessing and prayer to God. There are to be no barriers; therefore, the individual wears no jewelry, scent, bandaids, nail polish, or clothes. A "*mikveh* lady" supervises the process to make sure that all of the person's hair is submerged and that her arms are outstretched without touching the sides. It is not so difficult to reveal yourself in front of the *mikveh* lady, alone, but Daniela arrived with an entourage. This very private person found herself submitting to a very intimate experience in front of the *mikveh* lady, her interpreter, and the *mikveh* lady's 6-year-old son, who came along when his babysitter didn't show up. Nevertheless. Daniela dunked three times and recited the *brachah* and the *tefillah* (prayer). The conversion was complete, but the metamorphosis had just begun.

She needed to complete the package. Newly converted, she wanted to indeed become a "daughter of the commandments." She joined an adult Bat Mitzvah class, once again at Tifereth Israel. There were seventeen women in the class, participating for a myriad of reasons. Three of them were deaf. They met twice a month for almost two years and studied basic Judaism, theology, Torah study, and Jewish feminism. Their teachers, Madeline Nesse and Cynthia Peterham, personalized the study by encouraging the woman to choose which areas and customs they would adopt into their new conservative lifestyle —which traditions fit with who they were and what customs were most meaningful.

During these discussions, she realized that she needed a name. The name her parents had given her no longer fit. She picked the first name, Daniela, because it means, "judged by God." The last name,

Ioannides, was her grandfather's last name. He and her grandmother had always been supportive, but there was more to it. When her grandfather, a Greek immigrant, had arrived in the United States, he faced the same prejudice that many new arrivals feel when they first enter the country. In order to "fit in" or assimilate, he changed his family name to a more American name. Finding her own way and not looking to "fit in," Daniela took back her grandfather's name. She took the name as a symbol of changing into a new path in which she would mold her life with her own desires and free will.

During the process of its study, the large class attacked the logistics of dividing up the service. The deaf women had to decide how they would approach their parts, what mode of communication would work most effectively. The three decided they would recite their Torah readings in spoken Hebrew. For the two prayers that Daniela would lead, she would do so with American Sign Language, enlisting the sign language interpreter to voice those parts out loud.

On the morning of May 1, 1999, the seventeen women, in an array of finery that included multicolored *tallit*, *kipot*, and hats approached the *bimah*. With some trepidation, they took turns coming forward to sing, chant, or recite their assigned parts. Daniela's first part was the signing of *Ahavah Rabah*, which is a prayer that talks about God's love for the Jewish people. During the Torah reading, Daniela came forward and recited her *aliyah* in spoken Hebrew. Near the end of the service, Daniela led the next-to-last prayer, the *Aleinu*, signed with the fingertips of both hands resting on one shoulder—translated loosely as "responsibility." *Aleinu* impresses on the Jewish people their responsibility for praising God for His singling us out and making us special. Daniela stood proudly, eyes shining, beckoning the congregation to join her in their united responsibility of thanking the Almighty.

It was a very public prayer from a very private woman, expressing more than just words on a *Shabbat* morning. They were words of thanks from a woman who takes her "responsibility" quite seriously. From a sleepy New England town, via a long journey, Daniela Ioannides claims her right to be counted among the singled out and the special. She searched, studied, and accomplished goals that she set a long time ago. She is not complacent, however, and strives to learn more and more. From a spark that was ignited in a middle-school girl, a flame burns brightly in the woman she became. She feels a deep love of Judaism, a strong sense of connection to her roots, and a desire to share and inspire other Jewish deaf women to achieve more as Jews. When Michelangelo looked at a block of granite, before he ever applied his chisel, he could envision the statue of David that he would carve. By virtue of her birth, Daniela was like that smooth, untouched block of stone. But her exploration, examination, and education enabled her to emerge as the person she was meant to be.

11

SUNSHINE

Carrie Linden—November 30, 1991
(written by Carrie Linden)

Photo by Mark Rychel

We found a school in Cape Cod called Riverview/G.R.O.W. that is a post-secondary school. I learned skills on how to be independent. Then I went to school in Cambridge, Massachusetts, Lesley College/Threshold Program. There I am learning the skills I need for a job—Human Services, Early Childhood and Business Services. I took Current Events. That was a good, important class. I thought Adult Sexuality was good because I learned about the woman's and man's bodies. I also took a course called Medical World, which was important to learn to be in good health. I will finish my class work this year and next year will have a practicum and get on-the-job experience. I hope to get a job working in an office. I like Boston, but when I graduate, I will move back home to Ohio.

The story of my Bat Mitzvah is very special. But before I tell you that, I'd like to tell you a little about myself. I have Down's syndrome and it took me longer to learn things. My speech was not clear and I had to work very hard to speak clearly. I like learning new words. I remember looking at pictures and seeing if I could define what the picture was. I did that when I was about 4. Ever since kindergarten. I have been in a regular class. I remember liking elementary school. In second grade, Ms. Ashmun's husband was coming to school to play his guitar. Even though I was sick, I went to hear him sing "For the Longest Time" by Billy Joel, who became my favorite singer. I still love that song.

My favorite thing was doing puzzles when I was young (like 2). I started with 5-piece puzzles and now can do up to 1,000, but it's fun to do them with someone else. I collected stones, stickers, bouncing balls, and seashells. I started ice-skating when I was 8. I played the piano for thirteen years. I tried to get good, but it didn't work. I still like playing the piano, but I'm not as good anymore. I like to try lots of things.

I had a problem with going fast. Most of the teachers were willing to work with me. In the fourth grade we learned a unit on the Vikings. I was very interested and learned a lot. When I took the test, I didn't do well. The next morning my mom and I went to school early to talk to the teacher. The teacher asked me questions about the Vikings, and I could answer every one of them. I just couldn't always answer them the way they were written on the test.

I have two sisters, Kimberly, age 20, and Courtney, age 18. They play a big role in my life because they are my sisters and they both follow in my footsteps. No matter what, my sisters are always there for me when I need them. I like being the oldest. I have to do more things around the house. My parents count on me. I've taken on doing laundry, getting dinner ready sometimes, and cleaning up the house.

My Bat Mitzvah was at B'nai Jeshurun on Fairmount Road, Pepper Pike, Ohio. When I first studied for my Bat Mitzvah, the teacher had given me only a small part to learn. I kept telling people that I could do more, and I did. I wore a white suit in the morning and there were flowers on the *bimah.* I did most of the service by myself. My *parsha* was *Vayera*, and I chanted the *Maftir* and the Haftorah. It's important to read it perfectly and I did. My parents read Torah at my Bat Mitzvah. It was a big deal for my mom because she never did that before. I made a speech and talked about school and my classes. The rabbi's sermon was the story of my Haftorah and *parsha* and what it meant. At the end he talked about my relationship to my family and the people of the congregation.

I didn't feel nervous at all. I felt very proud of myself that I could learn all the things I did at my Bat Mitzvah. I felt really good about it all and felt very confident in myself for doing it. My friends were all at my Bat Mitzvah. Their Bat Mitzvahs were similar to mine, except

theirs were at different temples, but the same year as mine. They just came and danced. I remember getting some outstanding gifts, like jewelry, which was my favorite. I wasn't really hoping for anything that didn't come because I loved all the things I got.

The expectations I had once I had my Bat Mitzvah were that I had to take on more responsibilities around the house. I also had to become more of an adult and take care of my family and do more chores than usual, like the chores I did before I became a Bat Mitzvah and an adult. At my sisters' Bat Mitzvahs, they did most of the service, as I did at mine. And just like my parents read Torah at my Bat Mitzvah, I read Torah at both of my sisters' Bat Mitzvahs. My advice to anyone becoming a Bar or Bat Mitzvah is to try your hardest, try your best. That's good enough for me.

Every summer I go to the Tikveh program of Camp Ramah in Canada. A few years ago, one of the boys in our program, Brian David, had his Bar Mitzvah in front of the whole camp—600 people! All of the Tikveh campers helped Brian through the service, joining in the singing of the prayers. Brian said the *brachah*, and I read the entire Torah portion at his Bar Mitzvah. At my temple, I am often asked to read from the Torah.

I have always been small, 4'6" and it's funny because my date for the prom was 6'4"! We had a great time at the pre-prom and the post-prom parties and didn't get home until 4:00 in the morning. My mother and father had to wait up to drive us home. When I was a senior in high school, I prepared for a job after graduation. My sister Kimberly is one year younger. My mom was taking her to a college fair and I asked to go along. When I saw all the programs that were available, I told my mom that I wanted to go to college.

Oh, I forgot to tell you the best part about my Bat Mitzvah. The rabbi called me the nickname "Sunshine" and near the end of the service he said, "if you are part of Carrie's family, please stand up to do the special prayer *Shehechiyanu*." Everybody in the congregation stood up! It was special. We loved it.

12

EIM B'ISRAEL

Mothers in Israel—April 16, 1999

Photo courtesy of The Baycrest Centre

Even though the "official" part of the program was over, the group continued to meet once a month for the following year. With the age range of the participating residents being from 86 to 94, the group felt fortunate that everyone survived the program, in spite of several illnesses. However, a year after the Bat Mitzvah, two of the seniors and one W.A. member died.

One of the final speeches at the Bat Mitzvah ceremony was delivered by Edith Kursbatt, a very distinguished-looking 85-year-old with an elegant English accent. She concluded her comments with an announcement that her great-granddaughter would have her Bat Mitzvah the next day. Great-grandmother and great-granddaughter were celebrating their year of study and hard work one day and seventy-three years apart! Unfortunately, due to the distance, Mrs. Kursbatt was unable to attend. However, in spirit, she would join her daughter and granddaughter as they placed their hands on the head of this young woman, the next generation, their future, our future, and they recited together, "May God make you like Sarah, Rebecca, Rachel, and Leah . . ."

May God make you like Sarah, Rebecca, Rachel, and Leah.
May Hashem bless you and safeguard you.
May Hashem illuminate His countenance for you and be gracious to you.
*May Hashem turn His countenance and establish peace for you.**

On the eve of *Shabbat*, it is customary for parents, upon returning from the synagogue, to bless their children. For male children, the role models are Ephraim and Menashe, Joseph's children. And when the female children are blessed, we ask God to make them like our Matriarchs, Sarah, Rebecca, Rachel, and Leah. With this blessing, we ask God to bestow on our daughters, whether young or old, the strength, devotion, humor, patience, and unconditional love demonstrated by these beloved four women.

The study of our Matriarchs, with the culmination of a very unusual Bat Mitzvah ceremony, took place in Toronto, Canada. There was a joint program between the Women's Auxiliary and residents of the Terrace, a seniors' apartment complex at the Baycrest Centre of Geriatric Care. Modeled after a Bat Mitzvah program that originated in Montreal in a seniors' facility, the aim of the program was to provide the opportunity to enhance a specific learning experience related to spiritual growth and a deeper understanding of the Torah. A six-month program, incorporating weekly instruction, was set once they had the commitment of ten W.A. (Women's Auxiliary) members and ten residents.

The selection process of the senior residents was assigned to a therapeutic recreationist, Bobbie Cohen. Bobbie's initial role was to interview ladies from the Terrace whom she thought might be interested in such a program. She created an initial list of thirty women with the input from three of the social workers in the department. Criteria were established for participation: no extended holidays, the ability to learn new things, comprehension of the English language, the ability to do "homework," and naturally, an interest in this religious learning experience.

Several women declined immediately, others wanted time to "think it over," and several were immediately thrilled with the idea. Some of the concerns raised were: "I'm too old to learn"; "How much Hebrew do I need to know?"; "I'm not sure I could do this." Having the advantage of really knowing these ladies well, Bobbie knew who could handle the program, enjoy the process, and come out richer spiritually, while feeling deeply accomplished.

*The translation for the parental blessing is from *The Complete Art Scroll Siddur*, a new translation and commentary by Rabbi Nosson Scherman, Mesorah Publications, Ltd., 1984, page 355.

Before the senior group of ten made its final commitment, Bobbie arranged for a meeting with the instructor to answer people's concerns and to alleviate some of their anxiety regarding the amount of Hebrew required. The instructor, Dr. Rachel Turkiencz, director of Judaic Studies at Toronto Heschel School, met with the group members to respond to their very appropriate and relevant questions. They wanted a course outline. In addition, they wanted to know what Rachel expected from them and how she anticipated the interaction between the two groups. This meeting was a huge success and everyone "signed on."

The program started in October 1998 and was held once a week for an hour. The first meeting was simply an opportunity for the two groups to meet and introduce themselves. As it happened, the session was quite moving, as every woman introduced herself and gave her personal reason for being part of this special program. Several of the women were Holocaust survivors or daughters of survivors. Others came from Orthodox backgrounds, where there was no consideration of a Bat Mitzvah. Whereas, for others, it was a matter of economics—there simply hadn't been enough money to celebrate their daughters coming of age.

During the second meeting, "buddies" were chosen through a democratic process. The names of the ten W.A. ladies were placed in a basket and every Terrace resident picked a partner. It took time for the buddies to really come together. The Terrace residents weren't sure what to do with the W.A. ladies, and the W.A. ladies weren't sure how to act with the residents. This intergenerational program was more difficult initially for the younger women. The end result was that most of them treated the seniors as their mothers.

As the program progressed, the interest level and the commitment level increased from both parties. For many, the relationship extended beyond their study sessions, and the W.A. ladies invited their partners out to lunch and on shopping trips.

The course outline had the women examine in depth the four Matriarchs. The instructor provided large-print copies of the text that were read through and discussed at length, sometimes line by line. Rachel's teaching style involved thought-provoking methods that provided new insights into old familiar biblical stories. Personal interpretations and personal life experiences (mostly by the residents) were interjected. During these discussions and personal disclosures, the

group bonded and often the W.A. ladies couldn't believe the depth of questions and the sage perspectives from the seniors. Most of the residents would return to their apartments after each class and read the Torah. So many awakenings were occurring for them that each week they couldn't wait to get together. As the end of the six months neared and the Bat Mitzvah/graduation ceremony approached, anxiety levels increased. The format for the ceremony was that each participant would choose a Matriarch whom she most identified with and explain the reasons why. With so many in the group, each member was given a time limit of three minutes.

On the day of the ceremony, Friday, April 16, 1999, each woman was called to the Torah by her Hebrew name and the names of her parents. She was accompanied by her study partner, who remained with her during the presentation. Each participant first read the *brachah* before the Torah portion. That portion was then sung out by the *Ba'alat Korei* (Torah reader), Hanna Lockshin. The reading of the Hebrew was followed by each woman's personal commentary. Their perspectives were colored by time and experience. Some of the women who had left Europe and moved to this strange new land found their connection to Rebecca. Many of the women identified with Rachel (our Matriarch) as a devoted mother. Bobbie Cohen, who was first involved with the selection process, became an enthusiastic member of the "junior" group. She felt herself very drawn to the first Matriarch, Sarah:

> Of the four Matriarchs that we discussed from the Book of Genesis, I identify most with Sarah.
>
> As I stand before you today, it is obvious that I am expecting a baby. But, like Sarah, I thought that this would never happen for me. Years passed, doctors said that it would be highly unlikely, and my hopes vanished. Although I didn't travel through the land, I did travel through career and professional challenges.
>
> Just as I felt my life finally come together and with the acceptance of being childless, this wonderful miracle happened that has so affected my life thus far and will continue to do so. Like Sarah, I laughed inside myself with disbelief upon hearing the news.
>
> These past many months, being involved in this very special program has given me both spiritual and personal insight and growth. It has brought women of different gen-

> erations together not only to learn from the Torah, but also from and with each other. Many new friendships have developed, as well as a better understanding of each other.
>
> I feel truly blessed.

Bea Elkind, one of the senior members, was inspired by Sarah but for different reasons:

> The significance of Sarah giving birth at the age of 90 is a lesson to all of us that age does not prevent us from fulfilling our ambitions. Now in my senior years, together with my class, I have embarked on a whole New World, the study of Torah. Our age is an advantage for we can view Sarah's life with maturity not available to most teenagers. In our senior years like Sarah, we have had to make many adjustments and decisions. There are many beginnings. Just coming to share this wonderful community at the Terrace is yet another beginning. Watching our children and grandchildren as they make their way reminds us of the many times we, too, made many changes.
>
> Sarah's aging beauty is our aging beauty, and like Sarah we will hold to the belief that God will provide us with the strength to see our visions come true.
>
> May we go from strength to strength.

The ceremony was a huge event held at the Baycrest Centre. Each participant was allowed to invite 10 guests. Over 300 people filled the Terrace dining room! Everyone in attendance was moved by the profound and personal nature of the interpretations of the Torah stories. With their insight, these 20 women brought our Matriarchs to life. Following the formal presentations, they all shared in a celebratory meal.

One of the final speeches at the Bat Mitzvah ceremony was delivered by Edith Kursbatt, a very distinguished-looking 85 year old with an elegant English accent. She concluded her comments with an announcement that her great-granddaughter would have her Bat Mitzvah the next day. Great-grandmother and great-granddaughter were celebrating their year of study and hard work one day and seventy-three years apart! Unfortunately, due to the distance, Mrs. Kursbatt was unable to attend. However in spirit, she would join her daughter and granddaughter as they placed their hands on the head of

this young woman, the next generation, their future, our future, and they recited together, "May God make you like Sarah, Rebecca, Rachel, and Leah. . ."

13

SUCH A LOT OF FLOWERS

Stephanie Scibilia—May 24, 1997

When Stephanie graduates from high school, she hopes to pursue a career in botany. She's had plenty of experience irrigating and fertilizing her family's crops. But she learned other, more far-reaching, lessons on the farm. She learned how important it is to help others. When times are rough, you have to be there. And when things go wrong with farming, you need to be creative to preserve the business.

God created the Heavens and the Earth in six days and rested on the seventh, establishing the Sabbath as a day of rest. People look forward to that day of rest and rejuvenation, a time to separate the mundane from the holy. In *parsha Behar*, in the Book of Leviticus, God commanded that the land should be worked for six years, and in the seventh year the land, too, has a Sabbath, time off. This *parsha* was very appropriate as the Bat Mitzvah portion for Stephanie Scibilia, who knows firsthand what it is like to work the land. She and her family own, work, and live on a farm in New Jersey.

It was not atypical to find Jewish farmers in New Jersey. There used to be many, but they were egg farmers; they didn't work the land.

Stephanie has never seen any conflict between being Jewish and living on a farm. She feels a close relationship with our ancestors who lived off the land. She also feels a bond with modern-day Israel, since horticulture there is carried out actively and creatively, yielding lush vegetation that sprouts in the desert. In fact, the watering system known as "trickle irrigation" that the Scibilias use on their farm was developed in Israel.

Growing up on a farm has afforded Stephanie many benefits. The obvious advantage is feeling part of and appreciating nature. Since she and her sisters and brother started doing chores when they were very young, she learned responsibility early. When she was only 5, she didn't realize that she was "working"; she just thought she was having fun. She would pick fruits and vegetables alongside the migrant workers. As she got older, one of her jobs was to watch the stand, so she learned how to deal with money and her overall math skills developed quickly. She's also had an education in retailing. Stephanie has learned to be creative when selling their products. Always be friendly and the customer is always right!

"Whistle Stop Flowers and Farm" recently underwent a transformation. Formerly a vegetable farm, it now grows flowers almost exclusively. Being surrounded by a rainbow of colors has not diminished Stephanie's enthusiasm for flowers. She finds them not only beautiful, but also interesting. She grew up watching her father cultivate plants and was always amazed that so many varieties could yield from one species. When she wasn't working, she loved to take nature walks around the farm and just "observe" things. She has different work for different seasons. In the early spring she helps with planting the seeds and transplanting the crops as they grow. On weekends and in the summertime, she is a cashier at the farm's stand. And she is also busy in the early winter, because the farm grows and sells Christmas trees. In spite of working and playing field hockey in the fall and lacrosse in the spring, Stephanie is a straight-A student.

When it was time for Stephanie's Bat Mitzvah, she wanted something really big—but not a big party with extravagant, "showy" glitz. She likes being different, so she decided that she would read the whole Torah portion, because that was out of the norm for a Bat Mitzvah being called to the Torah for the first time. And with her sister Adrian's assistance, the two of them led the entire service. She wasn't nervous at all. She felt calm and confident. She wanted to stand out. The *parsha* was so appropriate; it was all about nature and agriculture. In her speech, she compared what she had just read to her life on the farm. How you have to respect the soil and take care of it. How her family followed the land and rotated the crops. She ended the speech with the thought that if you take care of anything, it will take care of you.

In keeping with her idea of doing something different, rather than decorating the *bimah* with flowers, she donated two four-foot trees that adorned the synagogue on the morning of the Bat Mitzvah. The trees were later planted in the local Jewish cemetery. The *bimah* was not completely without color. Stephanie's dress was covered with flowers and her *tallis* had been hand-painted in Jerusalem.

Although Stephanie had to learn the hard knocks of the farming industry, she has reaped the benefits by being surrounded by the best of nature's beauty. Flowers are meaningful. They are not only important to the atmosphere; they add life and color to the world. They're also symbolic. Red roses mean love, yellow ones are for friendship, daisies are happy, and others even represent sadness and death.

Modern-day agriculturists know the importance not only of rotating crops, but also of giving the land a "rest." Soil conservation is an ecologically sound practice. And interestingly enough, thousands of years ago in the Torah we were commanded to work the land for six years and let it rest on the seventh. The commentaries tell us this is more than "environmentally friendly" behavior. We are commanded to do this so that we will realize that God is Master of the Universe. It's a reminder that we really never "own the land." As a precious gift, however, it is ours to take good care of, and in turn, the land will take care of us.

14

THE BAMBOO CRADLE

Devorah Schwartzbaum Goldstein—May 1984

This story is a summary of the book entitled The Bamboo Cradle, *written by Avraham Schwartzbaum, published by Feldheim Publishers, Jerusalem/ New York, 1988, used with permission of the author and the publisher. Devorah Schwartzbaum Goldstein is married, lives in Baltimore, and, Baruch Hashem, has six children.*

Photo courtesy of Avraham Schwartzbaum

In the early 1970s Allan Schwartzbaum was a visiting American professor on a Fulbright Scholarship to the Republic of China. He held part-time positions in three universities, teaching sociology and industrial relations. Every Thursday at 5:45 A.M., he left the quaint hilltop quarters that he and his wife, Barbara, occupied in Tamsui, in order to catch a train to central Taiwan. He enjoyed sharing the ride with the many school children who were on their way to school. Although he smiled when he heard their laughter and watched their antics, he also felt a tinge of melancholy because they brought home his own situation. Married for seven years, he and Barbara shared an interesting and varied life, but, with the absence of children of their own, were not completely fulfilled.

One Thursday in the train station, Schwartzbaum purchased his ticket and was heading toward his gate when he noticed a small red parcel on a vacant bench. As he approached, he saw movement and tiny dark eyes met his own. He gently picked up the baby and a note fell to the ground. It read: "Whoever finds this baby—watch over her with kindness and compassion, and fortune will share your way." As a stranger in a strange land, he felt compelled to turn her over to the authorities, but also made sure he found out where she was taken.

When he returned home that evening, he shared the remarkable tale with Barbara, who listened with tears in her eyes. As they looked at each other, she spoke, mirroring her husband's thoughts, "We'll go to the orphanage first thing tomorrow morning."

When they arrived at the address they'd been given, they were surprised to see that it was a church. On the second floor, they opened a heavy door and found themselves facing rows of old-fashioned metal cribs, filled with crying infants. No caretakers were in sight. When someone finally entered, they asked about the baby who had been found in the train station. The little one was located, and Barbara and Allan realized that it was now up to them to make a monetary offer for her. Allan had $25 U.S. that he offered as a "down payment," with the promise of $200 more. He signed a paper, listing the amount of the forthcoming "contribution." Before release into the care of the Schwartzbaums, the tiny infant was given the name Wen Yu-Bing, meaning "Jade Ice." With the naming completed and fearing that the orphanage caretakers would change their minds, Barbara and Allan left in a hurry with their new daughter. Barbara vowed, as they jumped into a cab, that she would never again use the cold name provided by the orphanage.

Most couples have nine months not only to get used to the idea of becoming parents, but also for preparations. Even adoptive parents, during the interview stages, have time to get ready for their new children. Caught up in the moment, Allan and Barbara arrived home flushed with excitement, only to realize that now that they had a baby, they had none of the basics for a newborn. Their housekeeper, Mei-Mei, took over and while doling out sage Chinese proverbs, she went about rounding up the neighbors and collecting the necessities. Before long, baby clothes, diapers, bottles, and a bamboo cradle appeared in

their home. That evening, they bestowed a proper name to fit their beautiful new daughter, "Hsin-Mei"—which means "my heart is in China."

Although bringing Hsin-Mei to their Taiwan home was an unbelievably simple process, arranging to take her "home," back to the United States, became a tangle of red tape and cultural politics. Allan's grant would run out in a few months' time, and they were planning to leave for the States. Following what they thought was the correct protocol for arranging for their daughter's visa, they kept hitting brick walls. It wasn't until Mei-Mei reminded them gently of China's "favor economy" and encouraged them, with all of their contacts, to locate someone to intervene for them that a path opened. At the "eleventh hour," a visa was awarded and the Schwartzbaums, now three, boarded a plane for New York.

Both Barbara and Allan had been raised in culturally Jewish homes and, although not particularly observant, had strong positive feelings about being Jewish. They both had received a very basic Jewish primary education, consisting, for Allan, mostly of after-school preparation for his Bar Mitzvah and for Barbara, a cursory study of language and Jewish history. Back in the States, they realized that because of Hsin-Mei's racial features, people would always question her Jewishness. They decided to investigate what was involved with the conversion process for their baby. They started their inquiries with an Orthodox rabbi. The rabbi started with the straightforward logistics of the conversion process itself. It must be done with the approval and in the presence of a *Beit Din*, a rabbinical court comprised of three qualified men. Male children must be circumcised by a competent *mohel* and then immersed in the *mikveh*. Female children also require immersion in the *mikveh* (ritual bath).

Although the process sounded simple enough, the rabbi continued. "The conversion of a non-Jewish child is a complicated issue in Jewish law. To begin with the basic requirement is that the candidate for conversion obligate himself or herself to perform all the *mitzvos*. A child before the age of maturity is halachically (according to Jewish law) incompetent to make such a commitment." He added that he felt it was wrong, therefore, to convert a child knowing that she was being raised in an environment where the *mitzvos* were not followed, where the Sabbath was not observed, and the other precepts of the Torah were disregarded. He concluded, "If you and your wife wish to study and develop your home into one based on Torah principles, then we can take up the question of conversion again." Allan shook the rabbi's hand; he and Barbara thanked him for his time and left the office.

They decided that the next stop would be a visit to the Conservative rabbi. The story they heard in the rabbi's lavish oak-paneled study was quite different. All that was involved for Hsin-Mei's conversion was the completion of several forms, and if the parents wanted, the baby could take a dip in the swimming pool at the Jewish Community Center, which would serve as her ritual immersion.

Their third stop was to the Progressive congregation that they had visited once before on the High Holidays. The rabbi met them in the Quaker Church that his congregation shared until its building fund expanded. He was glad to discuss the conversion. He suggested that the parents prepare a presentation in their own words, perhaps including some slides of China, together with musical tapes. He also mentioned that he would try to find a Hebrew name that synthesized their daughter's Chinese and Jewish identities. When Allan and Barbara asked about the necessity of the *mikveh*, the rabbi told them that he never imposes that demand. On their way out, the Schwartzbaums questioned each other on the relevancy of slides of China to a commitment to Judaism.

Their investigation led to answers that described three completely different processes for what is involved in the conversion of their daughter. And so they remained as they started—two Jewish parents with a non-Jewish Chinese daughter. The weeks passed into months and the months into years. They remained unaffiliated, but attended special events at the Jewish Community Center and local synagogues. Much of their life revolved around the university and the local Chinese community. Their home became an open house for Chinese students studying at nearby universities and colleges. On a fortuitous encounter, Allan met the principal of the Hebrew Day School, who invited the Schwartzbaums to spend Shabbos with him and his family.

From that time on, they spent one *Shabbos* a month as guests of one of the Orthodox families in the community. With each visit, they learned some new practice that they then incorporated into their own observance of *Shabbos*. Slowly, their celebration of the Sabbath grew, with Barbara now baking her own challah and Allan reciting the *Kiddish* and walking the 3½ miles to the synagogue. They heard that

a new rabbi, one who had been ordained at Yeshiva University, had just moved to town and that he had a very "open outlook." Barbara and Allan arranged a meeting and once again broached the subject of conversion for Hsin-Mei. Rabbi Fried got right to the point: "As far as I am concerned, there are four mandatory criteria: you must keep the Sabbath, you must follow the laws of *kashrus* (keeping kosher), you must observe the requirements of family purity in your married life, and you must agree to provide your daughter with the best Jewish education available in the community." Allan asked, "What about the other 600-plus mitzvos in the Torah?" The rabbi answered succinctly, "Once you start to observe the four criteria, they will pull the other mitzvos into your life."

Without hesitation, Barbara said she was willing to study and learn about these laws. Her husband echoed her sentiments. Rabbi Fried sent them home with a set of books to read and study and the promise of a home visit to help them in converting their kitchen into a kosher one. He also arranged to meet them at the local supermarket and, step by step, go down the aisles and point out various categories of kosher food. Barbara started studying the laws of family purity with the rabbi's wife and, over time, they began living an Orthodox lifestyle.

Four months later, Rabbi Fried agreed to organize a religious court for Hsin-Mei's conversion. Allan was given permission to go into the *mikveh* with her, since the water was over her head. Hsin-Mei disrobed and her father held her hand gently. They descended the steps into the *mikveh*. Allan held his daughter and explained that she would dunk herself three times and that there was nothing to be afraid of. She looked up at him with trusting eyes and after each immersion was caught by the strong hands of her father.

When they left the *mikveh*, they were handed an official letter that attested to the immersion in a kosher *mikveh*, welcomed Hsin-Mei as "our own daughter," and declared to her "Blessed God, the father of Abraham, our father, guide her that she may follow and walk in your path. Amen." Ten days later, Hsin-Mei, now Devorah, turned 4, and eleven months later, Devorah's mother gave birth to her first son, Dov Chaim.

Allan Schwartzbaum said, "There is no doubt in my mind that the apparent miracle of Dov Chaim's birth, after twelve years of childlessness, was a direct outcome of my discovery of Devorah. Had I not found her, it is probable that Barbara and I would have continued as we were until the end of our days, because the fact is that we were not dissatisfied with our existence, we were not searching for our identity, we did not feel unfulfilled, except with respect to raising a family. But had we adopted a Jewish baby instead of a Chinese one, it is doubtful that we would have embarked on the long road to finding our heritage."

The birth of Dov Chaim was followed over the next few years by the births of his brothers, Dahveed, Shmuel, and Yehudah. The family moved for a while back to Taiwan so that Allan and Barbara could continue their academic pursuits. They then arranged for a sabbatical in Jerusalem. It wasn't until the sabbatical was over and they returned to the United States that they realized how much they wanted and needed to be back in Israel. A position became available at the State University of New York that had a branch in Jerusalem, Israel.

They arrived in January 1983 at the Ben Gurion Airport and this time, rather than visitors, they were immigrants. On all of the necessary paperwork, their names were recorded as Avraham and Rochel Schwarzbaum.

They were now settled in Israel, and it was less than a year before Devorah's Bat Mitzvah. Her parents recognized that this was an important milestone for her, perhaps more so than for other Jewish girls. She had been converted as a child of 4, and obviously did not make the decision independently. Now, coming of age halachically (according to Jewish law), Devorah would have a chance to make the decision on her own. Avraham had many questions related to the conversion and the need for "re-affirmation" at this time. They consulted a noted authority.

Rabbi Shlomo Zalman Auerbach responded to all of Avraham's questions with the following: "If a child has been continuously engaged in keeping *mitzvos* since conversion, there is no need to do anything special. If on the 12th birthday, plus one day, in the case of a girl, the child, aware that she was converted and with the option of rejecting Judaism, nevertheless continues in the usual manner to be *shomer mitzvos* (observe the commandments), the conversion becomes complete and permanent. There is no need for verbal declaration; there is no need for witnesses. If the individual wishes to make an affirmation, that is acceptable, but not required by *halachah* (Jewish law)."

As the time of Devorah's Bat Mitzvah drew near, Rochel and Allan realized that they wanted to share the *simcha* (happy occasion) with their parents. Since the trip was too difficult for their parents to undertake, the Schwartzbaums traveled en masse to Florida one week before Devorah's birthday. The celebration was to take place in the Jewish senior citizens' apartment complex in Orlando. Friends and neighbors of the elder Mrs. Schwartzbaum came out, Rochel's parents flew down from New York, and several other relatives flew in for the occasion. Everyone gathered in the main auditorium of the complex. The room became quiet as Devorah moved to the stage and addressed the assembled:

> Often when someone becomes a Bas or Bar Mitzvah, they travel to Israel to commemorate the event. I have come from Israel to Florida so that I could be with my grandparents who, along with my parents, have helped and guided me through my first twelve years.
>
> For every Jewish girl, turning 12 is something special; it's something every Jewish girl looks forward to. But because I was adopted and converted as a small child, becoming 12 is extra special. In my case, I am able to decide whether or not I want to remain Jewish. I can make my own decision. My parents told me when I was young that when I turned 12 I would have to make this decision on my own. I remember when I was small and wanted to get back at my parents for not letting me have my own way, I would yell, I'm not going to stay Jewish when I'm 12, just because of you!"
>
> Well, that time has finally come, and I don't even have to think about my decision. I want to remain Jewish. I can't think of any other way of life. I feel a special "*kesher,*" a connection with *b'nei Yisroel* (the children of Israel). When the Festivals come, I grow excited. On *Shabbos*, I feel different. On Rosh Hashanah and Yom Kippur, I daven (pray) to Hashem (God) and beg him to accept my *teshuvah* (repentance). I'm proud to be part of the *klal Yisroel* (the Jewish people). Just like Ruth said to Naomi: "Your people are my people, your God is my God."
>
> We live in confusing times. There are many things which make it hard to remain a strong Jew with *emunah* (spirit—true heart) in Hashem. I want to thank my parents again for being the strong, understanding people they are. I

> thank Hashem every day for delivering me to such wonderful, special people. They have always tried to show me the right way, the Torah way. It's impossible for any of us to know what the future holds, but I would like to make one promise to my family: I will never forget who I am—a Jew, a *cheilek* of *klal Yisroel*, a part of the Jewish people.

This story, with beginnings in a distant land, describes a journey that involves much more than crossing a geographic distance. Avraham Schwartzbaum elaborates on their spiritual voyage:

> The bamboo cradle that gently rocked our tiny Chinese daughter to sleep came to symbolize our own beginnings in the discovery of our heritage. In the land where bamboo fields whisper echoes of the sea, we heard a voice calling us home. We did not know that the voice came from deep within our souls. For the first time, we turned our hearts to God and He answered our prayers. The cradle swayed in the soft China breeze with a will of its own, just as events in our lives created their own momentum.
>
> From our bamboo cradle, we emerged into a world of timeless, ancient wisdom. We cut our teeth on Torah and learned to walk with the Prophets; the first words we uttered were words of devotion. Each day dawned on new revelations, and faith in the Almighty filled our lives with joy.

15

THE ROAD NOT TAKEN

Dr. Laura Selub von Schmidt—June 2, 2000

On December 26, 2001, Dr. Laura Selub von Schmidt carried the Olympic torch that made its way to the 2002 Winter games. Her selection for this prestigious honor is a testimony to her inner strength, tenacity, and courage.

Photo by John Griffin

"The Road Not Taken" is Robert Frost's somewhat haunting lament on making choices and living with the consequences. The poem seems to refer to major life decisions—a career path, picking the right mate or one at all, where to live. But every day we have minor "roads not taken": We turn left and not right, we take public transportation rather than drive, or we pack a lunch instead of eating out. The hundreds of decisions we make daily are for the most part inconsequential, except sometimes when they rock our world.

It was Thursday, August 20, 1998, and the last patient had cancelled. Dr. Laura Selub von Schmidt decided that in deference to her staff, most of whom had been with her for years, she'd close the office an hour early. The office of her dental practice was a state-of-the-art masterpiece that Laura had designed herself. In addition to beautiful physical surroundings, the level of care was something in which she took great pride. With that little extra found time, Laura decided that instead of going directly home, she would stop and have a manicure at a new nail salon that had opened up not far from home. She called her husband, Chuck, told him she would be home soon, and, set her Toyota Camry onto the Long Island Expressway. That's all that she remembers. The rest of the details were filled in a month later when she woke up from the coma.

Her Toyota was rear-ended by a large vehicle whose owner has yet to apologize or inquire about her health. Her unconscious body was removed from the car by the "Jaws of Life" and helliported to Nassau County Medical Center. Meanwhile, Chuck was waiting at home with their youngest son, Joseph. When his concern was replaced by full-blown worry, two plain-clothes police officers appeared at the home to inform Attorney von Schmidt as to the whereabouts of his wife. He rushed to the medical center where Laura was about to have brain surgery. When the surgery was complete, but she had not come out of the coma, a nurse looked at him and said, "What are you going to tell the children?" Chuck misunderstood and thought that she meant, How would he tell the kids about the accident. What she meant was, "How are you going to tell the children that their mother is gone?" When Chuck comprehended her meaning, he knew that he was going to tell them nothing of the sort.

When Laura remained unresponsive to the neurologist's stimulus of pouring ice water into her ear, he informed Chuck that he would return to administer a "brain death protocol." They advised her husband to turn off the life support. Even though the doctors used words like *never will*, *can't*, *won't*, *isn't*, Chuck couldn't or wouldn't give up. Besides, Chuck and Laura had made an informal pact years earlier during a casual conversation. They promised each other that at all costs, they would do whatever they could for each other and their boys to keep themselves alive. Chuck was not about to let the hospital staff "pull the plug" on his wife.

So, he set up watch at the hospital. His brother, George, stayed with Laura all day, and Chuck stayed all night. They played music, touched her, and wiggled her toes. While Chuck, a Cooper Union-trained artist, lovingly talked to his wife, he sketched her in the hospi-

tal bed and journaled her progress. In the morning, he ran home and got the kids off to school. Friends helped out with everything from car-pooling to actually taking over Chuck's legal practice. After a month, when Laura finally opened her eyes, she had no idea of the extent of her injuries. Her first words were "I have an appointment." She expected to bound out of bed and resume her life of maintaining a busy dental practice and taking care of her two sons, husband, and home.

She was moved from the hospital to a skilled nursing care facility called Transitions in Manhasset, where she remained for several months. While Laura recuperated, her oldest son, Justin, continued to prepare for his Bar Mitzvah. Many of the basic details had been taken care of prior to the accident, but wonderful friends pitched-in and made sure that Justin got to all of his lessons. On December 12, 1998, Laura attended her son's Bar Mitzvah in a wheelchair, wearing an outfit that her family had purchased for her. Justin made a beautiful speech and pledged part of his Bar Mitzvah money to an association for head injuries. Chuck delivered some clever lines. With the help of her husband, Laura walked up to the *bimah* to thank everyone not only for helping out with the usual details, but for being their lifeline when it was most needed. In April 1999, Laura was finally able to return home.

Chuck is not the only one in the family with an iron-willed spirit. Laura, who once spent her days caring for patients, now found herself on the other side of the fence. In spite of challenges with daily living tasks and a schedule that included therapy and managing an ocean-full of pills at appropriate intervals, Laura tried to turn her disability into something positive. She is at home more and can spend more time with her family.

Several years ago. Laura enrolled in her temple's adult Hebrew class at night and thought about joining the B'nai Mitzvah class. However, with an overwhelming work schedule, she felt that it was unfair to commit to anything else that would take her away from her family. Chuck, ever supportive, said that now there was nothing between her and a Bat Mitzvah. They spoke with the cantor and he recommended several teachers. Justin's fourth-grade Hebrew teacher, Gail Panaro, was available and interested, so the lessons began. Once Laura started working with Gail, her Hebrew started coming back. Within three months, she could remember most of what she'd learned in her adult Hebrew class. Then there was the problem of finding a date. With Bar and Bat Mitzvah students reserving their dates two to three years in advance, no Saturday mornings were available. When the rabbi suggested having the Bat Mitzvah on a Friday night, Laura agreed readily.

Once again, with Chuck's assistance and the use of her walker, Laura made her way to the *bimah* a bit shaky on the outside, but quite proud on the inside. For this occasion, her artist/husband made her a yarmulke—a beaded green turtle on lavender velvet. Maybe the turtle represents the fact that the doctor had told Chuck that Laura would never walk on the beach. Once again, Chuck proved the medical community wrong. If it was not exactly a leisurely stroll, more like a step, shlep, step, Chuck and his bride of twenty-three years were barefoot in the sand and smelling the surf.

Laura read from the *siddur*, sang the blessing before and after the Torah reading, read from the Torah with a *yad* that Chuck had made for Justin's Bar Mitzvah, and then moved most of the congregation to tears with the following address:

> The Torah portion that I read is called *parshat Bamidbar* in Hebrew, or "Numbers" in English. I have come to think of this book of the Torah as both historical and allegorical. One year and one month after the Jewish Exodus from Egypt into the desert, Moses was commanded to take a census of all Israelite males over the age of 20 who were able to bear arms. The total males of all twelve tribes numbered 603,550.
>
> Famous students of the Torah see the time spent by the Jews in the *midbar* (desert) as a time of maturation and growth. Time spent in the Sinai was strategic for the Jews. It represented a time in which each person learned to appreciate the beauty of nature and his or her dependence on and loyalty to the community. It was also a personal time of religious development.
>
> In our modest lives, we find that sometimes the best, most important, lesson we can learn is taught in a very different school. Sometimes we experience in life something that is nearly unbearable. Yet we find that somehow, amazingly, we have survived. We may lose something that seems almost precious, yet the epiphany enlightens us. We are alive. . . .

It is true that we don't know what we've got until we lose it. But it's also true that we don't know what we've been missing until it arrives. For nine years, I had been wanting to attend Rabbi Gellman's Torah class. After the accident, I had nothing to limit my attendance.

When the door of happiness closes, another opens, but oftentimes we don't see the one that has opened for us. My life before the fateful day of the accident seemed perfect. I owned a successful, high-quality dental practice; I had two beautiful sons, one of whom was to become a Bar Mitzvah at Temple Beth Torah only four months after my accident and whose Bar Mitzvah I was well enough to attend. And I had a wonderful, devoted, loving husband and we lived in an excellent town.

The happiest people don't necessarily have the best of everything; they just make the most of everything that comes their way. The day I had the accident was just another Thursday. When I awakened from the coma, one month later, I started and said to Chuck. "I have an appointment." The true pain and suffering came to me much later, as I realized that I was unable to walk and that I would not be able to continue my practice. The contrast between my old life, with its seemingly immense problems, and my new life, with its staggering dilemmas, truly boggled the mind.

The good parts of my new life dawned on me very slowly, too. Although I am not able to walk unassisted, and I have numerous handicaps that interfere with my everyday life. I am able to be at home when my children come home from school. And for the first time in my adult life. I am able to pursue my Jewish education, the way I want to.

Now I know what wandering in the desert is like. I feel as if I have not just read this portion of the Torah, I have lived it! Perhaps the trials and suffering of the Jews enabled them to receive the priceless gift of the Torah. Moses' census is not merely a counting of the population, but a creative structuring and organizing of the community. By numbering each person, individually, Moses encourages in each individual a feeling of pride and self-worth.

To all of you who could be with me tonight, may you have enough happiness to make you sweet, enough trials to make you strong, enough sorrow to keep you human, and enough hope to make you happy.

16

HONORING THE EVERYDAY: MY DAUGHTER'S *YIDISHE BAS MITSVE*

Meg Cassedy-Blum—April 1998
(by Ellen Cassedy)

Meg Cassedy-Blum is a senior in high school near Washington, D.C. She continues to recite her Yiddish women's prayers on some Saturday nights and still plans to become a teacher.

The light coming through the chapel windows grew dim. *Shabes* was ending. *Havdole*: the dividing of the holy day from the ordinary days of the week. My daughter Meg's Bas Mitsve ceremony was coming to a close. Quietly, my not-quite-13-year-old spoke the words of a *tkhine*—a Yiddish women's prayer:

Der liber heyliker shabes geyt avek
Di gute vokh zol undz kumen
Tsu gezunt un tsum lebn
Tsu mazel un brokhe . . .

(The precious holy Sabbath is departing.
May the good week come to us
With health and life.
With fortune and blessing . . .)

Meg sniffed the sweet spices and stretched out her hands to the flickering candlelight. Her year-long study of Yiddish and *Yiddishkeit* had reached its conclusion. At that moment—for her, for me, for family and friends—the secular and the sacred were intertwined.

Ten years ago, when my mother died, I developed an urgent desire to learn Yiddish. A craving. I couldn't save my mother from cancer, but maybe I could help to save this other precious Jewish thing. By grabbing hold of *mame-loshn*, I could hang onto something important about my mother.

She would have been surprised, to put it mildly. In the household where she grew up, in Brooklyn in the 1930s and 1940s, it was English—perfect English—that held the place of honor. Yiddish was about ignorance and poverty. My mother wasn't nostalgic. She used Yiddish only occasionally, to goof around. In the kitchen: "Hand me a *shisl* (bowl]." On the phone: "The woman's a makhsheyfe [witch]." At the window: "A *plokhe* [downpour]."

Now she was gone. I *had* to learn Yiddish. Feeling like a greenhorn, I signed up for evening classes. I plodded through textbooks and thumbed my Yiddish-English dictionary until the binding broke. I joined the National Yiddish Book Center and visited the Workmen's Circle bookstore. My Aunt Manya and Uncle Will, who still speak Yiddish at home, wrote me letters. I logged on to the Yiddish e-mail club, "Mendele," and sang along with Yiddish tapes in the car.

It started to happen. Little by little, Yiddish became a living presence in our household. I was thrilled to be able to stumble through some short Yiddish classics in the original. I got out a dusty old LP of Jewish folksongs that I remembered from childhood; if I concentrated really hard, I could understand the words. Now and again, a stray Yiddish phrase—one I didn't even know I knew—floated into my consciousness like a long-forgotten scent.

When it came time for Meg to prepare for her *Bas Mitsve*, I suggested that she, too, might like to study Yiddish. "Say yes.": I urged silently, and she did.

Why Yiddish in place of Hebrew? For some girls, learning to read from the Torah is an appropriate symbol of joining the adult Jewish community. In our family, on the other hand, coming of age as a Jew is about learning the ropes of secular Judaism.

Though Yiddish has at times been a part of the Jewish religious tradition (for example, in the *tkhine* Meg recited), for me it's most meaningful as a part of worldly or "everyday" Jewish culture. It's the vernacular Meg's foremothers spoke in the kitchens, lanes, and marketplaces of Poland, Latvia, Lithuania, New York, and Baltimore. It's the language in which great Jewish writers conveyed new humanist ideas to an audience of "common folk." It's the language that united activist Jews in movements for social change on both sides of the Atlantic. Studying Yiddish and *Yiddishkeit*, I hoped, would enrich Meg's connection to secular Jewish culture.

For me, secularism isn't simply a rejection of traditional religion—it's a system of belief in its own right. I'm proud that my parents—my mother Jewish and my father (as he puts it) "not"—brought me up to believe in the worthiness of human beings, to involve myself in the struggle for justice and equality, and to feel a strong connection to the Jewish activist tradition. I wanted Meg's *Bas Mitsve* study both to continue that tradition and to enlarge upon it.

My husband, Jeff, agreed. Raised in a Reform Jewish community in Baltimore, he deeply appreciates the values he learned in that community, but he never warmed to its rituals. As a boy, he would spend Friday nights at temple either counting the squares in the ceiling or flipping through the prayer book page by page, trying to find one page—just one—that he could fully believe in. (Given that he didn't believe in God, he found this virtually impossible.) He wanted Meg's Jewish education to be different.

Giving Meg a taste of the daily lives of her ancestors—in the *shtetlekh* of the Old World and the tenements of the New—felt to both of us like a political act. It meant saying that ordinary life matters. That each person matters. That the daily tasks of keeping house and making a living deserve a place of honor in Jewish history, alongside the actions of famous men. That to become a Jewish adult, Meg needed to study that history.

No doubt, my mother would have been amused. After all, she'd grown up struggling to *loosen* her own connections to Old World language and immigrant culture. Nonetheless, there we were, bent on passing along those very connections through a homemade course of instruction.

Through the Internet, we found a professor at the University of Maryland who'd grown up speaking Yiddish in Montreal. Over the next year, we shlepped Meg to Miriam's apartment on Friday afternoons. Miriam would buzz us in on the Intercom: "*Kumt arayn! Kumt arayn!* [Come in!]" With its Yiddish nameplate on the door, Yiddish theater posters on the walls, and shelves crammed with Yiddish books and tapes, her apartment was a Yiddish center all its own.

Meg was an eager student. She lapped up the alphabet and had no trouble with pronunciation. Like me, she enjoyed the feel of Yiddish in her mouth, loved learning what seemed like a secret code, and—thanks to the many similarities between Yiddish and English—was pleased to be catching on faster than she'd expected to.

Meg and Miriam baked cookies in Yiddish. They made cucumber salad in Yiddish. On one memorable Sunday, we all went to the zoo, entirely in Yiddish, to view the *malpes* (apes), *helfandn* (elephants), and *bern* (bears).

Bit by bit, we cobbled together a curriculum, drawing on materials Miriam was using in her college courses, books and films that Jeff and I had enjoyed over the years, resources I'd encountered in my own Yiddish study, and things we came across as we went along. Meg enjoyed songs, movies, and literature from both the Old World and the New, including Yiddish literature in English translation. It warmed my heart when one of her favorites turned out to be Peretz's classic "If Not Higher" (*Oyb nisht nokh hekher*), a fascinating encounter between a skeptic and a rabbi that I've always considered a profoundly humanist tale.

Miriam and I especially liked the Yiddish stories by women in *Found Treasures* (a recent anthology, in English translation) and *The Tribe of Dina: A Jewish Women's Anthology*. Meg did not. In fact, she hated them. She emphatically did not enjoy reading about suffering widows, orphans, and girls forced to marry against their will. Somehow these stories touched a nerve that made them, for her, more disturbing than the most chilling tales of the Holocaust.

From Meg's notes:

> A pregnant woman has a hemorrhage and dies. Her oldest daughter gets sick and almost dies. When she gets well, she understands that her mother is dead.
>
> I didn't like it. I don't want to read about dead mothers, or about a girl going far away and never seeing her family anymore. I'm not going away from home, I'm only turning 13. I want to read happy things.

Miriam and I sighed over the question of how hard to push Meg to grapple with the pain of Jewish history. Maybe not very hard, we concluded. Later.

We joined Meg in savoring the sunnier, more sentimental songs and stories. We watched *Mamele*, a poignant film made in prewar Poland, featuring the star of the Yiddish stage Molly Picon. We sang "*In an orem shtibele*" ("In a Poor Little House"), where, as Meg wrote happily, "In the little house, there is so much love that it doesn't matter that the family is poor"; for her, the song even seemed to suggest that "they are sort of more loving and close *because* they're poor." Meg learned to recite "*Di grezelekh blien*" ("The Grasses Grow"), a cheery children's verse. "The sun shines down on all of us" Meg interpreted, "and all we have to do is be good."

Meg's approach to Yiddish study was by no means only a nostalgic journey. Though she refused to listen to our earnest lectures about labor history, she devoured the materials we gave her about speaking up and fighting back. She loved *Bread Givers*, the stirring novel about the Jewish immigrant experience by Anzia Yezierska. as well as Meredith Tax's *Rivington Street* and *Union Square*, historical novels about Lower East Side life and union activism.

She read *New Yorkish* and *Other American Yiddish Stories*, translated by Max Rosenfeld; a favorite was "Equality of the Sexes," a piquant little tale by Avrom Reisen, published in 1916, in which Ida and Harry engage in a very modern argument about who should pick up the check at the corner restaurant. On a long car trip, we listened to a cassette of Jewish immigrant songs and stories by labor troubadour Joe Glazer. We watched the movie *Hester Street*, a sepia-colored tale of immigrant life, based on a novel by *Forward* editor Abe Cahan.

So far, so good. But as the day drew closer, Meg began to have second thoughts. It dawned on her that her *Bas Mitsve* was going to be

really different from everyone else's. Jeff and I reveled in how unique it would be. At not quite 13, Meg didn't.

In our first meeting with our friend Rebecca (a self-described "rabbi for the margins"), Meg spoke up. First, she nixed the idea of using the ceremony to make some big point about women or womanhood. Men were important, too.

All right, we could live with that.

Next, she wanted to include lots of prayers.

Prayers?

Prayers in Hebrew.

Why?

She didn't know: she just liked them.

As Jeff and I exchanged a nervous look, Rebecca grinned and promised to make Meg a tape of the *Sh'ma, Shehekhianu, Oseh Shalom*. . . .

A few weeks later, Meg dropped her next bombshell.

Would we mind if she studied the Torah?

Torah? At the Cassedy-Blum **Bas Mitsve**?

We went back to Rebecca to find out what her portion would be.

Something from Leviticus, it seemed. Something about how to sacrifice an animal. Something that read like *The Joy of Cooking* on how to roast a muskrat. But then Rebecca remembered: Since the ceremony was scheduled for the Saturday afternoon before Passover, it would be fitting to read from Exodus.

We reached an agreement.

Meg would read from the Torah, in Hebrew, about the Jews' last night in Egypt. Then she would present her Yiddish study of another, more modern, exodus—the immigration of a great multitude of European Jews to America.

Rachel, the Torah tutor, was an Israeli grandmother who couldn't fathom why on earth Meg was studying Yiddish. It didn't matter. A gifted teacher, Rachel showered Meg with praise, scribbled all over her Xeroxed Torah portion with a special system of colored markers, and assured Meg that she could pull it off, even though she had only two months to practice.

Soon our house rang with the sounds of Hebrew *trup*, as well as with Yiddish songs. Meg and I made a deal: I would refrain from making snide remarks about the Torah and Meg would practice her Yiddish without being nagged. I didn't nag about the Hebrew, either;

I never needed to. Reading from the Torah was Meg's own idea and her discipline. She practiced diligently every day.

"I studied Torah for many reasons," Meg wrote in her "commentary." "It helped me feel connected to Jewish tradition because I was doing something that has been done in rituals for many generations. I found it very moving that the Torah has helped people for so long. From the Torah, people have found the strength to triumph over many hardships."

I read that paragraph over and over, pondering my daughter's emerging views about what is sacred and why. I felt a little hurt, I suppose, that Meg reserved these special words for the hallowed Hebrew text, rather than for a homespun Yiddish folksong or a pithy short story. Yet I was cheered by the particular way that Meg had found to appreciate the Torah—a way she'd figured out on her own. What made the Torah holy in her eyes was that people had been comforted and inspired by it. This humanist approach had certainly eluded Jeff, the Atheist, at her age.

Slowly, I came to feel glad that Meg had insisted on broadening her Yiddish *Bas Mitsve* to include more traditional elements. How much richer this was than if she had simply gone along with what we suggested. She managed—gracefully—to assert what she needed, while also embracing what we wanted. Isn't that part of what coming of age is all about?

The day came. A hundred friends and relatives assembled at Jeff s family's temple in Baltimore—the very place where he had spent Friday nights counting the squares in the ceiling. Instead of the grand sanctuary, though, we gathered in a small, cozy chapel. It was time for Meg's Magical Blend—her personal amalgam of *Yiddishkeit* and Bible study.

To begin, the congregation sang two songs of welcome—the Hebrew "*Hiney ma tov*," which many knew, and the Yiddish "*Lomir alemen bagrisn*" ("Let's Greet Everyone"), from a secular songbook. In memory of my mother and Jeff's father, Meg lit candles and recited a lovely secular blessing in Yiddish, composed by Judith Seid. "*Zol di sheynkayt fun zeyr lebn balaykhtn di doyres*," she chanted. ("May the beauty of their lives shine from generation to generation.")

The Torah service, with all its attending pomp—*aliyot* and *tallit* and Ark and *yad*—followed. Meg recited in Hebrew, then began her remarks in English, interspersed with Yiddish poems and songs. She

started with a poem by early-twentieth-century Russian immigrant Eliezer Shindler:

> *Undzer yidish*
> *Undzer sphrakh*
> *Farmogt dokh.*
> *Oytsres gor a sakh. . . .*
>
> (Our Yiddish
> Our language
> Does indeed possess
> A wealth of treasures. . . .)

The treasures Meg chose to share ranged from the happy song about the joys of poverty to Peretz's "Bontshe the Silent" ("*Bontshe shvayg*"), a scathing tale that, in Meg's words, "tells Jews to wish for more than a good breakfast—to stand up for themselves instead of meekly bowing down." She read from a worker's letter to the *Forward* in 1908 about his struggle to fight back against a tyrannical boss. She read from Reisen's tale of the battle between the sexes, concluding that "we must continue to fight for equality, the way Ida did."

Meg wants to be a teacher. She was a teacher that day. Among those gathered in the chapel—Jeff's enormous Jewish family, my tiny one that ranges from Orthodox Holocaust survivors to devout Catholics, Meg's friends, our friends—few had any connection to *mame-loshn*. Meg was proud to introduce them to the joys of Yiddish.

Whether they followed the translations and transliterations in the program booklet or just let the sounds wash over them, many were moved. One man came up at the end of the service, wiping his eyes. "I'm going to have to send you the dry cleaning bill for my handkerchief," he told Meg. "You said that blessing just the way my mother used to." Great-great-uncle Will whispered the highest praise: "She doesn't even have an accent!" Even one of Meg's cooler teenage cousins pronounced the ceremony the best *Bas Mitsve* he'd ever attended. (Since then, we've fielded inquiries from a number of families who want to incorporate Yiddish and *Yiddishkeit* into their children's *Mitsve* ceremonies.)

From the outset, one of our goals for Meg's *Bas Mitsve* was to create, out of secular materials, a sense of sacredness. Yiddish helped us do that.

For me, Yiddish—the embodiment of the everyday, the profane—*is* sacred. In part, this is because for my generation—and for Meg's—Yiddish is exotic, endangered. No longer something taken for granted, it has become a precious thing, a treasure we must honor and protect.

Meg deserves the last word: "I'm glad I connected myself with both the religious Jewish language and the more everyday one. These languages came alive to me. I plan to pass on the knowledge of Yiddish to my children, who, I hope, in turn will pass it on to their children. *Sholem aleichem* and *shalom*!"

Credit: "Honoring the Everyday: My Daughter's *Yidishe Bas Mitsve,*" first appeared in *Bridges: A Journal for Jewish Feminists and Our Friends,* Volume 8, 2000. Reprinted by permission of Ellen Cassedy.

Explanatory note: This piece originally appeared in *Bridges: A Journal for Jewish Feminists and Our Friends*, Volume 8, 2000. For a sample copy, write to P.O. Box 24839, Eugene, OR 97402. Ellen Cassedy is a writer living near Washington, D.C.

17

FOR THE LOVE OF IRIT

Yoni and Suzi*—July 1998

Yoni and Suzi continue to grow and thrive in Eretz Israel, a land that has made an art form out of survival.

On April 12, 1984, the number 300 bus left Tel Aviv at 6:15 P.M., on its way to Ashkelon, with the seats filled to capacity. One half-hour into the trip, four men rose from different sections of the bus. One quickly stormed the driver and demanded that he change course and drive down the costal road toward Egypt. The others pulled out their weapons. knives, grenades, and homemade bombs and blocked the exits. With this display of power, they declared

---

*The children's last names are withheld due to the protective nature of the Israeli social service system.

their intentions of hijacking the bus and holding the passengers hostage. One gunmen shouted at a pregnant passenger, "You want peace? We do, too, but tonight everybody on this bus will die! Your soldiers are killing our children!"

As the bus raced down the highway at the gunman's insistence, the pregnant woman begged to be released. She was let out on the highway, where she promptly flagged down a truck and they notified the authorities. The Israeli soldiers then pursued the bus, which was traveling at breakneck speed and crashed through two roadblocks. The bus ended in a ditch when the soldiers shot out the tires. As it came to a stop, several passengers dove out the windows to safety.

The remaining passengers—scared, hungry, and several wounded—waited all night as the soldiers tried to arrange for their release. The hijackers in turn demanded the release of 500 Palestinians being held in Israeli jails. All through the night, there was a young soldier, 19-year-old Irit Portugues, who worked tirelessly to help her fellow passengers. An eyewitness shared the following tale:

> When the bus stopped at Dir-El Belach, there were already four people wounded. It is difficult to describe the shock, fear, and feelings of helplessness that caused a blurring of the senses and stiffening of the body.
>
> Ze'ev, who was a male nurse, began to devotedly tend the wounded, and Irit immediately volunteered to help him. Shoshana Hagi, who was severely wounded, suffered from breathing problems and excruciating pains in her legs. Throughout the ordeal, Irit dedicated herself to taking care of her.
>
> In addition to tending the wounded, Irit mediated between the passengers and the terrorists, and every request was passed on through her. She walked freely through the bus and came to an understanding with the terrorists that she didn't have to ask permission to do so.
>
> Irit took care that all of the passengers would receive water to drink. I didn't want anything to drink, but Irit whispered to me to spill some on the seat so that if the terrorists would use the inflammable material that was in their possession, the damage would not be so great. Irit asked them to bring blankets for the wounded, helped to provide toilet facilities, and wandered through the bus looking for ways to help.

> At 2:00 o'clock in the morning, I asked her to sit down and rest, but she replied that if she rested she would collapse. In spite of this, after a while she complied with my request and sat beside me for about half an hour. We spoke in a whisper. Irit told me about her family, of her father who always brought her to the junction, and how she happened to get on this particular bus. From time to time, she would say how much she missed her boyfriend and wanted to see him. She also told me that she threw away the sign of the intelligence unit she belonged to.
>
> At the moment they brought coffee, Irit passed from seat to seat handing out coffee to passengers. She used her hand to put sugar in every cup since there were no spoons. A few moments before the rescue I saw Irit helping one of the passengers, as she was accustomed to, in the front of the bus.

On the scene all night, Defense Minister Moshe Arens said, "We don't give into terrorist demands." At dawn, the Israeli soldiers ended the siege with thirty seconds of gunfire, leaving the four hijackers dead. There was only one Israeli casualty, Irit Portugues.

Nellie and Moshe Portugues, Irit's parents, had immigrated to Israel in the mid-1960s from Argentina, feeling that their place was to help build the young Jewish state. They lived on a *moshav*, which is a community settlement. It is different from a *kibbutz*, in that people have their own homes and their own finances. However, each member of the community has a job that contributes to the communal good. Just a week before the hijacking, Moshe's job was to weed, plow, and tidy the section of the cemetery that was reserved for soldiers who fell in battle. He felt that it was important to make that area of the cemetery respectable, in case it was suddenly needed. He never suspected that his daughter would lie in the first grave. Irit was engaged to be married to the boyfriend she talked of missing on the bus. Instead of a wedding, her family held her funeral.

Nellie and Moshe were grief-stricken, but not bitter. "The fate of the Jewish people has always been one of suffering and tragedy," says Moshe. With their three surviving children, they looked to find consolation. However, they realized that they needed to find new meaning in their lives, and they offered their home for disabled foster children. In rapid succession four young children, all with Down's syndrome, were placed in their home. Having come from an institution, the children were not toilet-trained and were involved in self-stimulatory behavior. So often, disabled children are provided just with the basics. Nellie and Moshe wanted to provide more than food, clothing, and shelter for these children. They wanted to share their love of art and music with Yoni, Suzi, Tom, and Dana.

With their love and guidance, the children not only were educated, but were also provided with lessons in art, music, and computers. Raising children is very costly, especially when the social service system provides minimal assistance. Only with the help of friends like Monica and Ira Stern of Philadelphia could the Portugues family afford to grant these extras. Monica and Ira met the Portugues family when they spent a year living on the *moshav* in the early 1980s. When Monica and Ira learned about Irit's tragic death and then the placement of the four foster children, they set out to help in any way they could. Ira, a high school math teacher, enlisted the help of his cousin Skip Greenberg, and they trained to run the Tiberias marathon in Israel. As they trained, they recruited sponsors and collectively raised over $10,000, which they delivered to Moshe and Nellie for their children.

The Portugues family lives a very secular lifestyle. However. when it came time to arrange for schooling for their "second family," they found the best program for special education provided by an Orthodox day school. There, the children followed a dual curriculum and were educated in both secular and religious classes. At the school, as designated in the course of study. Yoni and Suzi prepared for their Bar and Bat Mitzvah, which would happen together, since they were close in age. Yoni learned how to put on *tefillin* and how to say the *brachah* before the Torah reading. They waited to celebrate the joint B'nai Mitzvah until the summertime, when their good friends, the Stern family, would join them for a visit. The auditorium in the school was set up as a synagogue, and all the seating was arranged: men on one side and women on the other. Several of their classmates were in attendance, as were the rabbis and teachers of the school. Yoni was called up to the *bimah*, and despite his slight speech impediment, he said the *brachah* in a loud and clear voice. As it was an Orthodox service, Suzi had no official role; however, it was made quite clear that this celebration was for her as well. When the davening was over, a lovely meal was served and a clown came in to entertain everyone.

With the emphasis on extracurricular activities in art and music, Yoni and Suzi developed into talented musicians—not just in compar-

ison with children with Down's syndrome, but in general. A year after their B'nai Mitzvah, they were invited to play for the president and first lady of Israel, Mr. and Mrs. Ezer Weizman. Yoni is an accomplished violinist, and Suzi is multifaceted, with skills on the violin, keyboard, and xylophone. The concert was lovely and was received with thunderous applause.

When the Portugues foster children become 18, they are required, just like nondisabled young men and women, to serve in the army. There is a special unit for disabled soldiers. After that, if they wish, they will qualify for independent housing or they may choose to remain with their foster parents. Moshe and Nellie tried to instill in all of their children the knowledge that they have a right and the resources to make the best choices. They provided Irit with the spiritual and emotional strength to act in the most humane manner in a time of crisis. And they feel confident that Yoni, Suzi, Tom, and Dana will be instrumental in planning their own course. From the tragedy of Irit's death came the inspiration to share her joy of life and love of music with four disabled children who might otherwise have remained institutionalized. Irit's life was a source of pride to all of the Jewish people, and that pride has been perpetuated by all of her brothers and sisters.

Author's note: This story was shared by Monica and Ira Stern, with permission by Nellie Portugues. The background information on the hijacking was found in a *New York Times* article by David K. Shipler, April 13, 1984, pp. Al, A7, and *Newsweek*, "Terror on a Hijacked Bus," by Angus Deming and Milan J. Kubic, AprIl 23, 1984, p. 45. There was also a story written by Simon Grlver entitled, "Irit Portugues: Teenage Victim" and an eyewitness account by a fellow passenger on the bus.

18

WOMEN OF VALOR

Sarah Danzig—January 25, 1998

Photo by Moskow Studios

Sarah often goes back to Children's Hospital, but now to visit other kids with cancer and ply them with lollipops (which sustained her at one point) and balloons. She applied to be part of a program with NCSY which pairs 25 "typical" teens with 25 developmentally challenged young adults and sends them to Israel to work together. Sarah's application essay focused on the challenges that she had faced in her life and the understanding she has gleaned from them. She was accepted into the program and will spend six weeks this summer in Israel. Rivka, in her role as social worker, also continues to be involved with cancer and its effect on the family. She runs a very powerful phone group for parents of children with cancer. Maybe it's the anonymity of the phone or the comfort of sitting in your pajamas in the privacy of your home that enables parents to bare their feelings and, more important, to support each other through tough times.

Sarah Danzig was 5 years old when her family spent Thanksgiving vacation in Washington, D.C. They went swimming and when they got out of the hotel pool, her mother noticed blood coming out of her daughter's ear. They sought medical help and were told that it was an infection. Sarah started on antibiotics. When they returned home to Philadelphia, they went to their regular

pediatrician, who felt that infection was the correct diagnosis, but because the situation was not resolving, she switched antibiotics. As the $70-a-bottle medication failed to work its magic, Sarah became more and more uncomfortable and kept crying to her mother that her ear hurt. They were referred to an ENT specialist, who told them that the infection had cleared, but he could see a benign cyst in the ear. They scheduled an out-patient surgery for what was expected to be a minimal procedure. Sarah's Dad went to work, and her mother, Rivka, anticipating a pretty straightforward day, took her daughter by herself to Children's Hospital of Philadelphia.

When the surgeon came out to the waiting room and Rivka saw his face, she knew that much more than just a benign cyst was growing in her daughter's ear. Instead, she was diagnosed with Rhabdomyosarcoma—a malignant tumor eating through the bones of her ear and pressing on her brain. Rhabdomyosarcoma—a huge word for a tiny little girl. With the diagnosis of cancer, they were assigned an oncologist. Cancer treatment occurs over a long haul; therefore, the match between doctor and patient has to be a good fit for the treatment to be effective. Their first oncologist forgot that a little girl was attached to the disease and turned out to be unsuitable for the Danzig family. They switched to Dr. Jean Belasco, who is a wonderful doctor, a caring human being, but, more important, a mentsch. The diagnosis coincided closely with Sarah's 6th birthday, and she had tickets to performances of the *Nutcracker* and *Beauty and the Beast.* When scheduling Sarah's additional surgery, Dr. Belasco told Sarah and her mother that she had to go and see those two shows before she underwent her treatment. Sarah, already on morphine and seated in the third balcony, had the pleasure of seeing the Sugar Plum Fairy and the Snow Queen before she went back to CHOP (Children's Hospital of Philadelphia).

Dr. Rivka Danzig and her husband, Dr. Neil Danzig, both originally from New York, were postdoctoral students at Hebrew University in Israel. Their plan was to come to the States, earn a few dollars, and return to Israel. They were offered several jobs in different parts of the country, but they chose Philadelphia. Rivka, with a doctorate in social work, taught at the University of Pennsylvania and worked for Jewish Family Service. Her husband, with a Ph.D. in talmudic studies, taught at the now defunct Dropsie College, the Reconstructionist Rabbinical College, and more currently at the Jewish Theological Seminary.

Their plans for a speedy return were foiled when Rivka became seriously ill, and they were forced to remain in Philadelphia. The Danzigs, a strictly Orthodox family, believe strongly in God's strength and power and pray not by rote, but with *kavannah*, a full heart and reverence. Rivka said that God sent them to Philadelphia, so that they would be there before Sarah was diagnosed. The protocol for her kind of cancer was developed at CHOP. The experts for treating her tumor were already there.

The cancer treatment was aggressive. It involved surgery, chemotherapy, and radiation. Except for an isolated day here or there, Sarah and her mother remained at Children's Hospital for almost a year. They were helped greatly by Bikur Cholim, a voluntary organization that cares for the sick—and for those who are taking care of the sick. A meeting was called, and Rivka met with fifty to sixty women in her friend's home. This legion of women identified the needs of Rivka and her family and set up committees. With Rivka living in the hospital with her little girl, the needs were great and varied. As the Danzigs were an Orthodox family that kept kosher, the group needed to provide food for Sarah and Rivka, as well as for her husband and the two boys at home. There were drivers who arranged for transportation and drives held for the donation of blood and platelets. There were people saying *tehillim* (Psalms recited on behalf of the sick) and people cooking and delivering food. Some lovely souls made the boys' lunches, inserting special treats every day while their mother and sister were in the hospital. And there were monetary contributions to help defray the cost of the treatment.

Rivka could have quit working, and that unemployed status would have made them eligible for aid. However, for her own mental health, she needed to leave the hospital for a few hours two or three times a week. For young children (and adults, for that matter), being in a hospital can be very scary. Being separated from a caretaker for even a short time is often frightening. So, Rivka slept on a narrow window seat next to Sarah's bed. When she learned the system, she realized that she could request a cot. Rivka's very good friend Dr. Elaine Zackal came every morning at 7:00 A.M. and sat with Sarah, so that Rivka could take a shower and get dressed. Cancer and its treatment has a way of rendering the patient and the family members powerless. In small and maybe seemingly insignificant ways, the individuals often try to gain some control over their lives. As an Orthodox woman

who covers her hair with an array of colorful headcoverings, Rivka made sure that her scarf always matched her outfit. With little control over the external events of their lives, at least she could still coordinate what she looked like.

Rivka also did a little work in the hospital. While Sarah was a patient, two families from Israel brought their children to Philadelphia for treatment. They spoke no English, so Rivka, fluent in Hebrew, was often called to translate between the doctors and nurses and the families, sometimes in the middle of the night. Sarah befriended the two children and was devastated to learn that while the one child survived (and they remain friendly to this day), the other youngster did not.

Sarah missed most of the first grade. Before she was diagnosed, she fortunately learned the basics of reading in both English and Hebrew, although during her treatment she didn't feel much like pursuing academics. During the summer between first and second grade, one of the teachers came to the house voluntarily and caught Sarah up on her Hebrew subjects. Sarah entered second grade, bald and emaciated, with a tube in her chest that provided IV feedings all night and self-administered morphine during the day. With the cancer and the treatment attacking her body, she was often in tremendous pain. However, she went as often as she could and covered her head with a variety of pretty hats.

While Sarah received IV treatments, the port in her chest was kept open. As the need for it diminished, the port was taken out. One great advantage was that Sarah could finally go swimming again. Her mother fretted about how she would handle the exposure of her bare head, since she couldn't wear a hat in the pool. She went to the store and bought a beautiful flowered bathing cap, so that Sarah could slip off the hat and slip on the cap. Sarah went to the pool with her friends, two girls from a set of triplets (the third is a boy) who were in her class. There is a Hebrew expression that translated means, "They bought their share in the world to come in one moment," referring to an act of great kindness. When Sarah shyly slipped off her hat, getting ready to quickly cover her head, the sisters sweetly and naively stroked the new peach fuzz that was sprouting on Sarah's head and told her how soft and beautiful her new hair was. Sarah chucked the bathing cap and swam with her head "au natural."

One by-product of the cancer, which resulted from a combination of the chemotherapy and radiation, was that Sarah's signature long, beautiful red curly hair never grew back. She has tried a succession of wigs, but as they were not really made for children, they would end up askew when she jumped rope or ran around and that made her feel worse. Sarah told her mother, "People will just have to accept me as I am." As an Orthodox young woman, she will cover her hair when she marries.

Two other related organizations are important to Sarah and her family, Chai Lifeline and Camp Simcha. Chai Lifeline assigned a "big sister" to Sarah. Rivky Schwartz, a young lady from Detroit, developed a strong and important phone relationship with Sarah. And every summer, for two weeks, Sarah attends a Glatt kosher camp in Glen Spey, New York, called Camp Simcha, for kids with cancer. She has met children from all over the world.

Sarah has two older brothers, David and Hayyim. The day before David's Bar Mitzvah, his grandmother (Rivka's mother) was killed in a car accident on the way to Pennsylvania. The gala celebration had to be canceled, and a very quiet *minyan* was held in the house the next day. For Hayyim and Sarah's B'nai Mitzvot, there was a "no-holds-barred" attitude. Sarah had survived to live to see this day! It was a miracle. There was reason to celebrate.

The Bat Mitzvah was really a community celebration of Sarah. It was a glorious formal event, with all those who helped her in attendance. She is a community child and was surrounded by those who had given her their time, love, and the basics of blood, platelets, food, and money. They celebrated in style at the Wyndham Hotel, where David's Bar Mitzvah was supposed to be held and where Hayyim's Bar Mitzvah was held in full regalia.

Sarah had studied with her mother and learned about the meaning of a prayer from Proverbs entitled *Aishet Chayil*, "A Woman of Valor."* It is a beautiful allegorical set of verses that are a tribute to the perfect wife and mother and is supposed to be recited by a husband when he enters his home after *shul* on Friday evenings. The deeper meaning extends to the Torah, the *Shechinah* (God's holy spirit), and the Sabbath; nevertheless, it is a tribute to women because they were

---

**Author's note*: Information on *Aishet Chayil* was learned from *The Complete Art Scroll Siddur*, a new translation and anthologized commentary by Rabbi Nosson Scherman, Mesorah Publications Limited, 1984, pages 358–359.

chosen as the vehicle through which to deliver lofty spiritual ideas. Sarah shared her speech about "The Woman of Valor" with poise, aplomb, and a level of maturity indicative of the experiences that had forced her to "grow up." Even the musician hired for the affair cried with the rest of the crowd through Sarah's speech. When she was finished, the family came together and said the *brachah* of the *Shehechiyanu*, thanking God for allowing them to reach this season. Upon everyone's hearing the blessing, there was a collective, joyous response of "Amen."

The afternoon was a collection of special moments. Sarah's brothers took her old school photographs that had been enlarged and told cute stories about each time period of her life. Since it was an Orthodox event, there was separate dancing and Sarah danced with Dr. Belasco, her oncologist. Chai Lifeline flew in Rivky Schwartz, her big sister, to share the big event. Everyone was laughing and crying, and a sense of love and elation permeated the room.

Sarah could not have picked a more appropriate topic to discuss on the day of her Bat Mitzvah. Having experienced the rigors of cancer treatment, she doesn't ask, "Why me?" but rather, "What can I do for you?" Being the recipient of abundant kindness has made her all the more sweet and gentle. Rising to the occasion and facing all that was asked of her, Sarah emerged stronger, braver, and with a continued unyielding faith in the Almighty. Though not yet a wife and mother, she is nonetheless an Aishet Chayil, a young woman of valor.

19

A GREAT MIRACLE HAPPENED HERE

Lucy Goldhair—December 11, 1999

Lucy is in high school. She loves nature, animals, and anything related to science.

The traditional dreidel has four Hebrew letters, one on each side — *Nun, Gimel, Hay,* and *Shin*. They are an abbreviation for *Nes Gadol Haya Shum*, translated as "A great miracle happened there." This refers to the Chanukah story and the miracles it encompasses. A small band of Jews, led by Judah Maccabee, fought against the huge Syrian army and prevailed. When the victorious Jews went to reclaim their holy Temple, they found it desecrated and in ruins. In order to re-dedicate the Temple, they found a tiny bit of oil, enough to last for one day, and lit it. The oil burned for eight days—a visible, vibrant miracle. When we say, "a great miracle happened there," the "there" refers to Israel.

Lucy Goldhalr was born on the seventh day of Chanukah. Her Bat Mitzvah was celebrated on *Shabbos* Chanukah. The theme for the weekend-long celebration was *Nes Gadol Haya Po*, with *Po* meaning "here." "A great miracle happened here"—Lucy.

Lucy and her younger sister, Salle, were born with cystic fibrosis. Every morning since they were newborns, their parents, Debbie and Richard, have given the girls chest physical therapy for thirty minutes to help clear their lungs of the abnormally sticky mucous found in CF patients. This mucous, left there, traps germs and provides the perfect environment for them to proliferate. Along with the CPT, daily aerosolized medications help dilate airways, deliver on-site antibiotics, and thin the mucous. Digestion is also impaired because that thick, sticky mucous blocks the transport of enzymes from the pancreas, where they are produced, to the intestines, where the food is broken down. Taking enzyme supplements with all meals and snacks containing fat and protein is another part of Lucy and Sallie's daily routine.

At the Bat Mitzvah, during her speech, Debbie described Lucy's first few days:

> There is one image I would like to share with you. Nine hours after Lucy was born, she had her first surgery lasting eight hours. The next day, a second surgery, only six hours. On her third full day, I was standing by her incubator, watching her, stroking her arm. She had a diaper on, with lots of wires and tubes. It was late at night, quiet on the floor. The nurse came over to stand beside me. She had beautiful shoulder-length blonde hair, but was otherwise average looking. Later I found out her name was Terri. She stood beside me, with her hands clasped behind her—very close, but not touching. After a bit, she said very softly, as gently as anyone has ever spoken to me, "Have you held her yet?" I shook my head no. She said, "Let me show you." She brought over an easy chair they had for the parents. She showed me which wires could be detached for short periods of time and how to untangle the rest. She told me to sit and then she put Lucy in my arms. It was a beautiful moment that took me many years to understand. In that moment I learned what true *chesed*, kindness, is. In that moment, I felt the presence of God. Lucy was born on the seventh day of Chanukah. It was clear from the start

> that she was a miracle. At first, we understood the miracle to be that she survived more than thirty-six hours of surgery before she was ten weeks old. Later, we understood that the miracle was that she was born in 1987, when the level of cystic fibrosis care and research was charting new frontiers in the world of medicine. As the years have passed. though, our understanding of the miracle of Lucy has changed.

To add another layer of complications, at the age of 4, Lucy was diagnosed with pervasive development delay. She had the language skills of an 18-month-old. So, in addition to attending to the physical needs of their children, Debbie and Richard put their hearts and souls into Lucy's academic needs. Lucy was enrolled in a therapeutic nursery, with additional speech and play therapy. At one of Lucy's early evaluations, Debbie asked the doctor about Lucy's potential for a Hebrew day school education with a dual curriculum. The doctor's cruel response was that they would be lucky if Lucy learned to speak English, let alone Hebrew. At another hospital, they were told that Lucy was retarded. Devastated, they went home and thought about this diagnosis. Debbie was a special education teacher, and she knew these "specialists" were wrong. Defying these predictions, with the right intervention, Lucy is enrolled in a regular Hebrew day school program with a dual curriculum. She loves Hebrew and is a strong, voracious reader.

Then on January 4, 1999, eleven months before her Bat Mitzvah, Lucy was diagnosed with CF-related insulin-dependent diabetes. A few days after her diabetes was diagnosed, she sat on her hospital bed and asked her mother, "Why are people upset about this? I had one disease and now I have two." She continued, "If a kid had no disease, then he got diabetes, that would be hard for them. But I'm used to having a disease. This is not hard for me." Her mother disagrees. It is hard for Lucy. What is not hard for Lucy is doing it anyway.

The Women's Tefillah of Riverdale is a women's prayer group that davens together monthly. Each woman at the core of this group has her own story and reason for being there.The group relies on the halachic authority of Rabbi Avi Weiss and does not consider itself to constitute a *minyan*. Therefore, group members omit any prayers that require a *minyan*. Lucy decided that she wanted to celebrate her Bat Mitzvah by *layning* Torah as part of the Women's Tefillah group. Men may attend

the service, but it is the women who maintain the seats in the center and the men must sit behind the *mechitzah* (partition or curtain).

Lucy's Bat Mitzvah weekend celebration started on Friday morning in school. It was Lucy's official Hebrew birthday. Normally, the boys and the girls daven separately, but for this occasion, they davened together. Lucy gave a *D'var Torah* after the davening. She addressed why the dreams, both Joseph's and Pharaoh's, came in twos. If they each had only had one dream, it might be considered uneventful or unimportant. The fact that they had two dreams forced them to really pay attention. Then, in keeping with the tradition of Chanukah, Lucy passed out doughnuts to her classmates, teachers, parents, and Rabbi Weiss, their temple rabbi who honored them with his presence.

The rest of the day was spent in hectic preparation. But every task, even the most mundane, was filled with joy, and every detail turned out perfectly. Debbie had ordered special cinnamon babka to be delivered as hostess gifts to friends who were hosting out of town guests. The babka, gourmet and normally delicious, came out even more crunchy and sugary. Richard was pressed into service delivering these gifts. In the course of his service, he was supposed to drop Lucy off at the hairdresser to meet her mother, sister, and aunt, who were already there. In the tumult and confusion, Richard gathered up all of his parcels and made his way around town, neglecting to include the reason for all of the excitement—the Bat Mitzvah girl. When Debbie realized that Lucy was still at home, she called her other sister to please deliver her to the beauty salon.

There were deliveries of centerpieces and hostess gifts, table arrangements and seating charts, photos and finery. And as the sun began to set, and Debbie lit the *Shabbos* candles, a lovely calm settled over her and the entire house. She had taken care of all of the details and now it was here. She could do no more. What was to be done, was done, and all that was left to do was enjoy the moment, the hour, and the day. They walked to *shul* for *Shabbos* dinner in a slight drizzle and never felt the rain. Here Debbie Goldhair was peaceful and warm, as she was surrounded by the people she loved most in the world. She set the table in a horseshoe so that all the people she had talked about through the years, but who had never had a chance to meet each other, might take this time to get to know one another. One treat of the evening and the weekend was that Debbie hired a group of New York college students who belong to an acappela group called PIZMON. They normally do not work private parties, but because they realized what a special occasion this was, they consented to come. Coming from Orthodox backgrounds, they do not travel on *Shabbos*, so Debbie made arrangements to house and feed the entire group. The reward for this was beautiful music. They serenaded the guests throughout the wonderful meal.

The next morning, the whole group once again walked to the Hebrew Institute of Riverdale. The Women's Tefillah group met downstairs, while the regular services were held upstairs. Richard had an *aliyah* in the regular *minyan*, and the other men generally made a fuss over him. But the real celebration was happening downstairs. The Goldhair women entered the small sanctuary where some of the women chose to wear a *tallis* and/or *kipah*, while others did not. It was a service with very personal expression. Lucy's grandmother, Elayne, was the first on the *bimah*, called up to open the Ark. There was a steady stream of family members as Debbie; her sisters, Susan and Jaimee; sister-in-law Judy; and mother-in-law, Elaine, came to the *bimah* and either recited the *brachah* or actually read from the Torah. Since it was Lucy's special day, she was given two *aliyot.* When it was time for Lucy to *layn* from the Torah, her father, grandfather, uncles, and even the rabbi made their way downstairs and watched from behind the *mechitzah*. Taught by an expert, Esther Farber, Lucy chanted beautifully.

The service was followed by a *Kiddush* for several hundred people. Then the Riverdale congregation was treated to a concert by PIZMON. The music was beautiful and spiritual. Lucy provided another *D'var Torah* about the *parsha*. She was followed by her mother, who took the opportunity to share some of her reflections:

> I am so happy to be celebrating my daughter Lucy's Bat Mitzvah. Lucy, you did a beautiful job *layning* today. Whatever has been set before you, you have accomplished more than Daddy and I dared hope. Your voice is strong and clear, a testimony to your *neshamah*, your soul, which burns so brightly. How can I ever help you to understand what I felt as I stood beside you listening to you sing the words of Hashem, thousands of years old in a voice so fresh and vital, a voice that I gave birth to.

> During the past twelve years I have spent many hours fantasizing what I would say today. For a long time, my fantasy skirted around the facts of Lucy's difficult life. I wanted to talk just about her sterling character and endearing idiosyncrasies like all the other mothers who speak at their daughters' Bat Mitzvahs. But what I gradually came to learn is that Lucy is a complete package and everything that is hers has shaped her in ways I can only imagine. So, although I would like to give my daughter just one day without even one thought lighting on cystic fibrosis and diabetes, I am choosing not to attempt the impossible. . . . Hashem has given me a beautiful daughter, a miracle, and we have learned that countless doctors, nurses, neighbors, friends, rabbis, teachers, and family have given her to us as well, over and over again, every day.
>
> What is the Jewish concept of a miracle? A miracle is an event outside the natural order of the world as we know it, but requiring our participation, drawing us closer to Hashem's ultimately unknowable presence in our lives. So we reclaimed the Temple and lit the *Ner Tamid*, the eternal light, knowing that we had only enough oil to sustain the flame for one day. But the flame burned for eight days, enough time to press new oil. As children, we understand that this was a miracle. As adults, our understanding deepens to include the miracle of the human spirit, understanding the strength, courage, and faith it took to light the flame at all.

With the speeches completed, it was just time to celebrate. The social hall was transformed into a festive, gala atmosphere. The room looked gorgeous. The multicolored tablecloths had centerpieces to match, huge dreidels filled with books that were to be donated to the synagogue library. Each dreidel contained the four letters for the sentence "A great miracle happened here." To commemorate the Bat Mitzvah, Debbie and Richard presented Lucy with a tiny gold dreidel on a chain. Once again, the four letters stand for "A great miracle happened here," so that Lucy will remember that she carries the miracle with her—always.

20

FROM RUSSIA WITH LOVE

Natasha and Anna Oziraner—May 25,1992

Not until the twins arrived at the Scranton campus of Penn State did they really thrive. They joined clubs and activities and immersed themselves in campus life. By her sophomore year, Anna was the editor of the newspaper, a member of student government, a student representative on the faculty senate, and creator of the Multicultural Club. As a result of her activities and a high GPA, she was awarded the Walker Award—which is the most prestigious award university-wide and goes to the most involved student. Natasha maintained an honors status, served on the newspaper staff, and became equally involved. They graduated from Main Campus in the spring of 2001.

While the rest of America commemorates December 7th as Pearl Harbor Day, the Oziraner family attached a different significance to that date. On December 7, 1990, Natasha and Anna Oziraner, age 11; their brother Michael, eight years their senior; and mother, Eugenia Martinova, arrived from Moscow, Russia, at Kennedy Airport. They arrived on Friday night, and since it was Shabbos, they had to wait in New York City before boarding a small plane the next night after sundown. This little puddle-jumper

would take them to their new home in Scranton, Pennsylvania. They had no family there and knew no one. They had been classified as "refuseniks" in Russia. They had applied to leave and were refused permission. Even with the advent of Gorbachov and glasnost, or freedom, they were denied the right to leave Russia. However, after two years of waiting, the Oziraner family was granted a visitor's visa, allowing them to leave "temporarily." The excited foursome boarded a plane in Moscow and seventeen hours later touched down on American soil.

Scranton and the surrounding communities, nestled in northeastern Pennsylvania, have a Jewish population of only 3,000. The area boasts, however, the highest average per capita donations to the United Jewish Appeal in the country. A small population with a big heart! In spite of a diminutive local Jewish community, with mass emigration taking place from Russia, the Scranton Jewish Federation accepted hundreds of Jews for resettlement in the late 1980s and early 1990s. In some of the bigger cities, Russian immigrants got off the plane, somehow made their way to the nearby Jewish Family Service or HIAS (Hebrew Immigration Aid Society) office, were given a check to start them off, and were sent on their way. Not in Scranton! The new immigrants were met at the Scranton-Wilkes Barre Airport in person by the head of the Jewish Family Service, Tom Goldenson, usually with an entourage of children and other staff members bearing gifts and flowers. They were personally escorted to a clean, furnished apartment, complete with the beds made and a refrigerator full of kosher food.

It was no wonder, then, with the Jewish community reaching out so beautifully, that many of the newly arrived children attended the Scranton Hebrew Day School rather than the local public school. Natasha and Anna were old enough for sixth grade, but instead were placed in the fifth grade because they knew very little English, let alone Hebrew. The challenge was greater in enrolling these new immigrants in a school that provided a dual curriculum, but at the same time the atmosphere was warm, supportive, and cloistered. The girls were provided with a tutor, Mrs. Shira Silverberg, who patiently explained both the Jewish traditions and American customs. Even within the protective environment, there were times of great frustration that resulted in tears. The English language is filled with contradictions and exceptions to the rule. Anna couldn't figure out where the "t" sound came from in words like *dressed*—and where was the "t" sound in words like *fraction*. To this day, Anna hates to read out loud.

With the help of the tutor, the girls had an interesting advantage. Many of the Orthodox girls "lived" Judaism as a matter of course, without fully understanding the "why" behind the practice or celebration. The twins learned not only to observe the holidays, but also their history and significance. This positive exposure to the pride, beauty, and joy associated with their Jewishness was crucial for the girls. Growing up in the Soviet Union was difficult and sometimes heartbreaking for these two little Jewish girls. Some of their earliest memories of school include the taunts and teasing of the other children. Anna clearly remembers having to defend Natasha with her fists against the physical attacks of the other children. They were outcasts—pariahs. Despite being cultured, well mannered, musically talented, and intelligent, they suffered tremendous humiliation because they were Jewish.

Kids are cruel, but what is the excuse for the adults who treated Anna and Natasha's parents with no less disdain? One day, Eugenia walked proudly down the street on the arm of her husband, when an unknown assailant stuck her finger in Alexander's face and said, "I hate you, you Jew." While her husband looked dejected, Eugenia responded calmly, "You don't have to marry him, I already did."

Eugenia took the hits and remained determined to keep her pride, in spite of the country's effort to reduce her to something humiliating, shameful, and insignificant. Her husband, on the other hand, was perhaps thinner-skinned and allowed the insults to reach his core. He was a brilliant mathematician who had taught at the University of Moscow. He would curl up with one of his math books, rather than a novel, for relaxation. He loved the stable, constant, dependable world of numbers. When he peeked his head out into reality, he was inevitably greeted by a cruel society. It came time for his promotion as a published, well-respected member of the faculty. However, because he was Jewish, the university would not allow him to move up the academic ladder, and it fired him instead. Eugenia had been proposing emigration for a while, but his answer was, "If no one wants my brain here, who would want it there?" Completely depressed and seeing no alternative, Alexander took his own life on January 6, 1987.

Brokenhearted, his very strong-willed wife was even more determined to provide a better life for her three children. She filed for emi-

gration and was refused. Bearing the title "refusenik" made it even more difficult for the family to live. Their phone was tapped and they were harassed constantly. And yet Eugenia took on the system with a vengeance to make sure she got her children out. Consistently being denied the proper papers for leaving, she was shocked when the authorities finally approved a visitor's visa. Leaving behind all personal possessions, they took a few modest belongings, only as much as they could carry.

The girls had had a limited and clandestine exposure to Judaism, thanks to their great uncle Moshe. Every year at Passover, their large family had found some excuse to get together. While the adults would schmooze and catch up in the living room, Uncle Moshe would take the children into the kitchen and recount in exciting detail and colorful language the Exodus of the Jews from Egypt. To this day, they still remember his descriptive vocabulary and enthusiasm as he shared the story of our freedom. The girls also spent a summer with Uncle Moshe and watched as he davened every morning and said the *brachos* before eating.

This limited knowledge was expounded on and expanded in the Hebrew Day School, but the leap from a communist, nonreligious environment to immersion into Orthodox Judaism was a broad one and just one of the culture shocks that the family experienced. For their own religious activities out of school, they became involved with the Conservative congregation. Enough of the service was in English to give them a sense of spirituality. They went every week and became regular fixtures during the *Shabbos* morning service. It was in this synagogue, Temple Israel, that the rabbi approached the family and asked if the girls would like to have a Bat Mitzvah. "Yes, of course!" was the enthusiastic response.

For their part, the twins could already read Hebrew and were used to daily davening. They studied for several months with a very patient Cantor Wolkenstein and a very involved Rabbi Rone. The cantor remarked that he was thrilled to finally have two students who could actually sing. While the girls studied, the community, once again, pitched in and prepared for the celebration. There was a great feeling of communal pride . . . in a sense, our children had come home.

Outfitted in different colors of the same style of dress, sewn by their mother, Anna and Natasha Oziraner were called to the Torah in front of their newly acquired family and friends. While the girls were understandably nervous, their mother experienced different emotions. As her daughters led the prayers and took turns with the Torah portion, Eugenia's tears rolled freely, and she thought, "This is why we came here. At this moment, we are together—part of these people." Natasha remembered how different it was to be Jewish back in Russia, where they couldn't openly talk about it or practice the holidays. It was a very personal, emotional feeling as she read the Haftorah for the first time. She wished that her grandfather could have lived to see it. For both of the girls, the Bat Mitzvah meant that they were no longer just the two Russian girls, they were now part of the community.

The Hebrew Day School, although warm and nurturing, did not prepare the girls for secular high school. Going off to Scranton High in their *frum* wardrobe, the twins found themselves once again unpopular outcasts. To a more sophisticated crowd, their slight accents were charming and their musical talents (Anna plays the piano and Natasha plays the violin) enviable. They managed to find a few good friends, but still suffered through the same taunting and torment that they took as kids in Russia. This time, though, it was not necessarily their religion that made them targets, just that they were different.

It was not until the twins arrived at the Scranton campus of Penn State that they really thrived. They joined clubs and activities and immersed themselves in campus life. By her sophomore year, Anna was the editor of the newspaper, a member of student government, a student representative on the faculty senate, and creator of the Multicultural Club. As a result of her activities and a high GPA, she was awarded the Walker Award—which is the most prestigious award university-wide and goes to the most involved student. Natasha maintained an honors status, served on the newspaper staff, and became equally involved. They graduated from Main Campus in the spring of 2001.

Every year on December 7th, the day that they arrived in the United States, the family members sit down to dinner and list all of the accomplishments they have achieved during the year. This enables them to see where they are in comparison to that day, over a decade ago, when they stepped off the plane. It is always a reminder of where they came from and what they were. Michael graduated from college, has a good job, owns his own home, and is happily married to another Russian Jewish immigrant. After failing to secure a job in her field, engineering, Eugenia opened a lucrative cleaning and tailoring shop

and established a reputation for quality. Natasha and Anna take this day to look back at the dirt path they started on and look down at the paved road that stretches ahead.

21

THE QUEEN'S EQUAL

Rebecca Miller—May 22, 1999

Photo credit: Jim Nicholais

The Montessori school that Rebecca attended only went up to the eighth grade, so when it came time to pick a high school, she wanted to go to the regular public school. When the administrators saw her standardized test scores for reading and spelling, they wanted to put her in the lowest academic track. Rebecca pleaded with her mother to once again "believe in me" and help her talk the school officials into placing her in level-two classes, which is the regular academic track. With the aid of a resource room at study hall, a note taker, untimed tests, and her nightly study buddy (Mom), Rebecca is not just getting by, she is flying by. She made the honor roll first semester, with all A's and one B. Given the chance to take the information in her own way and with the strength of well-developed study skills, she is proving herself to be quite a good student.

When Rebecca Miller looks through the lens of her camera, she sees things, really sees them. She detects subtle changes and variations in light and shadows, patterns and perspective. She has a great eye for composition, color, and texture and can freeze time and motion. There is freedom with her camera. She can interpret what she sees with the independent eye of an artist.

It's a different story when she looks at the printed page. Rebecca is dyslexic, and reading for pleasure is an oxymoron. Although she possesses normal intelligence, for her, reading is a laborious task in which she must use endless flashcards, memorization, the tedium of sounding out words, and guesswork. She devotes hours every evening to homework. Compounding the dyslexia is an auditory processing problem that makes it difficult to process information or memorize through music or timing and rhythm. Rebecca's mother, Dale, first recognized there was a problem when as a toddler, Rebecca couldn't remember the words to "Happy Birthday" or nursery rhymes.

For elementary school, Rebecca attended a Montessori program that is noted for its short periods and hands-on approach to learning. There, Rebecca met with a level of success with her academics. Rebecca attended the Hebrew School of Temple Hesed in Scranton, Pennsylvania, and moved along with her peers. However, when it came time for Bar and Bat Mitzvah preparation and the program became more intense, the teacher noticed that Rebecca was having a difficult time. She called up the Millers and explained that because of the difficulty Rebecca and another young lady were having in the class, she would like to set up a special class just for the two of them. The teacher, Emily Trunzo, was tentative on the phone, fearing that she would offend the Millers with her suggestion. Offended? They were thrilled that Rebecca would receive the extra attention. Rebecca, who knows her own strengths and weakness, was glad for the additional help. She realized that just as in regular school, where she had to take the information home to review and reinforce it, mostly with her mother, she'd need someone to study Hebrew with also. Conveniently, Dale Miller had majored in special education in college, so her background, along with immeasurable patience, made her the perfect candidate for the hours of nightly homework she did with Rebecca. However, when it came to Hebrew, Dale had a deficit. With her own cursory Hebrew education, she didn't know enough to assist her daughter. Because Mrs. Trunzo was setting up the special class anyway for Rebecca and the other young lady, Dale joined them and increased its enrollment to three. It was no big deal for Rebecca to have her mother in class, and this way they moved along at a very slow pace, which they both needed, and then they could study together for homework.

Because of her intense involvement with Rebecca's work, Dale knew better than anyone the struggles her daughter faced with reading and memorization. The English itself posed enough of a hurdle, even before the Hebrew was introduced. Fearing that a very public Bat Mitzvah, with all that was required, would be frustrating and overwhelming, Dale tried to talk her daughter into an "alternative" ceremony. Dale tried to encourage Rebecca to have a special Bat Mitzvah in Israel. She was actually very colorful in her description of how the whole family would be there to celebrate in this very meaningful place. She really tried to "build up" the Israel trip. Rebecca wouldn't hear of it. "Who would see me in Israel?" Rebecca asked her mother one evening during one of Dale's continuous discussions of this "special" Bat Mitzvah. Rebecca's older brother and sister had both had their Bar and Bat Mitzvahs in Temple Hesed in front of the whole congregation, and she wanted nothing less.

The special class went very well and very slowly. The first year, they met every Thursday from 4:30 P.M. to 6:00 P.M., and they just worked on the reading. The other student moved along nicely. She couldn't read the Hebrew, but was able to memorize everything. With dyslexia, it is difficult to break words down. Rebecca had to learn how to read every sound. Determined to have her Bat Mitzvah in her own temple, she needed to prove that she was as good as everyone else. She thought that no one believed in her.

In the second year of study, they actually started learning how to read from the Torah. They divided the *parsha* so that Rebecca's whole family would each have an *aliyah*. This would be the first time since his Bar Mitzvah that Ken, Rebecca's father, would read from the Torah. Aaron and Jessica, Rebecca's older siblings, would each take a part. And since Dale was studying fervently right alongside her daughter, she would read from the Torah as well. At one point, Dale brought up the idea of having a joint Bat Mitzvah, but with all of the effort that Rebecca was pouring into her studies, she wanted the day to herself.

Somewhere along the way, Dale had approached Rabbi Peskind, the spiritual leader of Temple Hesed, and told him that she wanted a "bare bones" Bat Mitzvah, asking that Rebecca do only the minimum requirements. The rabbi looked at her and asked why she was setting limits here. He told her to let Rebecca set the limits of what she could and couldn't do. He was very supportive and empathetic because his own daughter has a learning disability.

Six months before the Bat Mitzvah, the classes were stepped up, and Rebecca went every day to work on the Torah reading and the prayers. In addition to Rebecca's studying with Mrs. Trunzo and the rabbi, Esther Adelman helped Rebecca with her speech. Since Rebecca couldn't memorize it with rhythm, it had to be read, but had to sound as if it flowed. Success varied from day to day, and no one knew until the day before whether she would actually be able pull it off.

Dressed in a cream-colored satin suit with matching flowers in her hair, Rebecca was cool and confident. She led the morning services, and then for the Torah reading, she watched as one after the other of her family members had an *aliyah* and read from the *parsha Naso*. When Dale finished her reading, she felt in her heart as if she had just become a Bat Mitzvah. Rebecca read from the Torah and then continued leading the remainder of the services. She delivered her speech and it flowed without flaw. When she looked out to smile at her parents, it was the first time she saw her father cry. Since Dale was an officer in the temple at the time, it was her job to present the Bat Mitzvah girl with her certificate. And much to her surprise, her daughter pulled out a certificate of her own. Rebecca presented her mother with an official Bat Mitzvah certificate, as well.

She did it! She did it all! There was nothing skimpy about this Bat Mitzvah. She did it, not because her mother or father wanted her to, but because she wanted it so badly. Her effort and drive were monumental, and the outcome was wonderful. She was given an out, which she refused to take, and although it took her longer, the end result was worth it. She was smooth and calm and proved that she was as good as everyone else (some say better!).

She still marvels that the Bat Mitzvah preparation for her friends was apparently "no sweat," whereas everything for her takes longer. At the same time she shrugs and says matter of factly, "This is what my life is." Although her mother will tell you that she works "like a dog," Rebecca feels that this is the way it is and if she wants something, she has to work for it. Beginning with her Bat Mitzvah, she felt that she had to prove that she was just as good as everyone else. In reality, she proved that she is a whole lot more.

22

MOTHERS AND SONS

Emily Trunzo and Craig Trunzo—May 27, 1988

Emily remains active with a variety of projects at Temple Hesed. One of her newest programs was awarded an honor. Emily paired homeless or needy children with members of the community who purchased new clothes and supplies for the first day of school.

Craig is a sergeant in the Air Force, stationed at the Pentagon.

HARRY AND JEAN WEINBERG

INVITE YOU TO
THE BAT MITZVAH OF THEIR DAUGHTER

Emily Weinberg Trunzo

WHO INVITES YOU TO
THE BAR MITZVAH OF HER SON

Craig Richard Trunzo

Emily Trunzo felt as if she had missed out on something. An important Jewish milestone had not been hers for the taking when she was a young girl, so she was reaching for it now. Back in her formative years, girls were just skipped over when it was time for Bar Mitzvahs, so this mother of three, at age 46, said to herself. "If not now, when?" And so, she decided to reclaim her right to become a daughter of the commandments.

Actually, timing plays a role in this story. After a rather circuitous route, Emily found herself at Temple Hesed, a Reform congregation in northeastern Pennsylvania. What started out as a temporary substitute position ended up becoming a permanent teaching job at the temple, first as a Sabbath school teacher and later with the Bar and Bat Mitzvah students. The spiritual leader of the temple, Rabbi Milton Richmond, was planning to retire, and Emily wanted to make sure that he presided over her long-overdue coming-of-age ceremony. There were delays and postponements, and before long, time was running out. Emily was preparing her son Craig for his Bar Mitzvah, and with very few dates available before the rabbi left, Emily approached him about sharing the date with her son. Although it had never been done before in this Temple (and probably in very few other places), the rabbi gave the idea the green light. Now, Craig is a very practical young man, and when his mother asked him if he were willing to share his Bar Mitzvah day, he immediately agreed. Craig has ADHD; one way that it manifests is in dyslexia. He didn't view his mom as taking

anything away from him; she would do half of the service, meaning that he wouldn't have to do everything himself.

At that time, Emily had not yet become the Bar and Bat Mitzvah teacher, so she enrolled in the B'nai Mitzvah class with the 13-year-olds. Emily had a stronger base than many of the other students, so once she got her part down, she used the time during the class to help the other kids. No one seemed to mind her presence in the class. She took the lessons as seriously as they did, maybe more so.

Craig's *parsha* was *Naso*, which deals with Samson. Samson's mother was barren, and an angel appeared to tell her that she would conceive. Her son would become a Nazarite, an elite group of priests who separate themselves and live by a strict set of rules. Her son, she was told before conception, was destined for greatness and would begin to free the Israelites from the Philistines.

Since Emily was a free agent, so to speak, and was not bound by the *parsha* corresponding to her birthday, she chose for herself the song of Deborah. Deborah was the first judge to be described as a prophet. She was a fiery and energetic woman who settled disputes and decided cases while sitting under a palm tree. At that time, the children read their Haftorahs. Emily differentiated herself in another way: She chanted her portion.

While Emily took her son shopping for the perfect Bar Mitzvah suit, her own mother took her shopping for her Bat Mitzvah dress. It was red and white and would be worn only once, for this special occasion. It was not sentiment that prohibited Emily from wearing the dress again. The dress-maker had measured wrong and made it too short.

In addition to Emily and Craig being called up to the Torah, they were each permitted to honor one other person by giving that person an *aliyah*. Twice divorced, Emily gave her *aliyah* to her father. Craig chose his "big brother," Richard Feibus.

During their speeches, Emily spoke with a lot of feeling about the importance of Judaism and tradition in her family. She remembers lighting candles with her grandmother. She emotionally told the assembled guests how, as a divorced single mom, she had raised her youngest son for the last thirteen years alone. How lucky that they have arrived together! Samson was the topic of Craig's speech, and he made an analogy between the problems Samson had and the problems

that he (Craig) has in school. And just as Samson learned patience and control, Craig, too, was learning the same lessons.

The Bar or Bat Mitzvah and his or her family have the honor of presiding over the *Shabbat* table—the blessing over the candles, wine, and challah. Craig said the *Kiddush*, the blessing over the wine. The rabbi thought that as an adult, Emily should find a special melody to sing while lighting the candles. Her inspiration came from a made-for-TV movie, *The Murder of Mary Flynn*. This is the famous story of the unjust lynching of Leo Frank for the murder of a young girl down South in the early part of this century. In the movie, Leo's wife brings her *Shabbat* candles to the jail and lights them with her husband in his cell. As she kindles the lights in this cold, dark, foreboding place, she sings the *brachah* in a beautiful melody. When Emily heard it for the first time, she knew that this was the tune she would incorporate for the B'nai Mitzvah. She memorized it and "borrowed" it when she lit the candles in front of the congregation.

As proud as Emily was of her son, that is how proud her parents were of her. Whether 46 or 13, she was their child who had accomplished something wonderful. Now, the downside of being both the parent of and the partner of the Bar Mitzvah boy is that Emily did all of the baking for the *Oneg Shabbat*. Also, since it was a joint celebration, the invited guests had the pleasure of sitting through two candle-lighting ceremonies—26 candles, 26 different cutesy rhymes about the significant people in Emily and Craig's lives, and 26 photo ops where the mother or son was sandwiched between relatives and smiled for the camera. In lieu of a big party, Emily rented a van and drove Craig and eight of his friends to a Yankees game.

Several years after Emily became a Bat Mitzvah, she was assigned the delightful task of teaching the Bar and Bat Mitzvah classes in her temple. She has an uncanny knack for varying her approach with each student. Some of the kids require one-on-one instruction, while other students thrive with group lessons. She is soft-spoken, incredibly kind, and tries to instill in her students the same pride that she felt on her special day. She remembers how nervous she was in spite of being an adult and tries to allay her students' fears by making sure they are completely prepared. She views her Bat Mitzvah as one of the most special days in her life, even more so because she shared it with her son.

23

THE HOUSE THAT DAD BUILT

Elizabeth Secor Skolnick—October 30, 1999

Elizabeth is a student at Poly Prep County Day School in Brooklyn. B'Nai Yisrael the synagogue that Lee Skolnick designed in Armonk, has won a Faith and Form Religious Art and Architecture Award and will be featured in a new book on Religious Architecture.

Photo by Marlene Lieberman

Standing at the *bimah* on her Bat Mitzvah, Elizabeth Skolnick looked as if she'd stepped into a painting. She was surrounded by nature. The rows of seats in front of her were made out of beautiful wood. And the wall behind her was completely made of glass, leaving Elizabeth framed by the trees outside and the fall foliage. The sight of this beautiful young woman ascending the steps to take her place as a Jewish adult left the observer feeling that she was taking her place in the world.

This lovely setting would be special under any circumstances, but more so on this occasion because the temple had been designed by

Elizabeth's father. Lee Skolnick, a Cooper Union-trained architect, had never before designed a synagogue. He specializes in museums, children's museums, and homes. He almost never engages in competitions for work, because his strategy for doing the best job is to establish an intense interaction with the client and listen to the person's needs. In spite of that, a design competition was held for a synagogue to be built in Westchester, New York. The architect was excited about the idea of designing a spiritual community center and was inspired by the site. Skolnick's firm, Lee H. Skolnick Architecture and Design Partnership, won the competition and the job.

The design and subsequent building of B'nai Yisrael became a very spiritual experience for Skolnick. He reached back into his old affiliations and knowledge gleaned from a childhood in Queens, New York, and rekindled those feelings. He wanted to create a place that was the embodiment of his background and memory. The whole process was unique and fed the experience as a soul-searching project. Skolnick had dealt with museum boards in the past, and now he learned to deal with a temple board. They all shared the same goal, however, of delivering something that would make everyone feel proud.

Skolnick looked to the rabbi for guidance. He wanted to know what was important and what was not. Skolnick questioned the rabbi on how he conducted the service, where people stood, and where religious objects were placed. Form followed function. On a typical Sabbath, only a handful of people came to services, and yet for holidays and special occasions, hundreds were in attendance. Skolnick wanted to design a sanctuary that accommodated either small or large groups. He also needed to design the building to anticipate an expansion of the temple that was predicted over the next few years.

Since Skolnick lives in Manhattan, it was easy for him to involve his family in this project, if only as observers. Lee brought his wife, Jo Ann, and their children, Elizabeth and Harrison, up on the weekends, and they witnessed everything, from the destruction of the old temple on that site to the full construction of the beautiful new building. They all felt that they were part of B'nai Yisrael, even though they lived in Chelsea (a downtown section of Manhattan) and belonged to the Village Temple. So, it wasn't completely far-fetched when they broached the subject of having Elizabeth's Bat Mitzvah in the newly erected sanctuary.

There were logistics to work out. Actually, there were a million little details and several large roadblocks. Even though both temples are Reform, their services are very different. They use different prayer books and music. The lion's share of planning the event fell to Jo Ann, and she approached each new snag with an even temper and steady resolve. As close as Lee had become to Rabbi Krantz of B'nai Yisrael, the Skolnicks wanted Rabbi Burt Siegel, the acting interim rabbi at the Village Temple, to preside over Elizabeth's Bat Mitzvah. Rabbi Siegel had not only converted Jo Ann, but he had officiated at their wedding and the funeral of Lee's father. They felt that since Rabbi Siegel had been drawn inexorably into their lives, it would be meaningful for him to preside over this special ceremony in their next generation. They also wanted to bring Cantor Levine, who had studied with Elizabeth for almost a year, and he in turn wanted his own organist. Bringing your own rabbi to another synagogue is like going to a restaurant and bringing your own chef. But Rabbi Krantz was very cool about the whole process and announced to Skolnick and his entourage, "My synagogue is your synagogue."

Next, they had to actually transport their guests from Manhattan to Westchester, a distance of about thirty miles. Many Manhattanites, relying exclusively on public transportation, do not own their own vehicles. Jo Ann not only hired a bus, but also stocked it with delicacies, making the trip quite pleasant.

Elizabeth felt very lucky to have her Bat Mitzvah in her "Dad's Temple." Rather than feeling detached because this was not their regular congregation, she felt that it was more special. She had watched the synagogue actually being built and felt as if she were a part of it. Lee's only fear was that somehow the day would become about him, and he didn't want to overshadow his daughter. His fears were for naught. A perfect balance was achieved. In one speech it was mentioned that Elizabeth's father had designed the synagogue, and the rest of the day belonged to her. Elizabeth, draped by the morning sun, led the entire service in a beautiful voice, all of the blessings, prayers, and the Torah and Haftorah reading of *parsha Vayera*. Since the portion is complex and contains many different themes, she chose to speak about the positive aspects of our Patriarch Abraham's generosity rather than about the destruction of Sodom and Gomorrah. During the service, Rabbi Krantz moved around the sanctuary, taking this unique opportunity to experience the different vantagepoints of his congregants.

Both parents came to the *bimah* to address the crowd. In his speech, Lee fondly recalled his parents and his grandfather—who had been an "architect," in a way, because he was one of the founding members of the synagogue in Queens where Lee became a Bar Mitzvah. Lee proudly included that Elizabeth was the first "Skolnick" girl to have a Bat Mitzvah. Like her husband, Jo Ann was filled with emotion. As was a mother's prerogative, Jo Ann shared some of Elizabeth's childhood moments that led up to the impressive young lady she had become. She emphasized how Elizabeth had displayed extraordinary dedication preparing for this day. Having converted, Jo Ann has tremendous respect for Judaism. Never feeling connected to the rituals she had experienced as a child, she now feels that Judaism mirrored her own feelings about life and all living things. She was so proud to watch her daughter experience a religious rite that was so meaningful.

When it was all over, Elizabeth experienced a feeling of relief, like a burden being lifted, but was a little sad that it was all over. It was also the greatest she had ever felt. She experienced a feeling of accomplishment after many months of hard work. Rather than the commercial enterprises that she had witnessed from some of her peers, her day was surrounded by special people in a special place. Everything was perfect. Her brother Harry—who was born with a rare genetic disorder that has caused multiple disabilities, including ADHD, impulsivity, and deafness—rose to the occasion on her day and sat through the service on the *bimah*, at her request, without making a peep. Even her favorite gift, which came from her friend Rosanna, was incredible. Rosanna wrote an essay about Elizabeth and presented it to her.

After the destruction of the Second Temple in Jerusalem several thousand years ago, the synagogue became the center of the Jewish community. It is a house of worship, a place to gather, and the site of ceremonies both joyous and sad. There are synagogues all over the world, some centuries old, that, while remaining true to the principles of Judaism, reflect the architecture and culture of their time and country of origin. But remarkably, whether it is a tiny *shteble* or a palatial structure, the *Shechinah,* God's Holy Spirit, finds a resting place there. As Elizabeth Skolnick descended the steps from the *bimah*, she was still bathed in the sunlight that filtered through the trees. Yet there was no immediate metamorphosis into adulthood, as some people had told her to expect. This was just the beginning of the process. Surrounded

by the beauty of nature, she stood in this place, this house of worship that her father had built, infused with spirituality, and felt very connected to the temple, her family, and the larger Jewish community.

24

EVERYTHING COMES TO HE WHO WAITS

Adelyne Rubinstein—March 20, 1999

Dressed in a lovely white suit, Adelyne had the pleasure of being called to the Torah in front of family and friends who thought enough of her to travel great distances to share the occasion. She had thought about becoming a Bat Mitzvah before, but something always thwarted her plans, whether it was timing or other commitments. Perpetually active in organizations, she has devoted a lifetime to volunteer work. Even now, in Florida, she has served as the president (for the past ten years) of the City of Hope, an organization that raises money for the hospital in California that treats children and adults with cancer and other debilitating illnesses. One lovely by-product of the Bat Mitzvah was that many donations were made to the City of Hope, Hadassah, and various temples in Adelyne's honor. She was thrilled that many people benefited from her simcha.

Born at the conclusion of the First World War, Adelyne Rubinstein has been a firsthand observer of the twentieth century. She has lived through Prohibition, the Great Depression, four wars, a walk on the moon, and technological advances that change by the minute. As an octogenarian, she bucks the stereotype. She is hip, active, and progressive. She chose her 80th birthday to become a Bat Mitzvah.

Adelyne started with a great role model, her mother, who was born in Russia. Her mother felt that a good education was as important for girls as it was for boys and continued her own studies by matriculating at the Community College of Rochester after she arrived in this country. As Adelyne grew, her mother worked hard to make sure that she had an education, even though it was a financial hardship. Though times were tough, she also believed strongly in attending and belonging to a *shul* or temple. And no matter how hard you had it, you could always give charity and help other people.

She went to Hebrew classes after regular school, Monday through Thursday. She was the only girl in the class and learned right along with the boys how to read Hebrew and study the *trup* (tune) that boys needed to know to chant their Haftorah. In those days, girls were not allowed to read from the Torah and/or become a Bat Mitzvah. Children didn't question their parents and when Adelyne's mother and father said "no" to a Bat Mitzvah, there was no further discussion. She was prepared enough, however, to have had a Bat Mitzvah right along with her male classmates.

Because her parents belonged to an Orthodox *shul*, there was no "Sunday" school program. Therefore, she attended the religious school at the Reform temple, where a very well-balanced Jewish education was taught in English.

After she got married, Adelyne and her husband joined the Conservative Temple Beth El in Rochester, New York, where they attended services every week and she substituted in the Hebrew school. Adelyne not only started the first Temple Library, she became its first librarian. Coincidental with her rise to Sisterhood president, the Conservative movement started allowing girls to participate in services, have *aliyot*, act as gabbai, and become Bat Mitzvah.

When Adelyne and her husband started spending a few months out of the year in Florida, they joined another Conservative temple—Temple Beth Israel. Over twenty years ago she had considered starting classes to prepare for her Bat Mitzvah, but the timing was wrong and her plans never came to fruition. In 1981, Adelyne moved to Florida full time.

In November 1998, the rabbi offered a class for men and women who wanted to become Bar or Bat Mitzvah. Prior to going to the first

class, Adelyne had a call from very close cousins who now lived in Tucson, Arizona. They were planning to come to Florida sometime in March, closely coinciding with Adelyne's 80th birthday, which was April 2nd. At the first class meeting, Rabbi Yaakov Thompson explained what he planned to do with the duration of the class. He then asked if anyone in the class would like to make a "public affirmation." If so, he would be happy to work with her. Six women, total, were in the class. One woman was slightly younger than Adelyne and the other four were old enough to be her daughters. The other women had limited, if any, knowledge of Hebrew. Being a compulsive person, Adelyne said right away that she would like to do it. The rabbi asked, "Do you have a date in mind?" Remembering the phone call with her cousins, she answered after consulting her calendar, "March 13th or the 20th." The other women were shocked that she could answer so quickly. When she explained that she had family coming at that time, the rabbi consulted his calendar and March 20th was available and confirmed.

So, without a lot of thought, here was Adelyne Rubinstein, age 79½, five months away from her Bat Mitzvah. She decided she didn't want to recite a Haftorah and prepared to read four portions from the Torah. She also told the rabbi right off that she didn't want to make the traditional "Today I am a fountain pen speech."

Unfortunately, Adelyne's husband had died in 1994, but she is sure that he would have been supportive and proud. When she told her daughter about her plans, Debbie said, "Go for it." Debbie and her friend Dave made out the invitations and sent them to relatives scattered in the four corners of the United States. At first expecting only local Florida friends and the Tucson cousins, Adelyne was elated to find that nieces and nephews were coming from California and that a rather large Rochester, New York, contingency would show up. Debbie's two closest friends (for forty years), their husbands, and several cousins and their children had decided to make the trek for the big bash.

The rabbi made a tape for Adelyne to study on her own, and he also studied with her quite diligently, one on one. Sometime in February he told her that she had to make a speech. She found the portion for that week uninteresting, but she did her homework, found research material, and was able to put something together. The Haftorah had not yet been assigned to anyone, so Adelyne decided to call young cousins from Rochester and Canada and ask them if they would come down and honor her with their recitation, since both young ladies were very well-trained.

Adelyne really did her homework and her speech was very profound:

> It is said that everything comes to he who waits . . . . I only waited sixty-seven years to become a Bat Mitzvah. Thanks to my parents, who felt that a girl should have the same Hebrew education as a boy, I had attended an after-school Hebrew class with all of the boys my age. I could have become a Bat Mitzvah with any of them, but in those days girls were not allowed to have that ceremony. Thanks to the Rabbinical Assembly, women are now given the same opportunities to receive aliyot and become a Bat Mitzvah. It is difficult at this age to learn to read from the Torah, but with sincerest thanks to Rabbi Thompson, who worked so diligently with me, I am here today. I would encourage more women who never had the chance, to join a class . . .
>
> Mere words cannot express my feelings at this time, when I look around and see my relatives who came from near and far to help me celebrate this important day . . . .
>
> *Shabbat Shalom.*

After it was over, there was a lunch, then later a dinner, and then another brunch the next day. In a moment of reflection, Adelyne couldn't believe that she had the nerve to get up in front of all those people and do this, but it was wonderful. It was wonderful because she had always felt a sense of awe for women, whether young or old, who had become a Bat Mitzvah. Maybe it was the need to affirm her Judaism by doing something for herself—studying and learning—as well as doing "charity" for others. The physical distance wasn't so great, but it took her sixty-seven years to walk up to the *bimah*, not only to say the *brachot*, but to read from the Torah. "Good things indeed come to he who waits."

25

WITH A LITTLE BIT OF SOAP

Elana Erdstein—May 21, 1992

Photo by Lifetouch Prestige Portraits

Elana Erdstein designed and executed her own Bat Mitzvah project and it, in turn, influenced her life. Her Bat Mitzvah was not the end of the story. Community service inspired a community activist and leader. Elana plans to become a rabbi when she graduates from Duke. She took something that she considered so obvious and so easy and impacted a population that is often ignored and disregarded. She collected and distributed tens of thousands of items and then taught others to do the same. She proved that adults don't make all of the "dents" and that one person, one little girl, can make a difference.

Elana Erdstein was 11 years old the first time she flew by herself from her Michigan home to Florida, in order to visit her grandparents. When she returned home, she recounted details of the trip, explaining one thing that had really made an impression on her. Her grandmother, prepared to welcome a young lady, had assembled a basket of sample-sized toiletries and placed it in the bathroom. Seeing the names of various hotels imprinted on the products, Elana came home and asked her mother, "Is everyone as cheap as grandma?"

She had this visual image of her dignified grandmother pilfering soap and shampoo from the Hyatt and the Sheraton. Her mother assured her that it was common practice to take the toiletries that were set out in hotel rooms, because by virtue of the room price, you had actually purchased them. This brief conversation ignited a tiny spark of an idea, which set into motion a project that would ultimately affect thousands, but none more than the little girl who conceived the idea.

Everyone needs a bar of soap! If most people took hotel toiletries and, like her grandmother, saved them and used them for special occasions, then maybe all of these people would be willing to donate them to others who didn't have the luxury of staying in hotels—the homeless and those living in shelters. Everyone deserves the dignity of his or her own bar of soap. It took a 12-year-old, as part of her Bat Mitzvah project, to come up with this idea. Elana learned that food stamps don't pay for toilet paper, toothpaste, and other basics that most of us take for granted as necessities, not luxuries.

She started off simply, by placing a wrapping paper-covered box in the temple after making an announcement about the project one week during services. Before long, the box was filled to overflowing. Then she sent out flyers and placed a few boxes in other strategic locations, such as the library and churches. Along with the boxes, she sent letters to hotel chains, asking for donations of sample-sized toiletries. She wrote to local television stations, asking them to do a public service announcement about the project. The response was overwhelming. Originally anticipating 1,000 toiletry articles, she ended up with well over 30 times that number.

The Erdstein basement looked like a warehouse. The filled boxes from around town were brought there for packaging and distribution. The donations from hotel chains were delivered there. The Erdsteins set up an elaborate sorting system. There were mounds of sample-sized toothpaste, shampoo, soap, and so on. There were stacks of toilet paper and diapers. When cosmetic companies launch new colors for the next season, they don't recall the already-distributed products. Rather, they leave the disposal of perfectly good, but one-season-old, colors up to the discretion of individual drug stores. So, in addition to amassing legions of articles for everyday hygiene, Elana collected some extras of nail polish and lip gloss.

Elana approached the distribution process with forethought and consideration. Rather than haul a box over to the local shelter and

deposit it on their doorstep, she called the shelters and asked them what they needed, trying to tailor her deliveries to fit their needs. It didn't make sense to bring a case of diapers to a shelter that housed only grown men. She also made an art form out of the packaging. Elana believed that the toiletries should be presented like gifts, not look like rejected, unwanted items dumped together in an unappealing fashion. So she made individual packages and wrapped them with colorful ribbons.

Anonymity is involved with the one of the highest levels of *tzedakah*, when neither the donor nor the recipient has any knowledge of the other. Elana felt that she didn't want to deliver the toiletry items with the recipients there, respecting their need for dignity and privacy. However, sometimes the recipients were the very people who helped her unload her mom's minivan. One evening, Elana and her mother, Janice, were bringing a delivery to a shelter in an unsafe neighborhood, outside of Detroit. Several of the residents were there to greet them and help bring in the boxes. Then, in a very touching moment, this band of unsavory-looking characters—who under different circumstances might inspire fear if you passed them on the street—insisted on walking Elana and Janice to the car to keep them safe.

In spite of Elana trying to maintain anonymity, one time one of the products' recipients actually tracked her down. In a shelter that houses victims of domestic violence, a mother escaped from her home at gunpoint with her three children, ages 17, 13, and 7. For years, the oldest daughter suffered silently about the sexual abuse she was forced to endure at the hands of her father. However, when he turned his attentions to her younger sister, she spoke up to protect the young girl. The father threatened them with a gun, but they got out without any physical harm. The older daughter, however, paid a deep emotional toll. In addition to her humiliation and shame about the disclosed abuse, she suffered terribly, feeling responsible for the break-up of the family and the reason for their living conditions. In the shelter, someone presented her with one of Elana's beautiful wrapped kits and offered to do her nails for her. This tiny gesture, receiving that little kit, meant to this girl "Someone thinks you're worthy." The girl's mother tracked down Elana to say that as a result of receiving the beautiful little kit, her daughter had started to turn her life around. The mother said that nothing was frivolous about the cosmetics. When you're on the skids, the gesture of someone giving you nail polish—normally an extravagance—becomes a lifeline. Once out of the shelter, the daughter returned to high school and tried to get on with her life.

One of the boxes that was set up in the community contained an interesting deposit. Someone had left a rather large supply of new condoms. Janice first turned this into a lesson for her daughter, explaining that perhaps some might think that poor people should not have children. Then she and Elana got creative with the distribution. There is a home for girls, ages 10–18, who have been neglected, abused, and/or placed there by the court; it is run by the Catholic League of Women. The emphasis in this home is on the girls and not on religious dogma. The home was thrilled to accept the donation, but, because of sensitive issues, came up with a brilliant way to make the condoms available. The employees started a rumor that several grosses of condoms were being kept in an unlocked desk drawer. In this way, girls who might need this ultimate personal-care product could just help themselves.

When Elana solicited the local Marriott, its management told her that she could come pick up a donation at the end of the month. When she arrived with her enthusiastic fresh face, the manager seemed somewhat abashed at presenting one meager box of sewing kits. She looked from Elana to her mother and in a hushed voice told them to drive around the back to the service entrance. When they did so, they saw a huge dolly loaded with big filled plastic bags. The manager had gone to the hotel laundry and just filled up bags with dirty towels. There must have been 400 to 500 towels. The manager had stolen her own towels! Knowing all the good use that could come out of this donation. Janice loaded up the minivan, washed all of the towels at home, and delivered them to shelters.

The program that Elana started ran so beautifully and smoothly that she was invited to a National Teen Summit to teach other kids how to set up a similar collection-and-distribution program. She made available, during the program and then later for anyone who requested them, "start-up" packets detailing how to begin. She found out later that someone in Hawaii had requested her information and had set up another program.

In the process of this mitzvah project, Elana actually had a Bat Mitzvah. And like her project, the service was unique and creative. Elana wrote her own "Gates of Prayer" *siddur* and incorporated readings that focused on peace, social justice, and the community. She and

her family included a detailed explanation of the service and the meaning behind it so that everyone felt welcome. Elana has never lost sight of what the Jewish community means to her. Rather than seeing her Bat Mitzvah as a burden and drudgery, she regarded it as a privilege. Judaism, with its history, culture, and community, is something to be cherished and protected. And then later, Judaism teaches, it is time to give back.

Elana ran the collection program all the way through high school until she left for Duke University, when it became physically impossible to continue. She tried to recruit a replacement, but never found another person with her dedication and drive. Even though the Detroit program is no longer active, Elana continued with other programs of social action. She runs the freshman community service program at Duke. Not looking for recognition and actually embarrassed by all the attention, Elana has been profiled on ABC Television and National Public Radio, and she was featured in several newspapers and magazines, including *Scholastic News* and *Reform Magazine*. Danny Siegel, author and motivator about mitzvah service, included Elana' s story in his book *Tell Me a Mitzvah*. She was also chosen as a "Giraffe" by a national organization that recognizes both children and adults for "sticking their neck out."

Elana Erdstein designed and executed her own Bat Mitzvah project and it, in turn, influenced her life. Her Bat Mitzvah was not the end of the story. Community service inspired a community activist and leader. Elana plans to become a rabbi when she graduates from Duke. She took something that she thought of as so obvious and so easy, and impacted a population that is often ignored and disregarded. She collected and distributed tens of thousands of items, and then taught others to do the same. She proved that adults don't make all of the "dents," and one person, one little girl, can make a difference.

26

MOTHERS AND DAUGHTERS

Merle Pranikoff and Kara Pranikoff—March 11, 1988

Kara recalls what an exciting time of life her Bat Mitzvah year was. While other kids dreaded the lessons, but loved the celebration, Kara enjoyed the preparation. She remembers getting into bed and practicing with her mother. The Bat Mitzvah was the first accomplishment they had achieved together. Now that she is grown and shares her story, the strongest reaction elicited is curiosity. As she looks back, it seems perfectly natural to have shared her special day with her mother. Kara recently participated in another ceremony and again picked a partner to share the day. But this partner will be lifelong—her husband. Her former "partner" has taken on the status of "mother-in-law" to Kara's newest partner. Having already shared the Bat Mitzvah with her mother, Kara will have to find other celebrations to share with her children. With the guidance of a strong role model and her own deep connections, Kara will find no difficulty in passing the legacy on to the next generation.

Whether seated on a padded rocking chair or crouched cross-legged on the floor, mothers around the world croon lullabies to their children. The languages are different, melodies diverse, and the voice quality ranges from bad to beautiful, but somehow, universally, mothers sing to their offspring.

So many of the songs start with a theme similar to "Hush, now baby. . ." offering peace, safety, and protection to the babe in arms. Mothers sing of promises and potential, hope and happiness, legacy and love. This private communication strengthens the bond between mother and child.

On March 11, 1988, Merle Pranikoff sang a very public lullaby, but this time not to, but with her daughter Kara. On this night they shared a Bat Mitzvah, and as part of the Friday night service, Merle chose a lullaby melody for the *Hashkiveinu*. While Merle sang, Kara translated. Normally not one to sing in front of people, Merle found herself swept away with the music and the meaning. Translated, this prayer implores God to allow us to lie down and awaken in the shelter of peace, not only for ourselves, but also for the House of Israel. Unlikely partners, Merle and Kara were the first mother-and-daughter team to have a Bat Mitzvah celebration together in Temple Shaarey Zedek in Buffalo, New York.

Never having had much of a religious education, Merle started taking Hebrew classes at the temple to feel more comfortable in *shul*. She had no hidden agenda of becoming a Bat Mitzvah. She wanted her children to have a good background, and in order to do that she felt that she had to study herself. It was an academic journey. She felt a strong connection to Judaism and wanted her kids to have that strong connection.

When Kara was in elementary school, she had heard about Camp Ramah and wanted to go there. Even though the family was not that religious, Merle looked into the camp and it just felt right. Kara started attending and has some of her most cherished childhood memories from her eight summers there. She remembers vividly the Friday evening service with the whole camp watching the sun set across the lake as they welcomed *Shabbat* with the singing of *L'cha Dodi*. Not only did she meet and make lifelong friends, but at camp she first started to develop a strong Jewish background.

When Kara began to prepare for her Bat Mitzvah, her mother went into her room one evening to kiss her goodnight. Merle smoothed back Kara's hair, gently kissed her forehead, smiled down at her and remarked how lucky she was. "I'm so glad you are getting a wonderful Jewish education. You know, when I was your age, I never had one and subsequently never had a Bat Mitzvah. How nice that you will have one."

A little voice from the bed said. "Well, do it with me."

Merle thought. to herself, "What a wonderful thing she just asked me to do! My daughter asked me to share this day with her." She couldn't turn Kara down.

Now, instead of studying individually, they continued their studies together. They picked and chose prayers that were most meaningful to them. The family attended the synagogue more often for the Friday evening services, rather than on Saturday morning, so they decided they that would hold the B'nai Mitzvah during that service as well. The rabbi said it was highly unusual, because there is no Torah reading, but since the whole affair was pretty atypical—a parent and child sharing the ceremony—he consented. Several cynics, of course, felt it necessary to share their opinions. They ranted to Merle, "How can you steal the thunder from your child!" But since it was the child who had initiated the suggestion and all of the people who counted thought it was a great idea, the detractors' comments went unheeded.

Instead of thinking in terms of stolen thunder, the naysayers should have focused on the close relationship between mother and child. They should have understood that the little girl realized that what she was doing was so special. She was continuing a legacy and joining a community of strong women. She felt that it was sad that her mother had never had the opportunity to become a Bat Mitzvah. Kara not only wanted her mother to watch her take place in this elite club, she wanted her mother to become a member, too. Rather than feeling that "her day" was diminished by this joint endeavor, Kara felt that it was enhanced.

In addition to the traditional service, which they split, they incorporated a few of their favorite poems. Because the Pranikoffs are a tightly knit unit, Kara's younger sister, Julie, and her father, Kevin, also sat on the *bimah* during the service and assisted by leading some of the prayers.

Then mother and daughter took turns making their speeches. Merle picked the familiar theme of *D'or L'Dor*, from generation to generation. But instead of focusing on what gets passed down, she talked about what she had learned from her child and why she was there, on this day. Kara was wearing a silver bracelet that symbolized the plight of the Russian "refuseniks" who were not permitted to emigrate. Holding up the bracelet, Kara talked about the separation of one family whose child was able to get out, while the father remained

behind. She talked about the closeness of her own family and how she hoped that one day soon the Russian family would be reunited.

One of the most memorable parts for Kara was that when it was all over—the kissing, handshaking, and Mazel Tovs—the four of them, mother, father, and two daughters, went home. They peeled off their finery, ordered a pizza, and talked and laughed for hours as they relived the evening, each filling in details that the others might have missed. Merle shared her tremendous sense of accomplishment. She voiced that if it were not for Kara's suggestion, she never would have contemplated becoming a Bat Mitzvah. She would advise others that rather than harboring feelings of regret, it is never too late for them to take on a challenge. She had set a goal and achieved it. She had learned Hebrew and our history, and that knowledge led to a deeper understanding and therefore a deeper connection.

Kara recalls what an exciting time of life her Bat Mitzvah year was. While other kids dreaded the lessons, but loved the celebration, Kara enjoyed the preparation. She remembers getting into bed and practicing with her mother. The Bat Mitzvah was the first accomplishment they had achieved together. Now that she is grown and shares her story, the strongest reaction elicited is curiosity. As she looks back, it seems perfectly natural to have shared her special day with her mother. Kara recently participated in another ceremony and again picked a partner to share the day. But this partner will be lifelong—her husband. Her former "partner" has taken on the status of "mother-in-law" to Kara's newest partner. Having already shared the Bat Mitzvah with her mother, Kara will have to find other celebrations to share with her children. With the guidance of a strong role model and her own deep connections, Kara will find no difficulty in passing the legacy on to the next generation.

27

CODA

Fayth L. Balsam—February 14, 1998

Fayth is a senior in high school outside of Philadelphia. Her sister; Alexa, is in the ninth grade.

Photo by Isaac Bensadoun

In musical terms, a coda is the final part of a piece of music, often distinctly different from the rest of the musical piece. The acronym CODA in the field of deafness refers to "Children of Deaf Adults." The two CODAs share a parallel definition, in that, musically, the ending is different from the rest of the piece, while CODAs are the offspring who are different from their parents, in that they are hearing, whereas their parents are deaf.

CODAs often share similar experiences by virtue of their parent's deafness and at the same time are as varied as the general population. Some CODAs, with American Sign language being their first language, embrace the field and become interpreters and teachers of the

deaf. Others, however, barely sign, rely on siblings to "interpret" for them, and are not active in the deaf community.

Fayth and Alexa Balsam are the two hearing children of Gay and Richard Balsam, who are both deaf. Fayth considers it a privilege to have grown up in her home. She is bilingual, fluent in both American Sign Language (ASL) and English. And living with people who are "different" has made her more open-minded, tolerant, and sensitive. Knowing sign language also helped her land a role on the daytime soap opera *One Life To live*, which led to other work in television.

Richard and Gay, like most parents, only want to provide the best for their children. They bought a cute little house in the Philadelphia suburbs. During their first holiday season, they realized that theirs was one of the only houses not decorated for Christmas. At school, the girls became friendly with non-Jewish children, who were the majority in the school system. Fayth and Alexa became confused, as other kids do when living as minorities. They asked their parents, "Why don't we have a Christmas tree? Why don't we get Christmas presents?"

Richard and Gay realized that although they provided a Jewish home, they needed to do more for their children. The problem was that as they started to look for synagogues, they found that most were inaccessible. They made inquiries and found that either the rabbi or the board of the synagogue were uninterested or unwilling to provide (pay for) an interpreter for services and/or Hebrew school. It didn't make sense to join a *shul* for their children's sake, if they, as parents, could not attend.

Then their friend Sharon Petroff, who is hearing but has two deaf daughters, invited the Balsams to come to her synagogue, Temple Beth Torah in the Northeast. The services are interpreted once a month and the board willingly hired an interpreter for Hebrew school for the two Petroff girls, Gabby and Laura. Excited by the access, the Balsam family found itself involved in a synagogue program, and Fayth and Alexa started Hebrew school. Gabby Petroff, the older of the two Petroff girls, was in Fayth's class and the two girls became best friends.

At the same time, Gay was having her own growth experience. Growing up, Gay knew that she was Jewish, but without any formal instruction had no clue what that really meant. She watched her brother, six years her senior, become a Bar Mitzvah, but she sat through the service without any idea of what was happening. Hungry to learn more, she jumped at the chance when a rabbi offered a Bat Mitzvah class to the Hebrew Association of the Deaf (HAD). Gay and two other women began to study with Rabbi Sonya Starr from Kenneseth, Israel and an interpreter, Lore Rosenthal, for seven months. It takes a very special interpreter to translate the Hebrew prayers and Torah portions into American Sign Language. That person must possess the knowledge to understand deeply what the prayers mean. Gay knew that the twice-weekly study sessions took time away from her family, but this was something she had always wanted to do. She also viewed herself becoming a Bat Mitzvah as a crucial role to demonstrate for her daughters. It was as if to say, "I didn't let anything stop me; don't let anything stop you."

During Gay's Bat Mitzvah service, she shared the following words in her speech:

> When the opportunity came up to take this class, I thought maybe this will help me better understand what was missing in my life as a Jew. I found that in addition to the rituals, customs, and traditions we observe and celebrate, a sense of being part of a larger "whole" developed. The missing piece in my life was understanding how God plays a part in our ancient history and in our present life. God is here for us in all ways, we just don't see or recognize it, since we are concerned only with ourselves and our immediate demands and needs.
>
> This course helped me to look beyond myself and better see this world in a more positive way as a Jew.

Several years later it was time for Fayth to prepare to become a Bat Mitzvah. Hers was to be the first in 1998 and the first with the new rabbi and cantor. Fayth studied long and hard with the prayers, the Torah reading, and what it all meant. For the actual Bat Mitzvah, the family engaged the services of the same interpreter, Lore Rosenthal, who was very special to the family and would now be interpreting the "second-generation" Bat Mitzvah in the Balsam family. Although Fayth signs fluently, she decided that she would worry about the davening and the Torah reading and leave the interpreting up to Lore. Richard and Gay were not the only two deaf people in attendance.

Gabby and Laura Petroff were there, as well as many good friends from the HAD.

Fayth was wonderful and her performance was seemingly effortless. Her friends from school couldn't believe that their deep and mysterious friend knew yet another language, Hebrew. They didn't realize all of the hard work, time, and effort that had gone into the "effortless" chanting.

Fayth has always been a very spiritual person. As she learned and studied more about Judaism, she shared what she learned with some of her friends. Many of them were in awe of all of the questions that Fayth asked. In some other religions, there is blanket acceptance—"That's the way it is." But in Judaism, she learned to ask, probe, and question. Fayth especially loved to have deep discussions with her friend Sarah, who unfortunately had lost her father to cancer. He had been very insightful, and Fayth feels good when she talks to Sarah, who reminds her of God's presence.

All of her research and studies led Fayth to sharing the following ideas with her invited guests:

> At the base of Mt. Sinai, God spoke to the Hebrews through lightning and thunder and announced His ten Commandments. The voice of God terrified the people and they requested Moses from there on to be the voice of God, enabling them to receive God's laws in a less threatening manner. This portion then continues with God explaining in detail how to handle situations with people, regarding personal relationships, servants, animals, working, and punishment of crime offenses.
>
> Most interesting of all is that the Hebrews received the major body of God's laws, to act and live in a civilized manner, before the tablets were made. It appears that the later delivery of the ten Commandments on stone tablets seemed more of a formality, sealing the "covenant" or bond between God and the Hebrew people.
>
> I think God wanted us to grow and learn and discover just how magnificent His world and His universe really is. This explains why doctors and scientists are challenging the known theories of life and existence and journeying into the unknown. What better way to marvel at just how unique we are and our universe truly is? This journey of self-discovery I realized I must take, not as a result of my

> Bat Mitzvah, but as a journey of self-discovery and awareness of God and myself.

Growing up belonging to two worlds, both deaf and hearing, may have added some confusion to Fayth's journey of self-discovery. However, proud of her dual heritage, she has chosen to embrace aspects from each culture and incorporate them into her life. She sings and she signs, and sometimes even signs songs. Her friends are both deaf and hearing, and she is comfortable in either setting. She is used to cuing into facial expressions, as well as into voice and intonation. And being bilingual has given her an edge in understanding the nuances of language. Having strong and loving role models—her parents—has enabled her to fit in anywhere and has given her the confidence to choose her own path.

PS: There must be something about holidays and the Balsam family. While Fayth's Bat Mitzvah fell on Valentine's Day, her sister Alexa's Bat Mitzvah fell on St. Patrick's Day. March 17, 2001. In addition to falling on a holiday, her Bat Mitzvah completes the circle (or square, if you think of the four of them), making her entire family B'nai Mitzvah, "sons and daughters of the commandments." Alexa shares some similarities with her sister, but she tends to be more headstrong. Her family thinks of her as a "lawyer-type" because she is always trying to find "loopholes," as well as making legal arguments. With her parents, she communicates by speech, sign, and expressive body language, so there is no way that she can be misunderstood. Her friends also think it's cool that she has knowledge in three languages (English, Hebrew, and sign language), and she just accepts it as a natural part of her daily life. For her Bat Mitzvah, Lore Rosenthal once again provided the interpretation. Alexa also shared some powerful words with her guests:

> Becoming a Bat Mitzvah has been an ongoing sense of wonder, discovery, and sometimes FEAR. But the more I learn, the more I wonder and want to learn even more. My Dad once told me, "It's not a matter of asking a question and getting an answer. True learning and thinking come when you let that answer lead you to more questions. This is what I call the ongoing journey to learn something new." I can't argue with that. But what's far more important is that for my journey, the first step starts with me.

28

SHEHECHIYAUNU

Rabbi Amy Eilberg—November 1967

Rabbi Amy Eilberg went on to become the co-founder of the Bay Area Jewish Healing Center, where she directed the Center's Jewish Hospice Care Movement. Nationally known as a leader of the Jewish healing movement, she lectures and writes on issues of Jewish spirituality and healing. She currently serves as a pastoral counselor in private practice in Palo Alto, California.

Photo by Cathy Gannes

Elizabeth Blackwell received her M.D. degree in 1849, becoming the first woman in the United States with a medical degree. Amelia Earhart became the first woman to fly solo across the Atlantic (1932). In 1981, President Reagan appointed Sandra Day O'Connor to the Supreme Court, making her the first woman justice. Dr. Sally K. Ride was the first American woman sent into space in 1983. And Amy Eilberg in 1985 became Conservative Judaism's first woman rabbi. All of these women gained notoriety by being the "first" in their fields. Even though it is now commonplace to see female doctors, pilots, astronauts, justices, and rabbis, we still owe them a debt of gratitude for their pioneer spirit, bucking the system, shattering the stereotype, and paving the way for other women to follow.

Sometimes we end up achieving goals in spite of our experiences, rather than because of them. Amy Eilberg's early Jewish background would not have predicted that she would eventually enter the rabbinate. Her parents, former Philadelphia congressman Joshua Eilberg and Gladys, a social worker, were deeply involved with Judaism, but more community-minded than ritually observant. Amy attended Hebrew school as a matter of course, rather than as a result of a passionate drive.

Growing up, their synagogue, Beth Emeth, in the Oxford Circle section of Philadelphia, did not afford women equal rights. Females were not permitted on the *bimah*. Women were gladly welcomed into the sisterhood or auxiliary, but were not permitted to hold offices in the general synagogue, Eilberg's Bat Mitzvah was "ordinary" for her day. It was held on a Friday night with some "creative adaptations," since the Torah is not normally read on *Erev Shabbat*. Because of the large community, four young ladies shared this Bat Mitzvah celebration. The Haftorah for *parsha Chayyai Sarah* was chopped into quarters and was read without a blessing (because that is only done on Shabbat morning); the girls each read one-fourth. The festivities culminated the next night with a small party. The whole deal was much smaller than her brother's Bar Mitzvah, which was held three years earlier and which led her to feel that perhaps her brother was favored.

Although Hebrew school and the Bat Mitzvah failed to evoke any spiritual enthusiasm in Amy, USY (United Synagogue Youth), only a short time later, became the impetus that would ultimately lead to life-altering experiences. Even though USY in the late '60s was not yet egalitarian, it nonetheless touched her heart. She was exposed to the magic of traditional Jewish practice in her teenage years. During those horrible/wonderful years, she was able to ask questions about how the universe is put together—and to seek out a connection with something larger than herself, even before she had the language to describe what was happening.

At the age of 14, she joined "USY on Wheels," which was a teen tour around the United States. As a group of forty, they davened three times a day, even if it meant pulling the bus over and davening *Mincha*

(afternoon prayers) on the side of the road. Everything they ate was kosher, so when they stopped to buy food, they all learned to check for the appropriate symbols of *kashrut* marked on the packages. The place that Eilberg observed her first traditional *Shabbat* was in the unlikely spot of Montgomery, Alabama. When Eilberg returned home at the end of the summer, she wanted to continue the practices that she had begun while on the trip, which included keeping kosher. She was so determined that her mother respected her decision and converted their kitchen into a kosher one.

Another formative experience happened while she was a college student at Brandeis University. Rabbi Al Axelrad, the rabbi at the campus Hillel, recognized Eilberg's passion and readiness to serve, for he also was passionate about identifying women as rabbis. He took her out to lunch and offered strong encouragement toward that end, even though at that time the Conservative movement had not yet approved the idea of ordaining female rabbis. Although women rabbis were already practicing in both the Reform and Reconstructionist movements (Sally Preisand was the first woman ordained a rabbi by the Reform movement in 1972, and the Reconstructionist Rabbbinical College ordained the first women in 1974, Rabbi Sandy Sasso), Eilberg's heart belonged to Conservatism and she was willing to wait. Upon completion of Brandeis, she enrolled in the Jewish Theological Seminary (JTS) in New York City. She was considered a Talmud major, even though she took many of the same courses as the rabbinical students. When she received her Master's degree in Talmud, the JTS faculty had still not yet sanctioned the idea of accepting female rabbinical students. Eilberg entered Smith College to pursue another degree in social work that she hoped could eventually be incorporated into her work as a rabbi.

Finally, after years of investigation, discussion, and debate, in 1983 the seminary faculty voted in favor of admitting women to the seminary rabbinical school. Normally a four- to six-year course of study, Eilberg re-entered JTS and completed the program in one year, since she had already taken most of the required courses.

Amy Eilberg would be the first! She was described by a professor as having the perfect intellect and personality to carry out this responsibility. This had been a long process and a great struggle. It was no easy task to persuade the leadership of the Conservative movement to accept female rabbis. Some of the faculty at JTS were supportive, while others were ambivalent about teaching a woman to become a rabbi.

Before 1985, ordination at JTS was part of the academic convocation. All of the degrees were awarded as part of the secular graduation, with ordination being part of the process. However, a change was in the air. The class of 1985—this was a spiritual event. The students created a ceremony prior to the academic awards, making the ordination a religious event. (The change in the ordination ceremony was not because a woman was being ordained. The change had been brewing very possibly due to increased spiritual sensibility on the part of the student body.) There was a great halachic (according to Jewish law) discussion about whether the class should recite the *Shehechiyaunu* as part of this service. The *Shehechiyaunu* is a wonderful prayer that thanks God for allowing us to experience "firsts." For example, we say the prayer when we wear new clothes for the first time or eat the first fruit of the new season. There was great debate about the appropriateness of including this prayer into the ordination ceremony. In the end, they included this beautiful prayer, but left it up to the individual graduates to make the prayer meaningful to themselves. If the students didn't feel that the prayer was appropriate for the service, then they were encouraged to wear some new article of clothing and have that in mind when the class recited the blessing. In unison, the Hebrew of the *Shehechiyaunu* rang out, which translates as: "Blessed are you Hashem, our God, King of the universe, Who has kept us alive, sustained us, and brought us to this season." At the end of the service, one classmate approached Eilberg and said rather humbly, "I want you to know why I said the *Shehechiyaunu,* I said it for you."

What started out as a religious service became a media event. There were lights, cameras, and reporters from television, newspapers, and magazines. After the service, an excited, effervescent Eilberg told the reporters, "This is the day that the Jewish leadership has opened its arm to the full equality and full participation of Jewish women in every arena of Jewish life."

Rabbi Eilberg's now wide-ranging professional experience has left her feeling that she knew something about Bar and Bat Mitzvahs. After all, she had either officiated at or attended many of these ceremonies. But when her daughter, Penina, approached her own Bat Mitzvah, Eilberg was completely over-whelmed by the power of the event. This was not just "one day." It was magical to hear her daugh-

ter's beautiful young voice as Penina practiced her *parsha* over and over again. As a parent, Eilberg had to stand back and watch her daughter, who was physically small of stature, step into a role of adult leadership. During the actual Bat Mitzvah, she was flooded with memories, almost like a slide show in her mind. She saw her daughter as a baby, taking her first steps, and the first day in kindergarten. As the newsreel in her head reached the present, it careened forward and Eilberg found herself thinking, "What will she be like in the future? What are her hopes and dreams?" Whatever those hopes and dreams are, Penina will benefit from the powerful, brave women who came before her and made her way easier. Or she will follow in her mother's footsteps, carving a place where no woman has gone before.

29

THERE CAN BE MIRACLES

Selena and Elianna Starr—December 5. 1999

The Starr twins are in high school in Connecticut.

Photo by Schaller Studios

Debbie and Howie Starr met as history majors in the '60s at Stony Brook University in New York. Together, they joined the VISTA program, living and teaching in the South Bronx. They were soulmates—sharing passions, interests, hopes, and dreams. They married young, and life was good as they went on with their respective careers. The only sadness in their lovely relationship was the absence of children to fill the house that they bought together. They started with routine doctor visits, but soon found themselves on the long, arduous, often heart-breaking journey of infertile couples. With traditional medical options failing, the Starrs applied for adoption with the Spence-Chapin Agency and requested twins. Having

been married sixteen years already they thought that twins would provide an instant family.

Infertility is a theme repeated throughout the Torah, and the resolution of our foremothers has served as an inspiration for modern women experiencing the same difficulty. Refusing to give up when medical intervention was unsuccessful, Debbie Starr resorted to a less technical approach. During a trip to Israel, she "called on" our foremother Rachel. Rachel, the beautiful wife of Jacob, watched forlornly as her husband's other wives produced son after son, while she remained childless. With the birth of her son Joseph, Rachel's own prayers were answered fifteen years into their marriage and again several years later with the birth of Benjamin.

Armed with the strength of the women who came before us, Debbie Starr embarked on a dangerous ride where she was the only woman among a busload of Arab men. Her destination—Rachel's Tomb. At this solemn place, Debbie poured her heart out to our foremother, who had experienced the same despair when she could not conceive and prayed for the same blessing.

The prayers were answered—Debbie conceived! Not only conceived, but she was carrying twins and possibly triplets. Her joy was short-lived, though, when several weeks into her pregnancy, after a blood test, the doctor called to inform them that Debbie had lost the babies. Howie took the call. He also took the call less than twenty-four hours later when the phone rang again. The voice on the other end said, "There are Korean twins available. Do you want them?"

Did they want them?!! In one day their despair rocketed into double joy. In a flurry of activity, they prepared for the arrival of their new daughters. Debbie's co-workers at the New York Board of Education bought a double stroller and many of the other essentials for the babies.

On March 27, 1987, there was quite a scene at Kennedy Airport. Twelve babies were carried off the Korean airliner. With limited social service staff, several of the passengers were pressed into service for the delightful task of delivering these children to their new families. The stewardess was yelling excitedly, "Who gets the twins? Who gets the twins?" Howie and Debbie Starr, along with their extended family, were grinning, crying, and smiling as they welcomed two perfect little girls.

Most children have a birthday when once a year they feel very special. Selena and Elianna have four such significant dates—birth date, arrival date, conversion date, and citizenship date. Debbie Starr knew that the girls will never "look Jewish," so she wanted to make sure that they would never encounter questions or problems related to their Judaism. Therefore, she arranged for an Orthodox conversion. At the age of 10 months, the girls were brought in front of a *Beit Din* of three Orthodox rabbis and then brought to the *mikveh*. At the age of 4, attired in red, white, and blue and proudly waving their flags, the girls became American citizens.

Debbie and Howie tried to maintain a connection to the girls' Korean heritage. The Starrs bought traditional clothing and took the twins back to visit Korea. They bought Korean tapes, books, and music and joined a playgroup for Caucasian moms with Korean children. But by the time the girls started school, they had lost interest. As students at Solomon Schechter in West Hartford, Connecticut, the girls instead prefer to focus on their Jewish education in an American day school.

In spite of their demure and quiet ways, Selena and Elianna seem to attract a lot of attention. They are quite lovely and, although not identical, look very similar. The attention is always positive and the girls have never experienced funny looks or rude comments, either at school or in the Beth El Temple, which has a membership of 1,200 families.

For their B'not Mitzvah, they chose a Sunday service so that religious friends and family would have no trouble with the traveling. Debbie and Howie also weren't sure how comfortable the girls would be during a regular *Shabbat* service. Not because they weren't prepared—both girls are excellent students—but because they are very quiet and shy away from attention.

The girls did everything. Selena did the first half and Elianna completed the services. They split the Torah portion, each girl read alone, and each delivered her own *D'var Torah*. A *D'var Torah* is an explanation of the Torah portion, with the addition of researched rabbinical interpretation and the application to our own life and times.

Selena chose to discuss the part of *parsha Naso* that introduces various laws, including those of the Nazirite. Samson, of the Samson and Delilah story, was a Nazirite, a group of special priests who "separated themselves unto the Lord." They did not drink alcohol or cut

their hair. After posing several rhetorical questions that she answered throughout her text, Selena concluded with the following:

> On a more spiritual level, isn't the path of separateness of the Nazirite practiced in order to achieve holiness? On a more modern level, isn't that the path of the Jew in today's world? Don't the prohibitions against work on *Shabbat*, the laws of *kashrut*, the restrictions against intermarriage all keep the Jew separate from the Gentile world? Is it not the case that the commandments are followed in order to produce *kadosh* (holiness) in our lives? The triumph of Chanukah was of observant Jews winning out over assimilationist Jews. The real measure of my becoming a Bat Mitzvah will be to continuously develop kadosh, holiness in my own life.

Elianna took a different approach with the same *parsha*.

> On this, the second day of Chanukah, my friends and family heard me chant a section of *parsha Naso*. The section I read dealt with the offerings brought by the heads, or chieftains, of the various tribes, at the consecration of the Tabernacle. One by one, on twelve successive days, the chieftain of each of the twelve tribes brought his own set of offerings. However, each set of offerings is identical to all the others.
>
> I think that perhaps the Torah wished to emphasize the importance and uniqueness of each individual, even when performing what seem like identical acts. Maybe it's only identical in appearance, but not in motivation, symbolism, or inspiration.
>
> Perhaps the message here is that although Judaism is bound by rules and structure—the seemingly identical lists of offerings—there is room for diversity of expression and belief. At the time of the dedication of the Tabernacle there were twelve tribes—today those divisions may be Ashkenazim, Sephardim, Orthodox, Hasidic, Conservative, Reform, and Reconstructionist, each group seeking meaning in its Jewish beliefs. Even the individual Jew seeks relevance in his or her proscribed practices and rituals. We need to seek meaning even as we observe identical ritual. As a twin, I have experienced firsthand the need to

> carve out one's uniqueness in what appears to be a duplicate situation.
>
> The celebration of Chanukah fits in perfectly with my becoming a Bat Mitzvah. Chanukah is about rededication to Judaism. As an infant I was converted to Judaism. This decision was made for me by my parents. Today, I stand before my family and friends, this congregation and God, and rededicate myself to Judaism, as I take on, by my choice, the responsibilities of becoming a daughter of the commandments.

Debbie rounded out the "formal" presentations of the service with her perspective on how they had arrived at this very special day.

> At 3 months old, the two of you, Youn Joo Kim and Youn Jin Kim, came into our lives. In a country where abortion is cheap and legal, your courageous and loving birth mother made a plan to relinquish you to an American adoption program. She gave you the gift of life, and she was determined to provide you with a loving and caring home. We have honored her trust and have cherished you from the day you were placed into our waiting arms. We thank God every day that she . . . gave us our most treasured gifts.

During the reception of the Bat Mitzvah, the girls chose for their first dance with their father and their Uncle Emery "When You Believe," © the theme song from *The Prince of Egypt.* The rabbi had talked about a miracle . . . not a remote, long-ago miracle like the Chanukah story, but one that took place far away and close by, uniting two continents. God heard the prayers of Debbie and Howie Starr and with His plan in His way answered them. One brave and loving woman bore twins, when she didn't have to, so that another equally brave and loving woman would raise them, love them, and cherish them. Two amazing girls, packaged in these beautiful souls on the other side of the world, transported home.

30

SOMETHING BORROWED, SOMETHING BLUE . . .

Katie, Eli, and Tali Perret-Jeanneret—May 1995 (by Katie Perret)

Eli Perret is now 21 and has just passed his second year at University in Dunedin, New Zealand, with flying colours in Spanish, French, and German. He is working occasionally as a translator, and hopes to make this his career. Tali Perret is now 19 and just completed her second year at university with flying colours in Psychology, English Literature, and her major, Theatre Studies. Tali has appeared in many productions this year for her courses, for lunchtime theatre, and in the local public theatre. Tali and I have both won roles in the forthcoming Dunedin Operatic Society production of "Fiddler on the Roof." Tali sings in a group called "Opera Alive" and I am teaching Drama and Dance at Columba College where I also teach English. I am also the head of the Intermediate Department. We are lay-readers at the local synagogue, and I am learning to chant Torah.

My children and I had been members at Beth Shalom in Auckland, New Zealand, since they were babies, but fate took us to Switzerland when they were 8 and 10 years old. They attended Hebrew School in Basel, in the northeast, at the beautiful Orthodox Synagogue there, and we attended *shul* both there and at the Progressive Synagogue, the J.L.G. in Zürich. This was one hour by train away from where we lived in Rheinfelden. As the time came to prepare for Eli's Bar Mitzvah, we were looking forward tremendously to sharing it with our new friends in Zurich. One terrible day, our beloved Rabbi Israel Ben Yosef passed away suddenly from a heart attack. I recall telephoning the family, which was on holiday in the Canary Islands, and crying into the poor hotel manager's ear for a rather pointless exercise in long-distance grief. But then came the next question: What to do about the Bar Mitzvah?

It did not take too long for me to determine that we would somehow do it together. We were, after all, well experienced in home schooling for our Jewish studies and had hardly ever experienced life in our Progressive *shul* in Auckland with a formally ordained rabbi. We were getting better at the totally different tunes in Zurich, and our German was okay enough since it was our fourth year there. I spoke to our friend Rachel, and she agreed to take the service and help us practice our portion. So, we were away!

Tali was going to be 12, I was 39, again, and Eli, nearly 14: synchronicity! A B'nei Mitzvah made in heaven. We were so excited and went back to cuddling up in the big bed, again, on Sundays and reading aloud to each other from our study books, including some beautiful fiction as well. It felt just right because that, in fact, was how we had spent a lot of their childhood, with me at the helm, but also an equal partner and very keen to learn more myself.

The great day came, and we invited our closest Swiss, English, and Dutch friends, who traveled on the train with us. We shared the service, and somehow through a blur of happy tears I also gave a *drosh* in German on the subject of "holiness" from the portion in Leviticus, *Kedoshim*. We were determined to try to have something from our lives in New Zealand in the service, so we decided to teach the congregation our Auckland tune for "*Sim Shalom*."

Eli wore his beautiful woolen *tallit*, handwoven by Ruth Ruberl, which we had bought for him when he was still a baby. His friend Anton sent him a lovely hand-felted *kipah* from New Zealand. Tali decided to wear the very old silk *tallit* that had belonged to a former member of the Zürich congregation, as a link with our European past and ever-present bone-tingling awareness of the Holocaust as we looked around us. I decided at the last minute to look in our "Jewish

Catalogue" and followed the instructions to make a new *tallit* for myself from a lovely South Seas piece of cotton in deepest blues and greens. I somehow managed to find the matching green cotton for the tzitzit, which made the choice perfect. Something old, something new, something borrowed, something blue.

There we were, with an astonishing variety of wonderful people, with Hebrew possibly the only language in common, surrounded by love and best wishes as we all stepped up proudly to become Jewish adults. Our friend Avi, from Yemen, was perhaps the farthest from former home and culture. But at a congregation such as the Progressive one in Zürich, we felt quite at home, because in New Zealand we also had learned to welcome many "strangers to our shores."

After the *Kiddush*, where we were so thrilled to see the usual special challot for happy occasions (someone remembered!), we had lunch standing around one big table, laden with "bring a plate" finger food (another New Zealand custom). We presented everyone who came to *shul* that day with a beeswax candle with our names and the date of our B'nei Mitzvot in Switzerland. We went for a walk around the Lake of Zürich, I insisted on having my photo taken next to the large green fiberglass cow that stands outside a Swiss handwork shop, in green and big yellow daisies, so that I could add, finally, "and something Swiss."

31

GOD BLESS AMERICA

Alexandra Nessa Berg—May 28, 2000

Alexandra Berg is a student at Central High School in Philadelphia. She excels in gymnastics and she qualified and attended national competitions at U.S.A.I.G.C. (Orlando, FL 2002). The little shul in South Philadelphia is still open.

Photo by David Ickes

Immigration into America at the turn of the last century conjures up a vision of men, women, and children lining the railings of huge steamers, muttering silent prayers of thanks as they pass the Statue of Liberty. Not all new immigrants saluted "Lady Liberty" as they entered the United States. There were several other ports of entry through which new immigrants made their way. The docks of the Delaware River at Washington Avenue in South Philadelphia were also a welcome sight for the weary passengers arriving in the late nineteenth and early twentieth centuries.

Brought over by his two older brothers who were already here, Leib Kalinsky arrived in Philadelphia in 1910. Leaving behind the oppression of Czarist Eastern Europe, he bounced down the gangplank at the age of 15, ready to embrace America as his home. It wasn't surprising, then, that before long Leib Kalinsky became Louis Martin. Taking an Americanized name only showed his respect and love of his newly adopted country. He never forgot his roots and where he came from.

South Philadelphia is famous for its rowhouses. In these houses in the late nineteenth and first half of the twentieth century, each new group of Jewish immigrants established its own *shul*. In its heyday, over 100 *shteble*-type *shuls* were set up in converted row houses. Louis Martin, like other Romanian "landsmen," joined Congregation Shivtei Yeshuron Ezras Israel on South 4th Street. He davened there daily until his death at 97 in 1992.

South Philadelphia at one time was a hub of activity for the Jewish community. Over 100,000 Jews made their way into America through Philadelphia and stayed right where they landed. It's all changed now. There was some upward mobility. The old generation died off and the population dwindled. Now other ethnic groups inhabit the homes that were formerly occupied by Jewish immigrants and their descendents. Out of the 100 row house *shuls*, one remains—the little *shteble* where Louis Martin worshiped. One reason for its survival is that the job of *shamas* (caretaker)—currently, Mr. Alvin Heller—has been kept in the same family for generation after generation.

Alexandra Berg was 5 years old when her great-grandfather Louis died. What she didn't remember firsthand was gladly filled in time and time again, as stories abounded about Great-Grandpa Lou. He was easygoing and good-spirited. He had a succession of jobs, but worked as a quartermaster until his retirement in the '60s. Most of all, he loved to sing. He occasionally found work as a cantor, but his singing didn't have to happen in a formal arena. He loved this country so much that on many occasions, he would break into "God Bless America." At funerals, unveilings, and even at the end of the seder, Louis would stand up and lead the family in this patriotic song.

As Alexandra approached Bat Mitzvah age, her father, David, wanted hers to be more than a time to honor and perpetuate tradition. Because David and his brother Mel grew up in South Philadelphia, they had their Bar Mitzvahs at Grandpa's *shul* on Fourth Street. Even though David's family has since moved to the Chestnut Hill section in the Northwest, they decided that Alexandra's Bat Mitzvah would also be the perfect time to remember the legacy of Grandpa Lou and pay respects to their South Philadelphia heritage by holding her Bat Mitzvah in the *shul* that he'd attended daily.

Because Congregation Shivtei Yeshuron Ezras Israel remains Orthodox, they set Alexandra's Bat Mitzvah on a Sunday, out of respect for the traditional worship. As it was an Orthodox *shul*, the men customarily sat downstairs, and through a large hole in the ceiling the women on the second floor could watch the service. For Alexandra's Bat Mitzvah, all of the participants, both men and women, sat downstairs, and the overflow or latecomers were relegated to the second floor.

The morning started with the showing of an award-winning documentary entitled, *Echoes of a Ghost Minyan*, by Longshore Productions. The film portrays immigration at the turn of the century and highlights all of the different rowhouse *shuls*, including the one that they were in. With the *shul's* antiquated electric system, it was no easy feat to wire the building in order to show the film, but they were successful. The Bergs chose to start the morning with this film to give those in attendance a feeling for what this place was like in years gone by—when every seat was filled and the room was alive, when the room was brightly lit and awesome, and when Lou Martin had davened there. You could almost feel his presence and the congregation experienced a sense of reverence, pride, and sadness.

The service that followed was egalitarian, eclectic, enthusiastic, and filled with high energy. There was a mix of a traditional service interspersed with Klezmer music, Joni Mitchell, and Shel Silverstein. Ben Laden, the Klezmer accordionist, wearing a sequined *kipah*, revved-up the group with the traditional *Hevenu Shalom Aleichem* and *Hava Negila*. When he unexpectedly broke out into "Oh, Dem Golden Slippers" and "Yes, Sir, That's My Baby," people started to dance in the aisles. The room was alive, and if there was ever a *Fiddler on the Roof*, they knocked him off!

In the Sephardic tradition, the *bimah* is located in the center of the room, with all seats facing in that direction. Alexandra ascended the *bimah* and read the ancient words from the Torah, while her guests followed along in equally ancient prayer books. Then she completed her Torah reading, she addressed her guests:

> When my great-grandfather, Louis Martin, escaped the oppression of the Czar in Eastern Europe, he came to a new

> land and eventually to this synagogue. Just as told by my Torah portion: The Jewish people, led by Moses, left Egypt and came to the desert—to a new land. They were instructed on building the *Ohel Moed,* their sacred place of worship from an ordinary tent. This very synagogue was once just a regular house, which then became the *Ohel Moed* in the new land.
>
> Just as the Jews had hope for freedom of worship when coming to America from Eastern Europe, we *must* make sure that no one will ever be slaves or prevented from having their freedom of speech and worship. They had hopes and dreams for their children to grow safely in a free country, and *we* are the children of those dreams.

When Alex finished, her father, David Berg, a professor at Community College and no stranger to lectures, shared an in-depth history of the Jews of South Philadelphia. Edna Berg, Alexandra's mother, who let her husband take the reins while planning this innovative celebration, talked briefly about her daughter's emerging autonomy and self expression.

As a matter of practicality, since they were already in South Philadelphia and in order to continue to honor their roots, the party was held right after the service at the nearby Mummer's Museum, with buses shuttling the guests. However, while the lights still blazed and the little *shul* was so alive, Ben Laden and Alexandra asked the group to stand and they led the emotional singing of "God Bless America" in both Yiddish and English. They sang it for Grandpa Lou, for all of the Jews, for the dream.

32

CLOSING A CIRCLE

Asnat Groutz, M.D.—October 9, 2000

Asnat Groutz is the mother of a gorgeous baby son, Ethai. (The original Ethai was one of King David's heroes.) She continues her OB/GYN practice, both hospital and clinical work, in Israel.

October 9, 2000

Dear Shay,

I'm so excited! I had a really wonderful day and I want to talk to you about it. Since I am hindered by the time difference, with me here in New York City, late at night, and you in Israel in the wee hours of the morning, I will commit my thought to paper while they are fresh, so you'll know how I feel. Where to start? I need to take you back in time . . . .

You know that we have never been religious. There is that strong line of demarcation between religious and nonreligious factions in

Israel and really very little in between. The Orthodoxy that I have observed represented religion as difficult, uninteresting, and inflexible. Either you got it or you didn't. Most of us preferred to grow up in *Gevatayim*, a small city outside of Tel Aviv, as nonreligious. However, being "nonreligious" in Israel is still associated with being Jewish. We have always kept Yom Kippur by fasting and on Pesach, we always had the seder. It's ironic that while many American Jews celebrate with great enthusiasm the other Jewish holidays, such as Succot, Rosh Hashanah, and Simchat Torah, we view them more as civilian holidays, without any emotional or religious feeling. We learn the Bible from the ages of 6 to 18, but it has never been part of my life.

While I was growing up, I anticipated my Bat Mitzvah at the age of 12. Like my peers, there was to be no religious aspect involved. The focus of the celebration is reaching the age of maturity and becoming a woman. It is a very important part of a young girl's life and is heralded in with a festive party that rivals many a wedding. My Bat Mitzvah was planned for October 9, 1973. There were no preparations on religious aspects, but there was work to be done, nonetheless. I had my speech ready to thank Mom and Dad for shlepping me to swim practice for all those years and sitting through all of my competitions, for all those years of piano lessons (smile), and, of course, your unconditional, limitless love and support. As you undoubtedly remember, the Bat Mitzvah never happened.

The Yom Kippur War started three days before, on October 6, 1973. In my opinion, this was the most difficult war in our history because we were surprised and unprepared. I clearly remember the war as if it were yesterday. I still shudder to remember when the first alarm sounded. It was 2:00 P.M. on Yom Kippur. We were all herded into the shelters. Rather than chaos, I remember the fear and the silence. In the initial stage of war we suffered many casualties and great losses. We watched Dad, a career military officer, go off to fight in the Sinai desert and on the Egyptian border. I was old enough to understand and worry about him, along with other family and friends who were involved in the fighting. And although Mom kept silent, I knew she feared for his safety as well.

I was 12. I was a kid, but I understood what "priority" meant for the first time in my life. I don't think during the war I even thought once about my "non-Bat Mitzvah." It didn't bother me. The war ended and it was clear that there was no place for celebrations. It was a very sad time. I never said, "What about my Bat Mitzvah?" I knew it was inappropriate. I don't remember any Bar or Bat Mitzvah celebrations the following year. No one felt happy or eager to celebrate anything.

But since the Bat Mitzvah is a major event in a girl's life, Mom and Dad wanted to somehow make it up to me. The following summer, August 1974, they took you, my baby brother, and me on our first trip to Europe. Leaving Israel for the first time, the first country that we touched down in was Italy. I adored the country, the people, and especially the food! I promised myself that I would go back someday.

So, why have I dredged up ancient history? You know that my two years of study here in New York will be over shortly and I will soon return to Israel. I came here two years ago because I needed a break from an overwhelming ob-gyn practice in Tel Aviv. Treating patients in both a public and a private practice was a lot like burning the candle at both ends. I needed to get out for a while and "re-group" (an interesting American term!), so I came to the United States to do what I do best: study. I came here for six months of research and to re-evaluate my life. I soon realized that six months was not long enough, both personally and professionally, and it expanded to two years. In addition, I came here to study with the best, Dr. Jerry Blaivas, an expert in female voiding dysfunction. I wanted to learn the most up-to-date practices and technology and bring them back home. In the process of my professional development, I had many wonderful experiences. Before I came here, I was warned that Americans, especially New Yorkers, were very unfriendly, and I would likely be lonely. Much to the contrary, I have made many good friends and have been "adopted" into more than one family. As excited as I am about seeing you soon, I dread leaving these people whom I have come to love, and I have been living in denial that I will actually be packing my suitcases and saying goodbye.

This year, for the first time that I can remember, my birthday fell on Yom Kippur—today. My wonderful friends invited me to B'nai Jeshuran, a wonderfully progressive synagogue in New York City. I experienced my birthday and Yom Kippur in the synagogue for the first time in my life. It was the first time that I spent all of Yom Kippur, from early morning until *N'ila* services, in a temple. I felt that I was undergoing such an exciting time. For the first time, I enjoyed these beautiful services. The music was so lovely, and it was as if many of the songs were a duet between the *chazan* and the congregation. We

sang together in one voice some of the most fantastic melodies I ever heard. The service was so personal. The Torah reading was divided between several disabled members of the community who had already become B'nai Mitzvah. The services were so inclusive. Then a woman, the child of Holocaust survivors, shared her story. It was so moving and personal. When my friends told me that we were going to the synagogue, I thought we would stay for only a short time, but we stayed all day. I observed all of the prohibitions and didn't drive, use the phone, and so on, and for the first time I was more religious than my friends!

Today was so beautiful and exciting because I experienced Judaism in a way that I never have before. I feel as if today I closed a circle in my life. As I said before, I never gave much thought to my Bat Mitzvah after it never happened. But today in the synagogue, my birthday, Yom Kippur, my Bat Mitzvah, the terrible unrest right now in Israel . . . I have found closure. I never had the celebration, but I learned all the right lessons. Even at the time, I knew that frivolous parties were bumped out of the way when there were more pressing issues, which for our country have become all too familiar. This year on Yom Kippur, I felt the *need* to be in the synagogue. It was such a revelation and one of the most exciting days of my life. I wonder if you are scratching your head and wondering, after my three years as an officer in the Israeli Air Force, medical school, residency, and practice, how can I find a day spent in the synagogue one of the most exciting in my life. I found something today. Amidst the songs, the music, the stories, the Torah reading, and the friendships. I found a place in me and a place for me. If I compare my life to a book, my "New York" chapter is one of the happiest, most fulfilling times of my life. New York City is now and forever a second home. I always knew I would not stay forever, and it is time to come home. But I return a different "Ossie" than the one who arrived here twenty-four months ago. Much in the same way as my round trip ticket, I have completed a circle and will make my way back home.

Love,

Ossie

33

MURDER SHE WROTE

Leora Rockowitz—November 16, 1996

Because of the commitments of high school, Leora has not had the opportunity for any theater in her junior year. She is, however, an anchor on New Rochelle High School's local television station and the arts editor of the newspaper. In spite of SAT preparation and a heavy course load, she still makes time for community service. Leora was elected to the New Rochelle Youth Council that aids in a variety of municipal projects. For her, the "Murder Mystery" was not so much about solving the murderer's identity as "Mrs. Green with the lead pipe in the Conservatory," but more about providing the forum in which to incorporate her mitzvah project. The teamwork, the clues, and the guesswork all made for an enjoyable party. And although making the sandwiches was great fun, the impact of delivering them the next day is what she remembers the most.

Leora Rockowitz loves musical theater and has personally graced the stage with singing roles in several school, synagogue, and camp productions. Therefore, none of her classmates at the Solomon Shechter School of White Plains were surprised when they received her Bat Mitzvah invitation beckoning them to "Leora's Broadway Celebration." Most of the kids figured that this was yet another disco party, with the only difference being that the dress code for this party was listed as "casual."

It was a "kids-only" party, with the few adults being Leora's parents and several of her aunts and uncles. The kids arrived and were milling around when they overheard a domestic dispute. It seemed as if Leora's relatives were hurling insults at each other.

"I can't stand how she looks!" said one aunt to another, pointing at a third. "Did you see that?'" screeched the offended relative to anyone who would listen. The bantering continued, escalating loudly until a shot rang out. The room was completely silent as a body lay still on the floor—dead.

Or so they thought for that long minute while everyone stood around, not knowing what to do. The silence was interrupted only when the "aunts and uncles" came together and announced that they were not really related to Leora; they were professional actors. This party was a "Murder Mystery," the death was staged, and it was now up to the unsuspecting guests to solve it. The kids were divided up into groups and worked together to figure out who was the victim, where she was going, and why she was "killed."

The boys got into this as much as the girls did, and they set about their task. To start off, they were given certain clues. Each time they figured out a clue and got closer to solving the mystery, they were given additional clues. They realized almost simultaneously that their poor victim had been on her way to make sandwiches for the homeless. If these young people wanted further clues, they would have to take over for the "unfortunate departed" and complete her job.

So, at that point in the party, they pulled out loaves of bread and jars of peanut butter and jelly. They liberally lathered the gooey stuff and then individually folded the PBJs into plastic bags. To secure the next clue, they prepared over 700 sandwiches that would be delivered the following day, because most food shelters don't accept donations on the weekends.

In spite of the lovely tablecloths now being covered with splotches of peanut butter and jelly, the teams continued to decipher clues to figure out who killed their victim and why. To keep it interesting, if you deciphered one clue in order to get the next, it didn't mean that you were on the right path. Only two of the six groups actually came up with the right solution. It seemed as if the mystery victim was an actress, and she had had an unpleasant dispute with a director about a role. They'd quarreled, and as things got out of hand, he'd "killed" her to prevent her from taking that part.

Leora's Mom, Julie, silently hoped that while the kids ladled out the peanut butter and jelly, they paused frequently to lick their fingers. The caterer, without explanation or remorse, had planned enough food for a party of five, not sixty. There were, however, plenty of Carvel ice-cream cakes, and no one seemed deprived or undernourished. In spite of the lack of food, the party was a wonderful success. No kids congregated in the ladies' and men's rooms, as is typical at many affairs. These kids were stimulated, enthusiastic, and worked together for the common goal of solving the mystery.

The Bat Mitzvah girl was also delighted with the results. She'd had a beautiful and very traditional ceremony the day before, where she was called to read from the Torah for the first time. It was for her to decide how much of the service she would attempt. She was very proud that she had read all but two *aliyot of parsha Toledot*, chanted the Haftorah, and led most of the davening.

For her party, she wanted something different that incorporated a "mitzvah" component. Her mother had seen an advertisement for "Murder Mystery" in the *Jewish Week*. The proprietor of the company, Art Feinglass, personalizes each "mystery" for the occasion. He came to their house, and Leora felt "powerful" because she made many of the decisions on how the skit would evolve. Because of Leora's love of theater, this party turned out to be a personal expression of who she is. She also demonstrated great maturity, in that she did not divulge to anyone the true nature of the party and acted all along as if the whole "murder" was a complete surprise.

The "mitzvah component" of the party was only partially realized with the preparation of the sandwiches. The next day, Leora, her mother, and younger sister Dahlia drove to Yonkers to deliver them to a homeless shelter. Carrying their shopping bags, they walked toward the building. Leora was unprepared for the onslaught of people who, while waiting to enter the soup kitchen, saw her approach with the fresh bags of food, came up to her, and asked repeatedly, "Do you have anything for me?" "Anything in there for me?" It drove the point home that after her beautiful Bat Mitzvah weekend, where she was showered with love, other people who live quite nearby have to wait outside in the cold to get their next meal.

Because of the commitments of high school, Leora has not had the opportunity for any theatre in her junior year. She is, however, an anchor on New Rochelle High School's local television station and the Arts Editor of the newspaper. In spite of SAT preparation and a heavy course load, she still makes time for community service. Leora was elected to the New Rochelle Youth Council that aids in a variety of municipal projects. For her the "Murder Mystery" was not so much

about solving "Mrs. Green with the lead pipe in the Conservatory," but more about providing the forum in which to incorporate her mitzvah project. The teamwork, the clues, the guesswork all made for an enjoyable party. And while making the sandwiches was great fun, the impact of delivering them the next day is what she remembers the most.

34

THE CHINESE BAT MITZVAH

Sarah Mittledorf—January 31, 1999

After an inspirational beginning, the program followed with the music, the poetry, the Chinese story, and the fables. The ceremony concluded with a recitation of the Kaddish, which Josh had been saying since his father died a little over a year before the Bat Mitzvah, and the singing of the Hatikvah (literally translated as "the Hope," Israel's national anthem). When the Bat Mitzvah was over, Sarah felt more connected to all of the aspects of her life, and she made a promise to herself to continue what she had started. She has kept up with her Chinese and started taking Judaism more seriously. Accomplishing the seemingly impossible, she has embraced all aspects of her heritages without rejecting any part. However, when pressed to define herself and while others wait to see which adjectives will take precedence over the others, she simply responds, "I'm Sarah."

THE LOST HORSE

A man who lived on the northern frontier of China was skilled in interpreting events. One day for no reason, his horse ran away to the nomads across the border. Everyone tried to console him, but his father said, "What makes you so sure this isn't a blessing?" Some months later his horse returned, bringing a splendid nomad stallion. Everyone congratulated him, but his father said, "What makes you so sure this isn't a disaster?" Their household was richer by a fine horse, which the son loved to ride. One day he fell and broke his hip. Everyone tried to console him, but his father said, "What makes you so sure this isn't a blessing?"

A year later the nomads came in force across the border and every able-bodied man took his bow and went into battle. The Chinese frontiersmen lost nine of every ten men. Only because the son was lame did father and son survive to take care of each other. Truly, blessing turns to disaster and disaster to blessing: the changes have no end, nor can the mystery be fathomed.

—Liu An

For Sarah Mittledorf, one part of her Bat Mitzvah preparation was to learn about Chinese folk tales and how they connect to Chinese culture. She learned that folk tales are one way people try to reinforce what they value. Chinese folklore is also created to show or teach people how to behave. Sarah picked several themes to emphasize through these stories: loyalty, respecting different perspectives, and how negative events can have positive implications and vice versa, as demonstrated in the previous story.

The second theme, "respecting different perspectives," can be a way to look at Sarah's whole Bat Mitzvah. Sarah is at the least a blend of a multicultural background and at best a stellar young woman who has affirmed all aspects of that background, rejecting none, and who draws strength from the different parts of her identity. Her mother, Alice Ballard, hails from an Old Philadelphia Episcopalian family. Although her family's name heads one of the oldest and most well-respected law firms in Philadelphia, Alice has jumped the fence and started her own firm, dealing solely with civil rights cases. Alice's coming of age was much different from her daughter's, in that she "came out" at a debutante tea, following the fashion of young women in her social circle. Sarah's father, Josh Mittledorf, who is Jewish, took on the nontraditional role of house-husband and as an accomplished musician can work out of the home. Theirs is a "Harvard marriage," and they will teasingly tell you it is filled with all of the snobbery associated with the smart, beautiful, and musically talented.

When they found themselves living in an old twenty-three-room mansion that they'd renovated, they wanted to fill it with sounds and laughter. Since Josh spoke Chinese and they had many Chinese friends, they started investigating the possibilities of adopting a baby from China. But at that time, in the mid 1980s, adoptions from China were still impossible. They learned that China has a well-defined "favor economy" system. Whereas many things cannot be purchased under communism for money, they can be bartered and traded for a favor. Alice found herself defending a Chinese professor teaching in a Philadelphia university who had been denied tenure, based on discrimination because of race and gender. This client was so grateful for the work that Alice did on her behalf that she was glad to use the favors owed to her to help the family adopt a baby from China—where, because of the "one-child policy," many women are forced to resort to infanticide or abandonment. Sarah was one week old when they found her, but it took four months to get her out of China. Her visa and passport required federal approval.

When they finally brought her home, they wanted to surround her with Chinese culture in the house. They arranged for a gutsy young woman from China to live with them as an au pair. The house is very ecumenical. The family fasts on Yom Kippur, Passover is viewed as political and personal liberation, and they celebrate the seders with the same four families. Both their Jewish and gentile friends gather for latkes (potato pancakes) on Chanukah, and the house is adorned with a Christmas tree and presents. In addition to the traditional and not-so-traditional observances of holidays, they will tell you that the family religion is really music. Everyone plays something, often together, and their house is indeed filled with music from Sarah's violin, Alice's piano, and younger sister Maddy's violin; Dad plays everything. Sarah shares a real connection with her maternal grandmother in their love of Bach, and they often play duets.

Although the family rarely went to the synagogue or church, its members were peripherally involved with the Folk *shul* in Philadelphia, a place that focuses more on the history and culture of the Jewish religion than on any religious dogma. Sarah noticed her friends preparing for their Bat Mitzvahs and thought it was very cool and inspiring. When her father asked her if she wanted to have a Bat Mitzvah, she said, "I need to think about it." Being a deep thinker, she took several weeks to mull it over and responded that she would like a ceremony, but it would be more meaningful for her to learn Chinese than to study Hebrew. Her parents agreed because they felt every 13-year-old deserves an opportunity to celebrate her cultural heritage, and isn't that what a Bat Mitzvah should be?

Xi Chen, already Sarah's violin teacher, was chosen as one of her mentors. Together, they researched stories that Sarah felt were connected to her family. She picked out themes that applied to her life and elaborated on them in her speech, which another mentor, Debbie Rogo, helped to write. One story she told in Chinese. And since music is so prevalent in their home, Sarah prepared two pieces that she played along with several good friends: the Mozart Clarinet Trio and Bach Double Concerto. Her grandfather, Fred Ballard, who in recent years has been infirm and homebound, not only came out for the event, but prepared a poem entitled, "Lines for Sarah," which he read during the ceremony.

While Sarah prepared for her "not" Bat Mitzvah, as they affectionately called this ceremony, it felt like a "project." But in the last few days before the ceremony, it started to take on a different meaning, something more special. In very good humor during the preparations, Alice felt as if this whole affair was a stretch for her. Alice was a 100-percent full-fledged, silver-spoon WASP, and her daughter was having a Bat Mitzvah! Alice did not participate in the planning and design of the concept, because she felt as if she didn't have any place. But she supported it tremendously and was very involved. She became the detail/support person. She worked with Sarah on her speech and music. She also attended to the invitations and Sarah's clothes. At one point, she asked herself, "Where do I fit in?" And she realized that the answer was that she fit in as Sarah's mom. During the ceremony, it really hit Alice hard: that the young woman standing in front of her, telling the story very comfortably in Chinese, was her daughter. This person whom she had known for the past thirteen years as her child was a separate adult. Sarah was now her own person. And this young Chinese woman happened to be Alice's daughter.

Josh, the architect of this ceremony, started off the festivities by greeting their guests with an introduction of what was to follow:

> In much of the American Jewish community, the Bar Mitzvah has been generalized into a ceremony to honor a boy at that terrible, wonderful age when children seem to oscillate every ten minutes from wisdom and maturity, to revolt against authority, to indignation, to painful self-consciousness, and back again. "And with this broadening has come the realization that girls; no less than boys, deserve this attention and celebration, and so was born the "Bat Mitzvah," derived from the Hebrew word for "daughter."
>
> In much of the American Jewish community, a girl's preparation for her Bat Mitzvah is derived from the traditional boy's role: study with a rabbi, preparing to recite Hebrew prayers and read a portion from the Torah. But our family has also benefited from experience with the *Folk Shul* tradition. In a Folk Shul, young men and women choose a mentor from among other parents in the community and undertake a Bar Mitzvah project, an individual course of supervised study on a topic of their own choosing. Five of Sarah's friends have paved the way for this event and showed us what creative and wonderful things can be done with this format. It was from them that our family learned what an opportunity a Bar or Bat Mitzvah can be for a communal expression of love and support in a young person's time of furious growth and occasional bewilderment.
>
> Certainly, in coming together to honor Sarah today, to acknowledge her talents and achievements, to express our joy in having her among us, we are fulfilling one essential mission of the Jewish tradition of Bar Mitzvah. And in creating this ceremony, in choosing and expressing elements that are most meaningful to our family, we have enriched our own cultural and religious experience.
>
> So let today not be a rebuke of any tradition, but an embrace of Judaism, an affirmation of the ancient struggle to re-interpret the law and make it our own. And let us acknowledge that in our family we do this in a way that also embraces the other rich heritages that are represented

> there: not just the obvious ones of Chinese ancestry, of Episcopalian religion, and the Society of Friends, but also the influences that have deep roots in our family history: progressive activism, love of music, and feminism. Let today's ceremony be a celebration of Sarah and her many and diverse heritages.

After an inspirational beginning, the program followed with the music, the poetry, the Chinese story, and the fables. The ceremony concluded with a recitation of the Kaddish, which Josh had been saying since his father died a little over a year before the Bat Mitzvah, and the singing of the Hatikvah (literally translated as "the Hope," Israel's national anthem). When the Bat Mitzvah was over, Sarah felt more connected to all of the aspects of her life, and she made a promise to herself to continue what she had started. She has kept up with her Chinese and started taking Judaism more seriously. Accomplishing the seemingly impossible, she has embraced all aspects of her heritages without rejecting any part. However, when pressed to define herself and while others wait to see which adjectives will take precedence over the others, she simply responds, "I'm Sarah."

35

THE PARTNER

Penina Gold—March 14, 1999

Penina Gold is a student at the Hebrew Academy of Nassau County. She volunteers weekly with the SMILE program, a Hebrew school for children with learning disabilities.

Every day during davening, when Penina Gold reached a certain *posuk* (sentence) in prayer *Ashrei*, there was something in the line that bothered her. It said, "Hashem opens His hand and satisfies the desire of every living thing." She wondered, "Why does it say that Hashem gives everyone his or her needs if there are poor people who don't seem to have their basic needs fulfilled, like food or clothing?" Her concerns grew when she felt that she could come to no resolution on her own, so she went to her rabbi to discuss the matter.

Rabbi Yehuda Kelemer, of the Young Israel of West Hempstead, discussed this concept in depth with Penina and shared some insights

of the great rabbis. He told her that a Roman General named Turnus Rufus once posed a similar question to Rabbi Akiva. He asked. "If God loved the poor, why does He not support them?" Rabbi Akiva answered him that by God not providing certain basics, He allows other people in essence "to step in and pick up where He left off," thereby allowing people to do good deeds.

In Penina's Bat Mitzvah speech, she further expounded on the idea:

> The deeper idea of Rabbi Akiva's response is that feeding the poor molds our character, elevates our *neshamos* (souls); and makes us a partner in repairing the world. The posuk in Ashrei says that God would provide enough of the raw materials by which to feed the human race. The more fortunate are called upon to ensure that everyone should be fed, which is God's original intention.

With the idea in mind that it was incumbent on others to make sure that poor people are fed, Penina, with the help of her family, embarked on her Bat Mitzvah project. Beginning a year before her 12th birthday, Penina drew up and distributed flyers in her school, announcing that she would collect non-perishable food every Friday. Once collected, the food would then be donated to a recently established kosher food pantry.

The idea caught on very quickly, and week in and week out the children of the Hebrew Academy brought in their canned goods, along with boxes of pasta, rice, and cereals. Once a month, when the decorated boxes were filled to overflowing, Penina's mom, Harriet, would pick her up at school, and together they would deliver the foodstuffs to the kosher pantry.

On occasion, Penina had a chance to actually work in the food pantry and see firsthand how valuable her work was. Grateful for the anonymity and glad that she never saw anyone she knew lest they feel humiliated, she saw real people, needy people, who would come to the shelter to pick up food basics to feed their family. It was quite humbling for her to realize that while her mother prepared beautiful meals at their home, especially for *Shabbos*, some people were dependent and grateful for just the bare necessities.

Penina's project continued throughout the year, up until her actual Bat Mitzvah. There were never any official calculations, but this one little girl collected and distributed an estimate of several thousand pounds of food! Enough to help feed quite a few families over the course of that year.

In continuing her theme of *tzedekeh* or charity, at her Bat Mitzvah party, the centerpieces were cans of food that served as anchors to colorful balloons. They were donated to the food pantry after the festivities. Instead of T-shirts, Penina gave her friends *tzedakah* boxes from Israel made in the olive-wood factory. They serve as beautiful reminders that it is "better to give than receive."

At the Bat Mitzvah, as she continued her speech, she played the "devil's advocate" and posed the following question to her guests: "How was Rabbi Akiva so sure of this concept? Maybe the poor are deprived of food as a punishment for their sins?"

In order to answer that, Penina studied a section on the Book of *Yeshayahu* and found some answers.

> From this verse it is clear that it doesn't matter if the poor are good or bad. We are not supposed to judge people when it comes to hunger. No matter what, we should give them food. We learn this approach from our fast days. Why do we fast? We fast to be able to feel the hunger of the poor people. Once we feel how it is to be hungry, we want to feed those people who constantly live like that. You would not like it if somebody came over to you and started to offer you food, and then said: wait a minute, you are a bad person—I don't believe you deserve this. The bottom line is: If you see a poor person, don't stop to think whether he's a good person or a bad person. Feed him because we are fulfilling Hashem's will that no human being should go hungry.

Those are very powerful words from one so young. How many times do we walk down the street jingling the change in our pockets and step over people sitting on the street or sleeping on steam vents. We rationalize that they are there, somehow, by their own accord and that if we offered them money, they would just use it for drugs or alcohol anyway. But somehow a compassionate 12-year-old recognized that it is not up to us to decide if a person is "worthy" or deserves to be fed. Just do it! After all, it says in our daily prayers. "Hashem opens His hand and satisfies the desire of every living thing." But in order for His work to be carried out, it means that those of us who are able

must open our own hands, along with our hearts and sometimes our wallets. Collecting one can of food at a time, Penina demonstrated that as she reached the age of accountability, she is not only a daughter of the commandments, but a partner with Hashem.

36

A CUP OF TEA

Janet Ruth Falon—March 1984

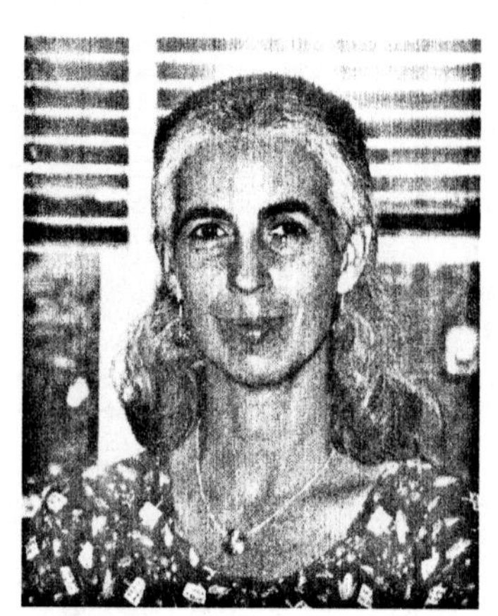

On the road to becoming a Bat Mitzvah, she gained a best friend. Over all those cups of tea, the two women, teacher and student, forged a friendship that has only become stronger over the years. From the Bat Mitzvah, they went on to share in each other's wedding, children, professional accomplishments, and personal sorrows. From the writing of a routine article, Janet Ruth Falon was able to rewrite her own history, filling in the missing pieces, but incorporating so much more with a sense of fulfillment, pride, and peace.

It started with a newspaper article. Not one that she read, but one that she wrote. Janet Ruth Falon was a freelance journalist writing a story for the *Jewish Exponent* in Philadelphia. The topic was adult Bar and Bat Mitzvahs. For her research, she turned to a friend from college. While growing up in Queens, New York, Janet's circle of friends celebrated their coming of age with Sweet 16 parties, rather than with any religious rites. Yet as a student at Boston University, she gravitated to the Hillel on campus. There she experienced a wonderful Jewish education at the hands of her newly found

Orthodox friends. In spite of graduation, those friendships were long-lasting and far-reaching. Therefore, when Janet was asked to write the piece on Bar and Bat Mitzvahs, she turned to a rabbi at Penn, Michael Kaplowitz, who was a friend from her days at BU. Mike was glad to provide background information for the story. The article was written and published in the paper.

Then the phone call came. A rather irate voice on the other end said. "I'm the teacher of the adult Bar and Bat Mitzvah classes. You should have spoken to me before you wrote the article." As a journalist, a practical person, and not one to miss an opportunity, Janet politely listened to Cheryl Skolnick, this lone and loud voice of displeasure. Even though the article had already appeared, Janet was very interested to hear what Cheryl had to say. After some probing questions, Cheryl enthusiastically described the class. Seizing this *bashert* moment, Janet blurted out, "I've always wanted to do this! Can I be in your next class?"

This was not the first time that Janet had thought about becoming a Bat Mitzvah. Infused with positive feelings about Judaism that peaked during her Hillel days, she had promised herself that she would one day become a Bat Mitzvah and accomplish that goal before her 30th birthday. She picked that milestone because you can't predict your marriage date or the birth of a child, but 30 comes whether we want it or not. Now, at the age of 29, a phone call from a disgruntled reader was the impetus that led to a class, a teacher, and the beginning of accomplishing her goal.

The ten students of varying backgrounds attended the class together. Then each was assigned a coach. In addition to having Cheryl as the main teacher, Janet found herself fortunate in having drawn Cheryl as her coach as well. Their one-on-one sessions took place in Cheryl's apartment, always beginning with the same ritual of preparing tea. They'd complement their studies with good conversation and cup after cup of tea.

Because the dates of adult Bar and Bat Mitzvahs are often arbitrary and not bound by a *parsha* that coincides with a birthday, Janet was given *parsha Pekudei*, the final portion in the Book of Exodus. *Pekudei* details the building of the Tabernacle under the supervision of Moses, while the Haftorah parallels the building of the Temple under King Solomon. Janet was well prepared from the class, the coaching, and the individual studying of the tape that Cheryl had made for her. She had the *parsha* down cold!

Janet and two other members of her class became B'nai Mitzvah on a breezy morning of March. For the occasion, taking place at the Penn Hillel, Janet wore a red corduroy dress. It was as if by this choice of a bright and bold outfit, she was shouting out to the assembled community, "Here I am! It's my turn. I am taking back what was denied to me as a child. As a woman I am reclaiming this rite, making myself a part of the larger Jewish family."

An interesting thing happened when she reached the *bimah*. As Janet stood in front of the Torah, everything else receded. It was just she and the words. She was unaware of the people at the service. All that mattered was the well-worn parchment, the bold hand-written letters, and the time-honored words that flowed forth from someplace deep down. It was a wonderful spiritual experience that was broken only when she was pelted with candy upon completing the Haftorah.

When the Jewish people crossed the Red Sea safely and then witnessed their enemies perish in the same water that minutes earlier had provided a safe haven, they probably gave a collective sigh of relief. We can imagine our weary ancestors taking a deep breath and settling into complacency, for the first time in many years feeling safe. But it was Miriam, the sister of Moses, who stood up and shouted, "Wait a minute! Did you just see what happened!" She roused her sisters, and, spurred on by her enthusiasm, the women sang and danced in celebration of their redemption, in honor of not only witnessing, but participating in a miracle—and most of all, with thanksgiving to the Almighty for choosing and cherishing the Jewish people. Janet Ruth Falon's Bat Mitzvah party, hosted by a friend, rang with the same celebratory feelings that Miriam and the other women had expressed. Feeling very spiritual and a sense of mastery of her fate, delighting in the company of friends who knew how much this meant to her, and satisfied with the accomplishment of a goal, Janet and the women (and men) sang and danced all night long.

As a freelance writer and writing teacher, Janet felt the freedom to write about Judaism differently, her way. With a stronger sense of ownership, she recently completed a book on liturgical readings entitled *In the Spirit of the Holidays* that she hopes will be published in the near future. The Bat Mitzvah has allowed Janet to be more creative in interpreting Judaism in her writing.

Janet attends the Bat Mitzvahs of her friends' daughters with a mixture of supportive sisterhood and envy. These young women have an opportunity to become B'not Mitzvah at the "right time," two decades before she ever did. And yet she hopes that this ceremony is as meaningful to them as it was and still is to her. Forget the party, forget the gifts, this was a spiritual experience that she counts as one of the top ten days of her life. This was a chance, as a woman, to be equal and pay herself back.

On the road to becoming a Bat Mitzvah, she gained a best friend. Over all those cups of tea, the two women, teacher and student, forged a friendship that has only become stronger over the years. From the Bat Mitzvah, they went on to share in each other's wedding, children, professional accomplishments, and personal sorrows. From the writing of a routine article, Janet Ruth Falon was able to rewrite her own history, filling in the missing pieces, but incorporating so much more with a sense of fulfillment, pride, and peace.

37

A PRIVILEGE

Barbara Birshtein, Ph.D.—December 1980

Now at Beth El Synagogue, Bat Mitzvahs are as common as Bar Mitzvahs. When Birshtein's daughter Rachel was called to the Torah for the first time, both her mother and father were able to join her on the bimah and share in the reading of the Torah portion. The same will occur for the Bat Mitzvah of their younger daughter, Susan. Even though it has become commonplace for young women to be called to the Torah, Birshtein feels strongly that it is not something we should take for granted. It is still a privilege.

Barbara Birshtein grew up in Clarksburg, West Virginia, birthplace of Stonewall Jackson. Her father, Samuel Joseph, felt a strong connection to the historic figure on many levels, but in a small way because they shared the same initials. There were about 100 Jewish families and an active Jewish life in this small town, located 100 miles south of Pittsburgh. Birshtein' s early years were safe and comfortable, nestled in her large extended family. The family inhabited four houses, all on the same corner. Birshtein, an only child, lived with her parents in one, her grandparents lived around the corner, and the other two houses were occupied by aunts, uncles, and cousins. Not

only did this large family share the holidays, but they were also forever popping into each others' homes.

Birshtein's grandfather, George Rosen, was a well-learned man and the patriarch of the family. When Birshtein's male cousin was preparing for his Bar Mitzvah, their grandfather taught him his lessons. With her interest in learning, plus the rare opportunity to study with her grandfather, Birshtein sat in on her cousin's tutorial. She did not know she was supposed to be "seen and not heard." Always a quick student, she couldn't keep herself from answering the questions posed to her cousin. It seemed, however, that her cousin, a bright boy, needed a little more time to formulate his answers, and with her quick replies, he didn't have a chance to think through the questions. Birshtein's mother quietly took her to the side and asked her to refrain from participating and to allow her grandfather to study alone with the boy. The Bar/Bat Mitzvah issue aside, she felt wistful at the loss of the private study time with her grandfather.

Not long thereafter, the rabbi of their congregation received a small gift from Birshtein's Norfolk grandmother with the request that he (the rabbi) give this token to Birshtein at an appropriate time. The rabbi approached Birshtein, explained about the gift, and asked her if she would like to have a Bat Mitzvah. At that time, the late 1950s, a girl had never become a Bat Mitzvah in Clarksburg. Aware of her grandfather's reluctance, Birshtein chose not to have the ceremony.

Her quick mind, even without a Bat Mitzvah, was put to use as a student at the University of Michigan and then at Johns Hopkins, where she received a Ph.D, as a scientist, specializing in immunology. Way back in junior high school, her science teacher had recognized her strengths and recommended that she start thinking about an advanced degree. With her Ph.D. in hand, she joined the staff of the Albert Einstein Medical School in New York City, where, to this day, she teaches medical and graduate students and runs her own laboratory.

It was one of her students who ended up impacting and changing her life religiously. One of the Ph.D. candidates, an Orthodox woman, was involved with the establishment of a Women's Torah Service and invited her to attend one *Shabbat* morning. Birshtein, who was "shopping around" for a synagogue and had not yet found a place where she was comfortable, readily agreed. That was the beginning. As a child, she had attended their Conservative Temple regularly, but this service allowed her the first opportunity to see the Torah up close.

Because the service was originally set up as a Women's Torah Service, only women were in attendance, allowing everyone—regardless of her religious connection—the access and freedom to participate. As the group grew and the diversity increased, there were women from a wide range of backgrounds whose husbands and boyfriends also wanted to worship. The service, which eventually evolved into an egalitarian one, ended up excluding the Orthodox women, who could no longer pray in mixed company. Birshtein, however, stayed with the group.

The small congregation, like Cinderella, depended on the kindness of "fairy godmothers." The chaplain at Einstein, Rabbi Marciano, made it possible for the group to meet in one of the chapels. His son was a medical student at Einstein, which may account for his indulgence. Rabbi Avi Weiss, the rabbi of a Riverdale congregation, loaned them a Torah each week, which required someone picking it up on *Erev Shabbat* and then returning it on Sunday. After years of the "take-out" Torah at the Women's Minyan, a more permanent scroll was donated to the small group.

No rabbi was in charge, but the young people in this knowledgeable group, many of them students at Einstein, were very comfortable taking turns reading the Torah and leading the davening. There was no formal or official list about who did what and when, but week after week, individuals took turns davening. It was a very safe, inviting atmosphere for people to learn in, so that they, too, would eventually take a turn *layning* the Torah, chanting the Haftorah, or leading the davening.

Almost as easily and naturally as Birshtein had become a member of the group, she decided that she would like to have a Bat Mitzvah. It wasn't about finding glory or being "showy." Birshtein is a scientist, and her life revolves around exploring and learning new things. She wanted to learn how to read from the Torah, so that she, too, could take her turn and lead the services. She picked a date in December, around her birthday, making her *parsha Vayeshev*. One of the postdoctoral students taught her the trup (tune) for the Torah reading and made her a tape, so that she could practice independently. During Thanksgiving break, she made the long trek back home to Clarksburg to spend the holiday weekend with her family. Excited to practice her

Torah portion with her father, she found that he knew only how to chant his own Haftorah portion and didn't know the *trup* in general enough to offer specific teaching.

Regardless of familial participation, Birshtein felt as if this was a very big deal, and she crammed a lot of hard work into a several-month time period. When she felt that she really knew the Haftorah, her "teachers" informed her that she had to learn the blessings before and after the Torah reading as well. She was overwhelmed for the moment and felt unprepared to learn, anything more, but the man she was dating, Dr. Howard Steinman, who later became her husband, "stepped up to the plate" and taught her how to sing the *brachot*.

For the *Shabbat* service when Birshtein became a Bat Mitzvah, no more than twenty people were in attendance, which was typical for a Saturday morning. Nonetheless, it was warm, cozy, and welcoming. As a professor, Birshtein was older than most of the other members of this disenfranchised group, with some of them being her students. Neither age nor status merited any attention. Although nervous, she did a beautiful job and everyone in the place was beaming. She was so proud of herself when it was over, because she had done something hard and had done it well.

Over the next few years, Birshtein, too, rotated in leading the services. When she and Howard married and had their first daughter, Rachel, they came back to this small group to name the child. Although they had moved to the suburb of New Rochelle and joined a large Conservative synagogue, Beth El, women were unable to have an *aliyah* and read from the Torah back in the early '80s. As a wife, mother, and Bat Mitzvah, Birshtein wanted to participate in the services when her daughter was named.

Now at Beth El Synagogue, Bat Mitzvahs are as common as Bar Mitzvahs. When Birshtein's daughter Rachel was called to the Torah for the first time, both her mother and father were able to join her on the *bimah* and share in the reading of the Torah portion. The same will occur for the Bat Mitzvah of their younger daughter, Susan. Even though it has become commonplace for young women to be called to the Torah, Birshtein feels strongly that it is not something we should take for granted. It is still a privilege.

38

COCOON

Karen Binney—December 13, 1997

With the M.B.A. and the Bat Mitzvah completed, this very goal-oriented woman did not stop to rest. Karen accepted her next challenge. As she did with everything else, she set her mind to it and lost 150 pounds. Her very lovely Bat Mitzvah dress made its way with the rest of her wardrobe to a new owner. To help achieve her newfound physique, she set a rigorous course of physical fitness. She became so enamored with the process that her next goal is to become certified as a personal trainer. During the past several years, Karen Binney was not content to sit back and wait for her retirement. She embarked on several new endeavors to keep her life interesting. Exercise and good nutrition enhanced her body, the M.B.A. stimulated her intellect, and the Bat Mitzvah fed her soul.

When Karen Binney's son Barry looked up at her and asked if she had ever had a Bat Mitzvah, she had to answer, "No." The two were in the synagogue near their Charlottesville, Virginia, home, securing a date for Barry's Bar Mitzvah, when he asked the question. His response to his mother was '"Well, you should." And she thought, "He's right, I have to do it." Karen would've signed up right then and there, except that she had

just committed herself to a two-year M.B.A. program, which was a hefty task, considering she already had a full-time job as an Intelligence Research Specialist for the Army. However, she made a commitment to herself that when she finished the degree program, she would start her Bat Mitzvah lessons.

True to her word, with her M.B.A completed and a year off to recuperate from the rigors of studying, Karen was now ready, at the age of 51, to take on this next challenge—becoming a Bat Mitzvah. The will was there. She even picked a date at the end of the year, December 13, because it was available on the calendar and the rabbi would be in town. But as she saw it, there were several stumbling blocks: she couldn't sing, couldn't read music, knew nothing about the *trup* (the tune for chanting the Haftorah), and the biggest stumbling block was that she could barely read Hebrew. Nonetheless, beginning in April of that year, Karen started studying with a very knowledgeable good friend who had a beautiful voice, Heena Reiter.

The process was painstakingly slow. By August, both teacher and student realized that there was a problem and were considering alternative ways to run the ceremony. Since the Hebrew was barely coming along and the tune nonexistent, they thought that maybe they should just do the whole thing in English. And when they were just about ready to "shift gears," Karen went away for a week to a Jewish Renewal Retreat in the Catskills. The concept of Jewish Renewal has been around since the 1970s; it is an egalitarian cross-section of Judaism that incorporates social action. At the retreat, Karen shared her trouble with learning the Haftorah and asked for the help and prayers of the people in her "family" group.

Upon returning home, just about two weeks after the retreat, somehow everything clicked! Possibly, it was the tape of the Haftorah that Heena had recorded for her at two different speeds. Or the nightly practice of one and a half to two hours. More mystically perhaps, the collective prayers of the people from the retreat, as well as her own, were heard. Whatever the reason, the music, the trup, and the Hebrew miraculously fell into place.

Having mastered the Hebrew and the *trup*, Karen next had to decide how she would approach the *D'var Torah* (speech about the portion of the Torah). The *parsha* for that week was *Vayishlach* from the Book of Genesis. There were four major events told in *Vayishlach* related to our Patriarch Jacob and his twin brother, Esau. Karen decided to focus on the apparent "lie" that Jacob told Esau when he said he would meet Esau in the town of Seir when he had no intention of going there. She investigated the commentaries and studied their explanations, and then she wrote her own *midrash.* A *midrash* is a story, a fable, or an interpretation concerning a part of the Torah. *Midrashim* are often used to demonstrate a point or emphasize a lesson that may not be as clear when read from the original text.

On the day of her Bat Mitzvah, Karen shared the davening and reading of the Torah portion with her mentor, Heena. It was during her *D'var Torah*, delivered before she chanted the Haftorah, that she really distinguished herself. There obviously had been no cameras during biblical days, so to know what our forefathers looked like, we can only rely on the description in the Torah text. Probably more than with any other character, the physical attributes of Esau are most clear. "While Jacob's skin was smooth, his brother, Esau, was hairy." Not only hairy, but red. While Jacob was described as beautiful, it is harder to get a mental image of him. Somehow it is easier to picture Esau as huge, red, gruff, and hairy. For her *midrash* Karen wrote a conversation between Jacob and Esau. In presenting this part of the *D'var*, she invited a friend—a man with auburn hair, a ruddy complexion, and a beard (an Esau look-alike!)—to read Esau's part. It was very effective and went in part like this:

> After Jacob says he will follow Esau to Seir, Esau starts to walk off toward his home. But after a few paces, he stops, turns toward Jacob, and, smiling, says, "Jacob, I have grown wiser while you have been gone. I have become a little more like you, relying less on strength for everything. and more on my wits, my intuitiveness. You are lying to me. My brother, my brother, why do you lie to me again? Why do you try to deceive me?"
>
> Jacob, with honesty and sadness, says: "It is not that I do not believe you or trust you in your welcoming me home. It is that I do not trust myself! Did we not fight even in our mother's womb? I was fighting for the birthright God promised our mother that I would have. But you, you were always stronger, and you forced your way out first. I tried to pull you back, but I wasn't strong enough. I have to use my guile, my wits, while you have the strength to do anything. How I envied and still envy your strength and your prowess: but even more so, the love and pride that

> always shined in our father's face when he gazed upon you. Only God knows what I would do if I lived near you every day. If we live one amongst the other, I fear that one or both of us will not survive, will not accomplish our birthrights. I show you my love and respect for you by staying away from you."

With all of her research, it was Karen's contention that Jacob had "lied" because he felt that it was permissible to "modify one's words" in the interest of peace. And more than fear of being killed, he was distressed at the prospect of killing others. Golda Meir expressed identical feelings years later when she said, "We are angry with our enemies not only for killing our sons, but also for making our sons kill." Karen went further and analogized the long-ago struggle between brothers to the continuous strife between nations in the Middle East.

> And even now, Israel and Edom (the descendants of Esau) are still fighting, one by strength and one by guile, but sometimes switching their tactics like a long-ago decreed dance . . . Hopefully, peace will be accomplished in the near future and then this will be the LAST battle EVER between Jacob and Esau.

After she chanted her Haftorah, she received several blessings, one from her mother, one from the rabbi, and one from a group of four friends, two male and two female. These four people surrounded her and, with their *tallitot* spread between them above their head, blessed her with the "Angel Song," © written by Debbie Freidman, which is normally sung at bedtime to ask the angels to bless us and keep us safe overnight. They prayed that "God's angels will surround you at His command: Michael, performing His unique miracles; Gabriel, the emissary of His almighty power; Uriel, who bears the light of God before you; and Raphael, who brings you healing from Him. And above your head is God's *Shechinah*, Holy Spirit." It was one of the most awesome times of her life, surrounded by four very close friends, encased like a caterpillar-moth in a cloud of *tallitot*, and TRULY surrounded by angels! Earthy ones as well as Heavenly ones! All that she could see were her friends and their *tallitot.*

Since it was a time of receiving blessings, Karen wanted to offer one of her own at the end of her speech to her friend and mentor Heena and Heena's husband, Steve. They were going to Israel to partake in

the Compassionate Listening Tour, which is a group that travels several times a year to meet with Israelis and Palestinians of all political views to foster communication and understanding in a peacemaking effort. With the services concluded, Karen celebrated with her family and friends, some of whom had traveled quite a distance to share this day with her. Her brother trekked cross-country from California, a cousin came from Phoenix, and one of the women from the Jewish Renewal Retreat (whose prayers may have contributed to the success of the day) made her way from Indianapolis.

With the M.B.A. and the Bat Mitzvah completed, this very goal-oriented woman did not stop to rest. Karen accepted her next challenge. As she did with everything else, she set her mind to it and lost 150 pounds. Her very lovely Bat Mitzvah dress made its way with the rest of her wardrobe to a new owner. To help achieve her newfound physique, she set a rigorous course of physical fitness. She became so enamored with the process that her next goal is to become certified as a personal trainer. During the past several years, Karen Binney was not content to sit back and wait for her retirement. She embarked on several new endeavors to keep her life interesting. Exercise and good nutrition enhanced her body, the M.B.A stimulated her intellect, and the Bat Mitzvah fed her soul.

39

B'NAI MITZVAH

Jennifer Woda, Daniel Charlick, M.D., Zia Fuentes, et al.—June 16,1984

Photo credit: Roy Woda

Jennifer Woda is an opera singer with the Cleveland Opera.

Daniel Charlick, M.D., is an orthopedic surgeon practicing in Lexington, Kentucky.

Zia Fuentes was a senior manager at a large firm and currently resides in Laguna Beach, California.

The Beachwood High School auditorium was abuzz with people on Saturday morning, June 16, 1984. These were the families and friends of six young people, four girls and two boys, who were about to celebrate their B'nai Mitzvah. These six youngsters had grown up together as part of the Cleveland Jewish Secular Community's youth program. Rather than celebrate with individual Bar and Bat Mitzvah, the ritual of the community was to celebrate with several small group Bar and Bat Mitzvahs, throughout the year, for those students who chose to continue their studies and enter the world of Jewish adulthood together.

The inside cover of the B'nai Mitzvah program explained:

> The Jewish Secular Community consists of individuals and families who wish to emphasize the humanistic aspect of their Judaism. To this end, both child and adult educational programs exist to deepen an understanding of our heritage and to foster a commitment to and identification with

> our people. We encourage all members to actively participate as we joyously celebrate holidays and creatively carry on traditions.
>
> We seek both a heightened awareness of our own identities and a deepened sense of community. We examine our particular Jewish perspective in the light of its broader relationship to the larger community. Jewish values and ethics are cornerstones of our philosophy. We transmit these values through the study of our Jewish civilization, including its history, culture, language, literature, music, and events of current importance.
>
> One of the most significant rites of passage in our Jewish culture is the B'nai Mitzvah. It marks the symbolic transition from childhood to adulthood. As secular Jews we see it as a time to evaluate who we are. Preparing and celebrating the B'nai Mitzvah offers us the opportunity to survey the sum of our parts in terms of our Jewish heritage, our personal histories, our immediate goals, and our hopes for the future. It is also a time to set the course of our lives in a purposeful direction. We celebrate this transition with the approval and support of family, friends, and community.

Every year, those involved with the B'nai Mitzvah—the students, their parents, and their teachers—came together, decided on a theme, and wrote their own program. They drew on the programs they had seen in prior years. It was a combination of a skit, songfest, and collection of inspirational readings. Often, some type of multimedia presentation was incorporated as well. The theme of this year's program focused on three questions:

1. Where do I come from?

2. Where am I now?

3. How am I going to live my life?

Lots of hard work and almost a whole year of preparation went into the ceremony. Everyone was involved with the research. To answer the first question. "Where do I come from?" the students wrote to their grandparents, aunts, uncles, and cousins, asking for advice, special anecdotes, and photos. They put together a slide show of family pictures from all six families, dating back to the late 1800s, with a voice-over of the children describing their relatives and the struggles they had faced as immigrants coming to America. The effect was to stress the cultural differences, due to the places of origin, and the universal similarities of family life and human existence.

To answer questions two and three, the kids started with a values survey. Both parents and children prepared a list of values they had and thought their parents had and then compared the two. It was fascinating to all involved to see how many similarities there were and quite striking to note the differences. They took this information and created an ethical will that was incorporated in the program. They wanted to stress that what is valued most are not material possessions, but the ethics and morals that are passed down.

They found readings, related to the theme, by Anne Frank and George Bernard Shaw and contemporary Jewish and folk songs, then incorporated them, along with traditional prayers and blessings, into the B'nai Mitzvah ceremony. There were many rehearsals. It was a real boon that most of the kids could actually sing, enabling them to perform three songs as a small ensemble, complete with two- or three-part harmony.

On the actual day of the B'nai Mitzvah, freshly scrubbed and all dressed up, the six young people recited their parts, some individually and some as a group. Their parents were very much a part of the program. During one part, the parents recited in unison the list of values that the children had inherited, and then the children expounded on each concept. It was also a time for parents and children to share special feelings. The parents, one by one, stood up in front of their community, talked about their relationships with their children, and very publicly told their children how much they loved them. A second slide show of the kids growing up concluded the program. The kids accompanied the pictures flashing on the screen by singing "Flying Free." If enough "lumps in the throat" weren't generated by the parents' declarations, then the video presentation propelled the participants and many in the audience into free-flowing tears.

Because six members were in the B'nai Mitzvah class, each with their own families and invited guests, they did not celebrate together and were unable to attend each other's parties. When the ceremony

was over, they separated and all went their own ways to celebrate individually.

The six members of the B'nai Mitzvah class of 1984 are grown up now; some are married with families of their own. Although they went through this life experience together, their perceptions of the day vary. Three members out of the six shared their reflections.

Jennifer Woda is an opera singer with the Cleveland Opera:

> Even though my dad is Jewish and my mother is not, I was raised Jewish, but we never belonged to a synagogue. Other than the Secular Jewish Community, I didn't meet other Jews until high school. At that time, my Bat Mitzvah was the only one that I had ever been to, so I had no sense that this was "out of the norm." I thought it was terrific! It was definitely a "rite of passage," something to be valued. There was so much work in the preparation—maybe the equivalent of four or five term papers, some of which we actually had to write and hand in. The Holocaust was one of the topics I researched.
>
> The youth program was structured like Sunday School. Not everyone who started in class with us opted to share in the B'nai Mitzvah. It was a choice. Everyone took it seriously. The Secular Community embraces the culture, not the religion. You don't have to believe in God, although I do.
>
> As part of the B'nai Mitzvah year, we were all involved with "Service Projects"—each of us had to volunteer at an agency of our choice at least once a week. I worked as a classroom aide in the Jewish Day Nursery. I think it was that experience that led me to be a music education major in college.
>
> For part of the actual ceremony, each of us wrote a speech, our parents gave a speech, and everyone cried. The music was great. Most of us could really sing, and two of us were strong musicians. Music is definitely a way to approach God.

Daniel Charlick. M.D., is an orthopedic surgeon practicing in Lexington, Kentucky:

> The B'nai Mitzvah was a chance for us to think about what was important in our lives. We had a lot of control over

what went into the ceremony. It was a coming of age, with an accounting of what our parents tried to pass on to us.

Our B'nai Mitzvah involved as much preparation as a traditional Bar Mitzvah, and for me the ceremony was more meaningful. It was a time for introspection and insight into what it means to be an adult in the Jewish world. Despite the unconventionality of our format, we seemed to arrive in the same place.

In addition, it was great fun. We already knew each other since we had attended classes together, but we became good friends. While there was the serious side of values exploration, we also put on a "show." Each person had his or her own moment to deliver a speech. And when our parents acknowledged how they felt in front of everyone, it became very emotional. It was a time for families to really focus on their kids.

Zia Fuentes was a senior manager at a large firm and currently resides in Laguna Beach, California.

I never viewed the Jewish Secular Community as Judaism, rather more as "Jew"ish history, background, and a lot of music. But there was a heavy emphasis on the values of Judaism and on how you treat other people. There was almost no Hebrew, except perhaps for an occasional song. However, the people were fabulously warm. I loved the people and the friends I made in the strong youth group. The community was welcoming and the events were fun. I always thought of it more as a club than a religion.

For me, the B'nai Mitzvah was a matter of going along "for the ride." I was always ambivalent about the whole thing. I attended a traditional Hebrew school for a while, but when my family relocated to Cleveland, my mother joined the Jewish Secular Community, which did not offer classes in Hebrew. I remember looking up my Haftorah portion, which was not incorporated into the service, and I thought to myself, "That's what I am supposed to be doing." I have thought about doing it again, this time more traditionally, but I feel constrained by a limited Hebrew background. I never felt that I had a real "Bat Mitzvah."

The B'nai Mitzvah focused on the past, present, and future, emphasizing to the children both the burden and the blessing of their strong inheritance and charging them with the responsibility of this most precious gift. Toward that end, the parents offered the following to their young men and women:

> This day traditionally marks the end of your lives as children and the beginning of your rights and responsibilities as adults.
>
> We recognize that you are no longer young children, dependent upon us to make all of your decisions for you. While we do not necessarily see you as adults, nevertheless, today we must recognize your growing independence and allow you to make your own judgments and begin to live your own separate lives.
>
> Letting go is not an easy task for us, but today shall mark its beginning.

40

TRIPLE BAT MITZVAH

Jacqui Gordon, Adrienne Gordon, Marion Gordon Moskovitz—November 25, 2000

Photo credit: Murray Goldenberg

The Gordon/Moskovitzs are a very closely knit family. Perhaps their losses have kept them so tight. Like Naomi and Ruth, Marion and Adrienne came together out of respect, then adversity, and then love. Ruth turned her adversity into triumph and became the matriarch of kings. (Her grandson is King David.) Marion, too, refused to let adversity, ill health, and even death defeat her incomparable spirit. She has poured her love into her family, reaping the reward of close relationships with her children and grandchildren. She and her daughter-in-law Adrienne were unafraid of accepting a new challenge, and Jacqui was not afraid to share her most special day with them. The three of them did it together: "Wherever you go, I will go . . . ." With the strong love, devotion, and mutual respect that links grandmother, mother, and daughter, the potential for greatness is unlimited.

"Wherever you go, I will go. Wherever you live, I will live. Your people are my people. Your God is my God."

These beautiful sentiments are often incorporated into modern-day wedding ceremonies, as one partner pledges love to the other. In reality, the quote is from the Book of Ruth, which is read on *Shavuos*, and the words were spoken by Ruth to her mother-in-law, Naomi. Ruth's story is a tale of love and loyalty. Naomi, her husband, Elimelech, and two sons left Israel during the time of famine and went to the land of Moab. Living there, the sons met and married Moabite women. As time went on, Naomi's husband and two sons died in this land. Bitter and brokenhearted, Naomi prepared to return to Israel, alone. Naomi convinced one daughter-in-law that she was better off returning to her family. When Naomi tried to convince Ruth, her second daughter-in-law and a Moabite princess of great breeding, to return to her family, Ruth recites the famous words "Wherever you go, I will go. . . ," committing herself to her mother-in-law, but more important, to Judaism. By going with her mother-in-law, she also committed herself to a life of poverty and humiliation, for she was forced to scavenge in the fields, picking up what was left over, in order to feed the two of them. And yet the relationship between the two women grew stronger, cementing the bonds of love and mutual respect.

When she was a newlywed, only eight months into her marriage, Adrienne Gordon's mother died. Adrienne had always been close to her mother-in-law, Marion, spending a great deal of time with her husband's family both before and after the wedding. However, when Adrienne's mother died, the relationship with Marion grew stronger. Marion, like Naomi in the Book of Ruth, knew the tragedy of losing a child, because her oldest son, Jay, died at the age of 21 as a result of testicular cancer. And later, she, too, would know the heartache of losing her husband. But unlike Naomi, who experienced a period of bitterness over her grief, Marion Gordon refused to succumb to anything resembling self-pity. She continued to work and spent the rest of her emotional energy pouring love into her remaining three children, their spouses, and later their children.

In 1997, Adrienne Gordon had a nasty fall and shattered her ankle. She was confined to her bed. Whenever her daughter Jacqui arrived home from school, Jacqui brought the mail up to her mother, as was her habit. One day, among the circulars and bills, there was a notice that their temple was having Bar and Bat Mitzvah classes for adults. Jacqui said to her mother, "Why don't you do that?" Within a few min-

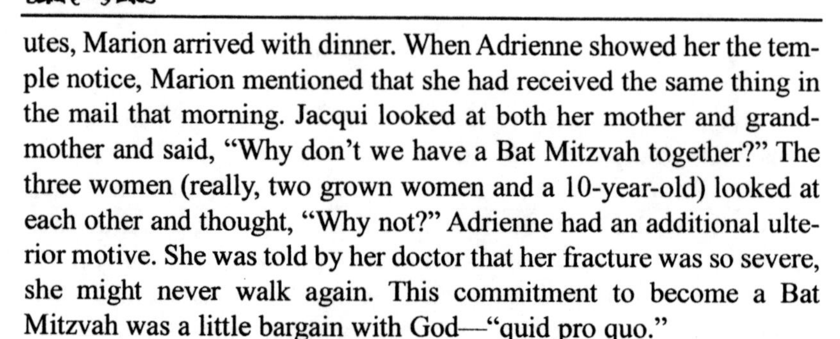

utes, Marion arrived with dinner. When Adrienne showed her the temple notice, Marion mentioned that she had received the same thing in the mail that morning. Jacqui looked at both her mother and grandmother and said, "Why don't we have a Bat Mitzvah together?" The three women (really, two grown women and a 10-year-old) looked at each other and thought, "Why not?" Adrienne had an additional ulterior motive. She was told by her doctor that her fracture was so severe, she might never walk again. This commitment to become a Bat Mitzvah was a little bargain with God—"quid pro quo."

Adrienne had attended Hebrew school as a kid and hated it. She didn't hate the subjects, but she didn't like the kids in her class and that colored her perception. She begged her father to allow her to quit, and he finally relented. Marion, on the other hand, had never gone to Hebrew school. During the Depression, her family moved from Michigan to Canada. When they returned to the United States, they enrolled Marion in the "Jewish school." Her parents were horrified when they learned that the school was based on communist ideology that was taught in Yiddish, not Hebrew. She was immediately withdrawn, and that was the end of her formal Hebrew education. However, when her brother was learning to become a Bar Mitzvah, a rabbi would come to the house to teach the lessons. Marion, always interested in learning, would stand on the sidelines while her brother was being instructed. She realized, somewhat wryly, that she enjoyed these classes more than her brother did. Her family has been Orthodox, Conservative, Reform, back to Conservative, and ultimately Reform, and Marion realized she likes them all.

So, with the goal of having a triple Bat Mitzvah, Adrienne and Marion needed to start with the very basics of learning the aleph-bet (the Hebrew abc's). All told, their Bat Mitzvah preparation took 2½ years. They went from the alphabet to actually studying the prayers and the Torah portion. Their teacher divided up the service. They were all going to chant from the Torah, one after the other. And they would do some of the davening individually and some together. Because it is such a large Jewish community, Jacqui would have been paired with another young lady for her Bat Mitzvah, and the service would have been divided in half. This way, the service was split three ways instead.

On the morning of the Bat Mitzvah, the three women appeared at Temple Beth El in Bloomfield, Michigan, in well-coordinated outfits.

Jacqui wore a suit in her favorite color, purple; her mother wore lavender; and her grandmother completed the trio with a purple suit that was trimmed in purple fur. On Jacqui's lapel was a brooch that had belonged to her other grandmother. The three entered the rabbi's study, wearing their new matching *tallitot* for the first time, and recited in unison the *Shehechiyaunu*, the blessing over something new.

When they entered the sanctuary (Adrienne was walking fine with her totally healed ankle), their guests were quiet, attentive, and quite impressed. Some family members had expressed concern that mother and grandmother would "steal Jacqui's thunder." In reality, the three women together made such a glorious sight that Jacqui's thunder was amplified, not stolen. The rabbi was elated that this first triple multigenerational Bat Mitzvah would happen as the temple was celebrating its 150th anniversary.

Randy Gordon, the man who binds these women together as son, husband, and father, helped during the planning stage, but also tried to stay out of the way. He left most of the preparations up to his wife and mother. During the service, however, he was called up to the *bimah* for an *aliyah.* With tears in his eyes, he also delivered a short speech. He would have felt proud if he were participating in a ceremony for any one of these women, but on this day, his pride and joy were tripled.

Usually, it is a parent who cries during a child's Bar or Bat Mitzvah. However, on that cold November day in Michigan, the roles were reversed as Marion's oldest daughter, Lynda, cried through the ceremony while watching her mother, sister-in-law, and niece simultaneously become "daughters of the commandments." Marion's second husband, Martin Moskovitz, was awed at the poise his wife displayed and shocked at how well she davened and read from the Torah. She has experienced a newfound respect among her peers, who recognize her wonderful accomplishment. Although accolades were showered on grandmother and mother, it was Jacqui, the youngest member of the group, who was described as being "fantastic." She demonstrated an uncommon grace and dignity—maybe because she was flanked by the two women who love her most in the world.

The Gordon/Moskovitzs are a very closely-knit family. Perhaps it is their losses that have kept them so tight. Like Naomi and Ruth, Marion and Adrienne came together out of respect, then adversity, and then love. Ruth turned her adversity into triumph and became the matriarch of Kings. (Her grandson is King David.) Marion, too, refused to let adversity, ill health and even death, defeat her incomparable spirit. She has poured her love into her family, reaping the reward of close relationships with her children and grandchildren. She and her daughter-in-law, Adrienne, were unafraid of accepting a new challenge, and Jacqui was not afraid to share her most special day with them. The three of them did it together. "Wherever you go, I will go . . . ." With the strong love, devotion, and mutual respect that links grandmother, mother, and daughter, the potential for greatness is unlimited.

41

NO LIMITS

Desiree, Serenie, and Yeshiva Cohen —April 30, 1995

Photo credit: Shana Sureck-Mei

When the ceremony was over and after the festivities died down, the phone started to ring and the letters arrived. An article appeared in The Hartford Courant about this very unusual triple Bat Mitzvah. Strangers called and wrote to her, saying how much they were inspired by what she had done. Many of the people were not even Jewish; they just admired her strength, courage, and devotion in completing a goal that she had set for herself. Although even the simplest physical tasks presented a challenge and everything took so much longer, Serenie still wanted to become a Bat Mitzvah. She says that Judaism is such a big part of her life. She just wanted to be counted. There were many times that Larry went to Mincha/Maariv services, only to return home because they did not have ten people to make a minyan. Serenie can now be counted. Before, she had always felt as if something was missing. And in spite of the wheelchair and her physical limitations, after the Bat Mitzvah she felt whole.

When she was in school, Serenie Cohen was a self-proclaimed troublemaker. Like many kids who find themselves constantly in the principal's office at school and then in the dog house at home, Serenie was looking for the attention of her often-absent father, who traveled for business. With one of her pranks, she certainly got her father's attention, but there were other consequences as well. When she was 11 years old, sitting in her Hebrew school class, she noticed that right outside the window was a tree that she could climb onto. She exited the class through the window and remained in the tree until her father was called and came for her. That required his leaving Washington, D.C., and flying home to Long Island. She defended herself with a declaration of the injustices of the classroom, claiming that the teacher wouldn't let any of the kids chew gum while he kept a wad in his own mouth. The principal did not buy this excuse and expelled the young girl, emphasizing that the only heights they were allowed to climb in the classroom were spiritual ones. Her prank—though successful, as it brought her father home—ended her Hebrew school career.

Unexpectedly, her climbing days, too, ended abruptly. As a college student at Southern Connecticut State, without warning she became blind and paralyzed. Rushed to Suffolk County Hospital, she was diagnosed with multiple sclerosis, a slow, progressive disease. She recovered from this first attack, regaining her sight and her mobility, but with each successive attack, the recovery was slower and a little more of her strength and movement were robbed. Remaining oblivious of the disease and its implications, Serenie went back to school to complete the first of several degrees. Her boyfriend at the time, Larry Cohen, was a little more aggressive in his desire to learn more about MS. Finding out about the debilitating consequences did not deter his amour, and he continued to propose marriage, until Serenie relented and agreed to marry him.

The marriage was blessed with three beautiful children. The two older girls, Yeshiva and Desiree, were only one year apart, and their mother dressed them alike until they finally rebelled. Somehow, their parents always assumed that the girls would celebrate their Bat Mitzvahs together. As honor students at the Solomon Schecter of West Hartford, Connecticut, the girls already knew how to daven, but they needed to learn how to read from the Torah. Somehow, in a moment of discussing "What if's?" the idea was raised that since Mom had never had a Bat Mitzvah, what if she joined the girls and the three of them celebrated together?

Larry went to Rabbi Hans Bodenheimer of Tikvoh Chadoshoh Synagogue and pitched this idea. This rabbi had been much more than

just a rabbi to the family. This *shul* was filled with aging congregants, many of them survivors, and when the Cohens first joined they were a young family with young children and everyone welcomed them. If they missed more than one week of *Shabbat* services, someone would call and ask how they were feeling. When Serenie's parents died, and she felt overwhelmed by the loss, Rabbi Bodenheimer consoled her with the idea that he would serve as a surrogate grandfather to her children. With the progressive nature of her illness, he was always there to be supportive. When Larry first asked the rabbi if he would permit this triple Bat Mitzvah, the rabbi's first response was, "Oh . . ." However, Rabbi Bodenheimer agreed, and Larry joked that he had no idea what he was getting into.

In the Passover *Haggadah*, there is the story of the four sons. In West Hartford, Connecticut, there is the story of the mother and her two daughters: one who thought she knew everything, one who thought she knew nothing, and one who was shy and quiet. There were sometimes arguments about who would do what, but Desiree, the younger of the girls, turned out to be the great compromiser. Because Serenie's Hebrew School days had been aborted, she had to start at square one in order to prepare. A good friend from the *shul*, Andrea Cohen-Kiener, came to the house once or twice a week and tutored Serenie for the service. Once a week, she studied with the rabbi, who gave her a tape to practice with on her own. Her husband was very supportive, but after a while he tuned out her incessant practicing. And her 10-year-old son, Judah, corrected his mother's pronunciation. Yet even with this goal set, she still had to contend with health problems.

Several months before their big day, Serenie was hit with an attack so severe that she wasn't sure she would recuperate enough to be present for her daughters, let alone participate herself. She was hospitalized with paralysis and couldn't move her legs. But once again, she came back from the attack—a little weaker, but ready to go.

A good family friend, Eva Pick, volunteered to take Desiree and Yeshiva shopping for their Bat Mitzvah clothes. After an exhausting outing, they returned bearing their finery. Since women are required to wear some kind of head covering on the *bimah*, Desiree set the pace when she showed up with a beautiful hat. Not to be outdone, Yeshiva returned to the store a few days later and found a hat of her own. Serenie, not one to be left out, went with Larry to secure a chapeau for herself.

The three women made a splendid sight. Somehow, Serenie's wheelchair faded into the background, and the flowers on the *bimah*, and the three excited women became the focus of the morning. They split up the service and each had an *aliyah*. Some of the prayers were led individually and others were said in unison. They each took a turn with their *D'Var Torah*. Both Yeshiva and Desiree focused on the Torah reading. Serenie took a different slant. Her speech was entitled "Thank You, God," and she began by emotionally thanking the Almighty for allowing her to reach this day. As she thanked all of her family members, but especially her two daughters for allowing her to share this day with them, she broke down in tears and could not continue. Her beautiful hat was used to shield her face. Her good friend and teacher Andrea stepped up to the *bimah* to continue Serenie's speech. The audience chuckled when Andrea read the part in which Serenie thanked Andrea for all of her hard work. In time, though, Serenie was able to compose herself enough to complete the recitation.

The *shul* was filled to capacity. One great honor to Serenie was that an Orthodox rabbi, the head of Chabad in their area, came and stood in the back of this Conservative synagogue. Otherwise, the sanctuary was filled with people who had touched their lives. The girls were so happy that their mother was well enough to be there that they certainly didn't mind her sharing this occasion with them.

When the ceremony was over and after the festivities died down, the phone started to ring and the letters arrived. An article appeared in The Hartford Courant about this very unusual triple Bat Mitzvah. Strangers called and wrote to her, saying how much they were inspired by what she had done. Many of the people were not even Jewish; they just admired her strength, courage, and devotion in completing a goal that she had set for herself. Although even the simplest physical tasks presented a challenge and everything took so much longer, Serenie still wanted to become a Bat Mitzvah. She says that Judaism is such a big part of her life. She just wanted to be counted. There were many times that Larry went to Mincha/Maariv services, only to return home because they did not have ten people to make a minyan. Serenie can now be counted. Before, she had always felt as if something was missing. And in spite of the wheelchair and her physical limitations, after the Bat Mitzvah she felt whole.

42

UP ON THE ROOF

Juliana Wurzburger—May 20, 2000

Juliana Wurzburger graduated from Penn State and is working in Manhattan.

Juliana Wurzburger arrived ten minutes late for the interview. She sputtered her apologies, tried to catch her breath, and shuffled her way into the chair, discreetly depositing her large bag at her feet. Her partner for the interview had, in contrast, arrived on time, was already seated, and appeared poised and composed. The interviewer posed the first and most important question, "Why do you want to go to Israel?"

Her partner, who had arrived first, answered first. She launched into a beautifully eloquent story of her family's Russian refusenik history and what it was like to experience the joys of Judaism for the first time when she arrived in America. By the time the first girl had finished her soliloquy, Juliana figured that she'd never be picked for this trip. She had nothing to compare to the heartbreaking tale with the happy ending that the interviewer had just heard. She was just a Jewish kid, with no Jewish background, who saw a chance to go to Israel and wanted to go.

As a student at Penn State majoring in advertising, Juliana was not involved with the campus Hillel. Almost none of her college friends were Jewish. But she did sign up for the Hillel list serve updates, just in case a program or activity caught her fancy. The subject line for this particular e-mail said: "Free Trip to Israel." Normally, her quick trigger finger was poised to hit the "delete" key, but for some reason she opened this message. It was an application from the "Birthright Israel" organization that offers free trips to Israel for young people between the ages of 18 and 26. The only criteria is a desire to make yourself more a part of the Jewish community. Juliana had never been to Israel. She filled out the application and sent it in. Despite her late arrival for the interview and her answers being delivered at her normal "warp" speed, Juliana was chosen with 61 other Penn State students to spend 10 days in Israel as part of the "Birthright Israel" program. All told, 800 college students would be on this trip, making a total of 6,000 students since the program's inception. The "Birthright Israel" philosophy is to promote Jewish peoplehood and Jewish renaissance with no *strings attached.* The ten-day trip to Israel is free for those selected.

Once in Israel, the students visited many important places. They went to Yad Vashem, Israel's Holocaust museum, Masada, the Golan Heights, and the Dead Sea and spent a few nights on a kibbutz. On their last night on the kibbutz, before they left for their last few days in Jerusalem, the Penn State group had a meeting. The program director, Ilana, mentioned that they would spend their one and only *Shabbat* in Jerusalem with many other students on the tour. She asked if any members of the group had never had a Bar and Bat Mitzvah. When four members of the group, including Juliana, raised their hands, she asked if they wanted to incorporate their Bar and Bat Mitzvah ceremonies into their Israeli *Shabbat.* The four readily agreed. Later, they had their own private meeting to learn the meaning behind the Bar and Bat Mitzvah ceremony and the phonetic transliteration of the Hebrew blessing before the Torah reading was distributed. In addition to studying the *brachah* all of those participating in the ceremony had to come up with a Hebrew name.

The *Shabbat* morning service was not a requirement for the students. And yet, there on the rooftop of the hotel in Jerusalem, overlooking the Western Wall, every seat was taken, and the overflowing crowd scrunched together on the floor. Those who would be called up to the Torah for the first time as B'nai Mitzvah came up in groups of four as their Hebrew names were called out. In unison, each group pronounced the blessing for the Torah reading, and then they individually made speeches incorporating a Jewish memory. The speeches varied in length and intensity.

Because she had neglected to pack anything fancy for the trip, Juliana, wearing black pants and a top, was called up to the Torah by her new Hebrew name, Adiit, which means "jewel." Since she knew of no other Hebrew name, one of the Israeli tour guides helped her come up with this Hebrew handle. In her speech she touched on many things: how she first got the e-mail and for some reason did not delete it, how she was ten minutes late for her interview and figured she would never be chosen, how her family was not religious and she had never gone to Hebrew school. Her biggest Jewish memory happened when her family moved from the Bronx to Houston, Texas, when she was still a little girl. Being new in town, she was all too grateful when three little girls invited her over to play. During her playtime, she told them she was Jewish, and they promptly told her that she had killed Jesus. That was her first encounter with anti-Semitism. From then on, she had never learned that Judaism was acceptable. It wasn't until this trip to Israel, where she saw so many beautiful things and so many people willing to share them, that she realized just how "acceptable" Judaism really is.

When the ceremony was over and despite great difficulty in getting an overseas connection, Juliana called her parents. "Hey, guess what!" was how she started the conversation. Her parents were so proud, they couldn't believe it. The Bat Mitzvah was definitely one of the best parts of the trip.

Back home in Glen Rock, New Jersey, Juliana's friends had called her a "fake Jew," probably because she was Jewish in name only. Deep down, she had never felt as if she were part of the community. A piece was missing; the pride in who she was wasn't given to her earlier. Once she came to realize what a Bat Mitzvah was, she realized that she should have had one a long time ago. Since the Bat Mitzvah, she has set up special expectations for herself, including going to temple more often and maybe even learning Hebrew. The best part, though, is not feeling ashamed about her religion. High on a rooftop, overlooking the Western Wall, she found a big part of herself there. Through this program, Juliana had more than just a Bat Mitzvah; she was given her birthright.

43

SPRING

Aviva Kempner—April 15, 1989

Photo credit: Merle Tabor Stern

The Life and Times of Hank Greenberg, *an Aviva Kempner film, released in 1999, won the 2000 New York Film Critics Award for Best Non-Fiction Film, and the 2000 Broadcast Film Critics Association Award for Best Documentary. It premiered on Cinemax in April 2001, twenty-five years to the date after her father had died in Israel. Just one more spring milestone Kempner is currently making a comic short,* **Today I Vote for My Joey**, *about Election Day in Palm Beach, when older Jews go to vote for Lieberman only to discover they have voted for Buchanan. It is a tragic comedy.*

Chaim Kempner, Lithuanian-born, arrived in the United States in late 1920s. Serving in the U. S. Army during World War II, he found himself after the war in Berlin, writing for the U.S. Army newspaper. He was working on a human-interest story about a Polish survivor of Auschwitz, Dudek Ciesla, who had been separated from his family during the war. In an emotional meeting, Ciesla was reunited with his only surviving sibling, Hanka. The sister, blonde and green-eyed, had managed to survive by passing as a Polish

Catholic in a forced labor camp near Stuttgart, Germany. In the process of writing the story, Kempner fell in love with Hanka, and the two were married shortly thereafter. Ten months later their daughter Aviva was born; her birth was marked with her first celebrity. She graced the cover of the Army newspaper, with the caption simply stating, "Miss 1947." She was the first American-Jewish war baby born in Berlin.

In an article that Kempner wrote that appeared in *Daughters of Absence: Transforming a Legacy of Loss*, Aviva explained the significance of her name:

> My mother decided to give me a Hebrew name in honor of my grandmother, who loved singing Zionist songs in the ancient language. My father's own lore about my naming was that he wanted a bris, a ritual circumcision for Jewish males, in Berlin. But since I was a girl, he opted for putting a Hebrew name on his daughter's German birth certificate as an ultimate act of cultural revenge.

When Aviva was three and a half, the family moved to Detroit, Michigan, where Chaim's brother Irving already lived. Before the war, Chaim had been denied entrance into medical school because of the quotas on the number of Jewish students. He did, however, graduate from the University of Pittsburgh and ended up in small business development. To earn a little extra money, he taught Yiddish and Hebrew, speaking both fluently. Although neither Aviva nor her brother Jonathan, who is a few years younger, learned Hebrew from their father, he did take them to Jewish cultural events and to the synagogue for the High Holidays. At home, Chaim instilled in his children a pride in their Judaism that was tied to a deep respect for justice and a love of freedom.

Growing up, Aviva and Jonathan knew that something was different about their family, more by an absence than by a presence. They had no grandparents. Although they had cousins, an aunt, and an uncle on their father's side, there was very little extended family on their mother's side. Their beautiful mother—now called Helen, because she took the name of her own deceased mother—lost both parents and a sister in Auschwitz. Chaim's mother had been in one of the many "roundups" and was shot by the Nazis. Like many children of survivors, Aviva and Jonathan became fiercely protective of their parents,

especially their mother, and tried to shield her from anything disturbing—including movies about the war. That didn't preclude their watching other movies. Mother and daughter would sit together on Sunday afternoons, engrossed in the cinematic splendor of love and romance. Somewhat "starry-eyed" from her idols on the silver screen, Aviva was hit very hard at the age of 13. While boys (and later girls) celebrated their Bar Mitzvahs, Aviva went through a different kind of rite of passage—her parents' divorce.

Staying close to home, Kempner completed both her under-graduate and graduate work at the University of Michigan. She then came east to attend the Antioch Law School. While advocating for Native America treaty rights, she had her first "epiphany." Kempner explained:

> Watching *Roots* in 1977 and *Holocaust* in 1978, I became intrigued about my own roots. During a 1979 Thanksgiving visit to Detroit, I leafed through Lujan Dobroszycki and Barbara Kirshenblatt-Gimblett's *Image before My Eyes*, a photo essay book on Polish-Jewish life between the wars. A burning desire to explore my family's past was kindled. After rereading Leon Uris's *Mila 18*, a book on the Warsaw Ghetto Uprising, numerous times, I felt struck to make a film about Jewish resistance against Nazis, a topic that became the focus of my life's work.
>
> My mother, who had successfully shielded us from her war stories, was horrified over my desire to explore the forbidden topic. Objecting vehemently to my career change, she claimed hold over the painful memories. She was claiming her perfect right to control her memories, as well as my knowledge of them. But I was determined that opening the Pandora's Box of those memories was exactly the path I needed to follow in order to grasp her pain. And possibly to lessen the inherited guilt of being a child of a survivor.

Having not a bit of experience in filmmaking, Kempner nonetheless knew the story she wanted to tell—the story of Jewish resistance during World War II. Kempner also knew how to surround herself with talented people who shared her vision. She asked Josh Waletzky, the talented director of the film version of *Image before My Eyes* (1980) to direct this documentary. In answer to "Why didn't the Jews fight back?" Kempner and Waletzky told a story of how ordinary, but very brave, young men and women risked everything and resisted while facing crushing odds. *Partisans of Vilna*, told mostly by the surviving members of the resistance movement, in either Yiddish or Hebrew with English subtitles, became the vehicle through which Kempner declared that she tried "to comprehend the pain of her mother's past and make up for the loss of her own family by creating celluloid substitutes to fill the gaps."

Her lack of experience was made up for in enthusiasm, and together, Kempner and Waletzky had an uncanny knack for weaving a story from dozens of interviews all over the world. *Partisans of Vilna*, a feature-length documentary film that was theatrically distributed, won a CINE Golden Eagle and First Prize at Anthropos. It was shown at the Berlin, Haifa, London, Toronto, and Troia Film Festivals. The film aired on PBS's *Point of View* (P.O.V.) and on European and Israeli television. The record based on the film was nominated for a 1991 Grammy Award.

In 1986, with her first film "barely out of the can" and about to open in Los Angeles, Kempner heard on the radio that Hank Greenberg had died. While Aviva was growing up in Detroit, Hank Greenberg was a legend and the baseball hero whom Chaim Kempner had always spoken about. Aviva had heard her father repeatedly tell the story of the special dispensation the rabbis gave to Greenberg, allowing him to play on Rosh Hashanah. But then, the story continued, on Yom Kippur in 1934, during the World Series, Greenberg opted for the synagogue rather than the ballpark. She heard this story so often that with "tongue in cheek," she will tell you that she grew up thinking that Hank Greenberg was part of the High Holiday Kol Nidre liturgy!

The spark for her next project on Jewish heroes was ignited. Hank Greenberg, the 6'4" slugger from the Bronx, not only broke records but destroyed stereotypes as well. Every condescending ethnic joke starts with "There was a little old Jewish man . . . ." With his good looks, boyish charm, and athletic prowess, Greenberg became a source of pride for Jews, young and old, all over the country. He was the first superstar Jewish ballplayer who played using his real last name. There were taunts, jibes, insults, and threats, and Greenberg took them all and took them out on his bat. He hit ball after ball out of the park and in 1938 was two home runs away from breaking Babe

Ruth's record of sixty home runs. There were conflicting theories that "they" (whoever "they" were) didn't want a Jew to break the Babe's record, and pitchers walked him rather than give him the chance to break the record. In a taped interview that was then edited for Greenberg's autobiography, Hank Greenberg, *My Life Story*, Greenberg denies those allegations.

It took Kempner thirteen years to raise the money to make this film. When she became disheartened from the struggle to complete this project, she was spurred on by the memory of her father, whom she describes as "an over-the-top fan." The film is a tribute to one man, Greenberg, who made a country *kvell*, in honor of another man, Chaim Kempner, who did not live to see the documentary, but whose beloved memory was a source of inspiration.

In the midst of all of her professional growth, Kempner was struggling with some spiritual issues. When she first moved to Washington, D.C., in 1973, she joined the Fabrangen community, which is a *havurah*.* She was a self-proclaimed "High Holiday" Jew. Her exploration of the Holocaust during the making of *Partisans of Vilna* forced her to realize that she had the responsibility to preserve the Jewish traditions that had almost been eradicated in Eastern Europe. At the age of 43, Kempner began preparing to become a Bat Mitzvah. In her Bat Mitzvah speech, she explained how she arrived at that moment:

> This past week I have been trying to formulate an explanation of why I decided to study for my Bat Mitzvah almost thirty years after the fact. I assure you that I constantly posed that question to myself hundreds of times as I struggled through my anxiety-ridden attempts to read or at least pronounce, Hebrew—a language with its own unique, difficult symbols and rhythms.
>
> In two weeks my brother and I mourn the 13th anniversary of the death of our beloved father, Chaim . . . . His burial was an Orthodox one, and as a female I was not allowed to participate. I can remember the anguish of burying my father and not being able to throw in any dirt or say a prayer. As a result I, for years, carried around in me pent

*A *havurah* is a group of people of similar interests who meet to study and pray together. It is less formal than an organized congregation, but the members meet regularly. Often the services are led by a lay leader or a member of the group, rather than by an official clergyman.

> up anger and hostility about, the religion. I only choose to identify with those strong intellectual, cultural, and political aspects of being Jewish that I had been brought upon.
>
> These hostile notions about our religious practices ended the day I responded to (Rabbi) Max Ticktin's challenge to have a Bat Mitzvah and began to learn about the history and traditions of Judaism. My anger subsided as I realized that I could turn around the exclusiveness and mystery of the religion by studying it head on. My past tears of sorrow over forbidden practices turned into tears of joy as I was empowered by the feeling of participating in the religion.

Children of immigrant parents always struggle to pronounce English correctly lest they incur the teasing of other children. Yet the pronunciation of Hebrew for her Bat Mitzvah was the most anxiety-producing for Kempner. The learning, however, was fabulous. Studying with her rebbe, Norman Shore, was a joy. It is interesting to note that even though Kempner makes part of her living as a public speaker, she worried mostly about mispronouncing the Hebrew. She was so unsure that she would be able to pull the whole thing off that she waited until very close to the actual day to invite her friends and family. (Even with the late notice, Kempner's mother and stepfather put together a party the evening of the Bat Mitzvah.)

For her Bat Mitzvah, in their father's absence, her brother Jonathan bought her the *tallis* that she would wear and served as a surrogate dad, going up to the *bimah* with her. Her father's presence was strongly felt, though. Kempner wore her dad's *kipah* and a Judaica charm bracelet that he had given her. If her father couldn't be there, she at least wanted his brother, her Uncle Irving, in his place. She picked the date—not one that coincided with her birthday, but rather the Saturday before Passover, when she knew that Uncle Irving (affectionately known as Po) and Aunt Hannah would be coming to town to share the seder with Aviva, her family, and two cousins who also lived in Washington, D.C. As they later found out, the date was *bashert*, because twenty-five years prior, Jonathan had the same Haftorah portion, *Shabbat Haggadol*, the Sabbath before Passover. On her fourth finger, she wore the aquamarine ring that her mother had sewn into the lining of her coat before she was deported. The ring had belonged to Aviva's grandmother. In some small way, the ring and this day were

for her grandmother, for her aunt, and for 6 million lost. Subtly, with this ceremony, she was declaring, "We have survived, and we will carry on."

She expressed some of these thoughts as she continued her Bat Mitzvah speech:

> I had documented the youthful resistance to the Nazis. But unless I attempted in my own life to continue with the cultural, political, and religious Jewish legacies I had learned about, then the Nazis had succeeded not only in killing millions but also in breaking the continuity of our rich traditions. That is why I decided to read some of the prayers in Yiddish today. I wanted to affirm the memory of the Yiddish culture that was destroyed. I also had learned that women in Eastern Europe, denied equal access to the synagogue, often read their prayers in Yiddish.
>
> . . . The Haftorah reading asks: "How shall we turn back?" For me, it is difficult to believe in the Messiah because of the Holocaust. But I can easily believe that this yearly identification with oppression is our salvation. On this day of my Bat Mitzvah I reaffirmed my commitment to "turning back" to the legacy of our past and revamping it for the future generations.

Aviva put those words into practice when she bought the *tallis* for her niece Aliza's Bat Mitzvah in the spring of 2001 and stood on the *bimah* next to her brother Jonathan when Aliza was called to the Torah for the first time. Interestingly, the spring season holds so much significance to the family—Kempner's mother, Helen, was liberated in the spring of 1945; Aviva and Jonathan had the same Haftorah portion, although twenty-five years apart, in the spring; and if the family got the right date (they didn't, only because so many children were having their B'nai Mitzvot that year), Aliza, too, should have shared the same Torah portion. And Aviva's beautiful Hebrew name, a source of pride to both parents, translates into English as "spring."

No matter at what age the Bat Mitzvah takes place, it signifies the ending of one stage and the beginning of the next, just as it is a connection between the past and the future. In spite of her many degrees and awards, upon completion of her Bat Mitzvah, Aviva Kempner felt as if she had religiously become a "woman" in much the same way her brother became a "man" after his Bar Mitzvah. There was this tremen-

dous feeling of being equalized. She had professionally started out in one field; then, somehow, a "lightning bolt" hit and Kempner's road forked, leading her in a different direction. This new path, a new career direction, led to the creation of beautiful, permanent works of art—two documentary films that honor real Jewish heroes. Audiences, both young and old, feel a collective sense of pride and loss in watching *Partisans of Vilna* and *The Life and Times of Hank Greenberg*. On a more personal note, Kempner honored her own mother and father in making these films. In some ways she incorporated the same process in her Bat Mitzvah that is responsible for the success of her work:

> I believe what compelled me was an unknown spirit within me. I often imagined it as a cupid hitting me with a bow. . . . It suddenly occurred to me that Elijah (the Prophet) was that cupid and he zapped me from his chariot. He wanted me to reconcile the history of the parents with the history of the children. I could recapture the world of the grandparents that I had never known. I, the child of the protesting 60s and 70s, had turned to the past to gather answers for the future.

44

ON THE WINGS OF EAGLES

Samantha Mandeles—July 15, 2000

Samantha Rose Mandeles is a little girl with big ideas. She describes herself as an "artist" and will tell you she has three passions—art, Taekwondo (she has a black belt), and acting. When she decided to "twin" with an Ethiopian Jewish girl in Israel, she did so with gusto.

"They flew on the wings of eagles . . . ." In just a little under thirty-six hours, between May 24 and 25, 1991, "Operation Solomon" brought almost 15,000 Ethiopian Jews out of the squalor of refugee camps and into the home of their forefathers, Eretz Yisrael, the land of Israel. Twenty-seven planes left Addis Ababa and returned to Tel Aviv in forty sorties.* Using cargo planes, with their empty hulls, hundreds of people were transported on

---

*Special Coverage—The Story of the Day: "Operation Solomon" 05.26.91. by Anat Tal-Shir (The Government Press Office: Hebrew Press), p. 12.

each flight. The uncomplaining passengers sat huddled and cramped on mattresses laid out on the floor, eating only bread and water.

The Information Department at the Consulate General of Israel in New York released the following:

> Friday, 4:40 in the afternoon. A white Boeing 707 Air Force plane lands at Ben Gurion airport and veers toward a side runway . . . . The sight overpowered all (who witnessed it): an entire community, beautiful, special, destitute, without belongings, touching in their poverty, their vulnerability, in (their) gratitude—coming here to find a homeland . . . .
>
> After the children descended the stairs from the plane, with a certain suspicion, the others (came). They appeared exhausted and frightened and only a few individuals managed to express happiness or relief. They escaped their country and arrived here without anything, only the clothes on their backs . . . . An old man who was sick was taken off in a stretcher. After him, a youth named Mukat clapped as he came down the steps and the crowd around him cheered. He bent down on his knees and kissed the runway."*

Small groups of Ethiopian Jews began arriving in Israel back in the 1950s. "Operation Moses" brought over 7,000 Ethiopian Jews out of Sudanese refugee camps and into Israel in a two-week period between December 1984 and January 1985. By 1990, there were 20,000 Ethiopian Jews in Israel. "Operation Solomon" increased that number by 15,000 in 1991.**

In the aftermath of the miraculous rescue of "Operation Solomon," the State of Israel began the task of resettling the thousands of new immigrants, a job that this tiny state knows all too well. During and immediately after World War II, there were refugee ships filled with Jewish people looking for safe haven. They were bounced from country to country and in some tragic cases ended up with their passengers disembarking in the only place that would take them, the concentration camps. With the establishment of the State of Israel, that fatal rejection will never happen again. Since its establishment in 1948, Israel has carried out other similar types of rescue operations

---

*Special Coverage—The Story of the Day: "Operation Solomon" 05.26.91. by Anat Tal-Shir (The Government Press Office: Hebrew Press), p. 12.

** The statistics were taken from Samantha's fact sheet.

for Jews from other countries, including Yemen, Iran, Iranian Kurdistan, Afghanistan, Iraq, Libya, Turkey, Egypt, Syria, Cochin, Maghreb, Romania, Ethiopia, Albania, and the former USSR.

Much less dramatic than the actual rescue is the more mundane, but equally important task of providing housing, food, education, and jobs to these new Israelis who are welcomed under the Law of Return. All of those things, however, require funding. One organization that has been supportive of the resettlement process (as well as involved with Jews still in Ethiopia) is the North American Conference on Ethiopian Jewry (NACOEJ), with offices in both Israel and New York City.

Laura and Mark Mandeles, of Fairfax, Virginia, have been members and supporters of NACOEJ for years. They value the work of this organization that strives to bring Jews who are "outside the fold" into the mainstream. When their daughter Samantha was preparing for her Bat Mitzvah at Temple Beth El of Alexandria, Virginia, and searching for a required *tzedekah* project, Laura remembered reading in the NACOEJ newsletter about its "twinning" program. As an American boy or girl is preparing for his or her Bar or Bat Mitzvah, this individual can apply to "twin" with a partner from the Ethiopian community who is the same age and may or may not be experiencing the same rite of passage in Israel. The Bar or Bat Mitzvah is given a beautifully designed *tallit*, handmade by Ethiopian craftsmen, and a certificate that is sent to the congregation's rabbi with the request that it be delivered on the day of the *simcha*. The "twins" typically write back and forth, getting to know each other while exchanging information on family, friends, and likes or dislikes. The small donation that NACOEJ accepts from the American families is used to buy books and supplies for the school of the Ethiopian youngster.

Once her application was accepted, Samantha began corresponding with her "twin," Sifra Birhanu. Samantha's letters were sent to Sifra via the New York NACOEJ office, where they were first translated into Hebrew and then sent on. Sifra's letters were likewise translated first from Hebrew into English and then sent to Samantha. Samantha learned that Sifra had arrived in Israel when she was only 3, accompanied by her parents and siblings. One of her older sisters is deaf.

Sam was not content to just write back and forth to Sifra. She wanted to do something for the Ethiopian community. Many of the

Ethiopian children received inadequate or little or no education, so once they arrived in Israel, they were forced to play "catch up." Now over 1,000 children are in after-school programs, where they are given the additional assistance they need to stay abreast of other children in Israel.

Samantha did extensive research on Ethiopia and Ethiopian Jewry. She made a colorful poster and put together a very impressive fact sheet with answers to questions such as:

- Where is Ethiopia?
- How did Jews come to live in Ethiopia?
- How did Ethiopian Jews come to Israel?
- Have all Ethiopian Jews left Ethiopia?
- What are some of the challenges Ethiopian Jews have faced in adapting to life in Israel?
- How are Ethiopian Jews different from other Israelis?
- What language do Ethiopians speak?

Sam then shared her research in a presentation to other classes at Temple Beth El and at the Gesher Jewish Day School, where she has been a student for the past nine years. Her presentation had the dual purpose of sharing information and also apprising her schoolmates of the needs of the Ethiopian Jewish population in both Israel and Ethiopia. Through her one-woman appeal, she collected enough school supplies to fill two suitcases!

Sam made a glowing Bat Mitzvah girl. She was too excited to be nervous. Every aspect of her service was fabulous to her, and she loved them all. One terrific bonus was that her mother, Laura, who learned the *trup* (tune) for chanting the Haftorah in an adult class and sometimes serves as a lay cantor, was able to teach the *trup* to Samantha. Laura actually did much more than that. She and her husband, Mark, live in a very eclectic world, having friends who range from Orthodox Jews to devout Christians. They wanted Samantha's service to be as meaningful as possible, so they created their own prayer book for their very unique service. Laura wanted everything transliterated so that all of their guests could follow along and join in if they felt comfortable. There was the traditional reading of the Torah and Haftorah portions; however, Sam wanted to chant more than was typically expected. They chose their own songs, making the service a

lot more fun and, according to Sam, "less boring." "I'm an artist," she declared. "I like to do creative things."

As for her twin, Sifra was there in spirit. While Sam wore a beautiful *tallit* given to her by her grandmother, the Ethiopian *tallit* was draped over one of the high-backed chairs on the *bimah*, typically reserved for people of honor. And there was a centerpiece with pictures of Ethiopian children who have made *aliyah* at the luncheon, to which the entire congregation was invited.

Although Sam was enthusiastic over everything—the preparation, the project, and the collection of the school supplies, the actual Bat Mitzvah with her first public reading of her Torah portion, and a party at which art supplies served as the centerpieces and the guests created their personal expressions of love and admiration for her—the best part was yet to come. Four days after the official Bat Mitzvah, Sam and her family flew to Israel to meet Sifra in person. They also wanted to hand-deliver the two suitcases of supplies. NACOEJ provided them with a letter to indicate that they were bringing these items in as gifts, not to sell. And in order to "guarantee" safe passage to Sam and her family, the students at Gesher Day School gave Sam and her younger brother Harry $5.00 each as *tzedakah* to give to the kids in Sifra's school. The premise behind that money is that if a person is traveling to Israel in order to donate charity, that individual will have a safe journey.

The Mandeles family traveled with a friend from Israel, and they realized that it wasn't that easy to find Sifra's immediate family, because there were several branches of her extended family. However, when they finally found her, they arranged to meet. Sifra waited downstairs to bring them up to her family's apartment. Dressed in Western clothes of a blue tank top and capris, Sifra was shy but really nice. As in the "Gift of the Magi," both girls had been practicing the other's language and Sam talked in Hebrew while Sifra responded in English. Although the communication was somewhat halting, Sam felt right at home. Sam brought her new friend a perfect gift for an adolescent teenage girl: a CD player with a Britney Spears CD. Sifra presented Sam with a beautiful embroidery, in an Ethiopian style, that had been made by her older sister. Though the gift was Ethiopian style, Sifra seemed every inch Israeli, and the Mandeles family observed that Ethiopians seem to be very much a part of Israeli society. The girls ended their visit with the promise that they will continue to correspond and to develop their friendship.

Although miracles still happen, we are unaccustomed to recognizing them in these modern times. In the days of the Exodus from Egypt, when miracles were much more commonplace (i.e., the ten plagues), some people got so used to them that miracles were almost taken for granted. The parting of the Red Sea must have been fantastic! We've marveled at the mere cinematic representations in Cecil B. DeMille's epic film *The Ten Commandments* and more recently in an animated depiction of the parting of the waters in *The Prince of Egypt.* And yet, when many of our ancestors crossed the Red Sea *on foot*, they reached the other side and did no more than catch their breath from the exertion. It took one lone little woman, Miriam, to rev up her sisters and remind them of what they had not only witnessed, but also experienced. Although technology has been stepped up a bit, and instead of a single staff being used to part the waters, Boeing 707s and Air Force Hercules planes carried out the miracle—a modern-day exodus—it was a miracle, nonetheless. In the words of those people who flew to Israel. "they flew on the wings of eagles to the Holy Land, to their families, to their people." On the wings of eagles they came back home.

For more information about twinning, contact: The North American Conference on Ethiopian Jewry, 132 Nassau Street, New York, New York 10038, 212–233–5200, fax: 212–233–5243, e-mail: *NACOEJ@aol.com*

45

SET THE NIGHT TO MUSIC

Amy Poran—June 25, 1983

Amy went on to graduate from the Hillel Academy, a Hebrew day school, and to this day she is grateful for the education that she received there. When she went on to high school, she was surprised at the distinction between her work and that of her classmates. While excellence was the norm at Hillel, many of her peers in high school were accustomed to mediocrity, at best. The education at Hillel served her well, as she continued on to major in biology at the University of Rochester and graduate from the SUNY Manhattan College of Optometry. She runs two practices in Brooklyn, New York, with her husband, who is an optician. And just as she promised in her speech at her Bat Mitzvah, she runs a kosher Jewish home. In her busy, hectic life, her home keeps her grounded so that she doesn't lose sight of what is important. Her Bat Mitzvah was ushered in with lights and music times two—the concert and the fireworks, plus the music and the flames from the Havdalah service. And the promise of the overflowing wine cup has been fulfilled, bringing her joy and spiritual abundance.

The *Havdalah* service is beautiful.* Every sense is stimulated. There is music from the singing of the blessings. We taste the wine, smell the spices, hold the candle, and watch the flames. We liken *Shabbos* to a Queen and we welcome her in grand fashion. As *Shabbos* ends, we must release the Queen with a royal

*Information on the *Havdalah* service was found in *The Jewish Book of Why* by Alfred J. Kolatch, published by Jonathan David Publishers, Inc., 1981; and in *The Complete Art Scroll Siddur*, With translation and commentary by Rabbi Nosson Scherman, published by Mesorah Publications. Ltd., 1984.

send-off and console ourselves with the loss. We do that with the *Havdalah* service. As the word literally means "separation," we distinguish between the holy, *Shabbos*, and the mundane, the rest of the week.

Amy Poran chose to celebrate her Bat Mitzvah by leading the *Havdalah* service. Her family and friends gathered on a warm June evening in Beth David synagogue. The men's section in the middle is flanked on both sides by an elevated women's section. While the men face the *bimah*, the women's sections face the center. Long high windows run the length of the sanctuary on both sides of the women's sections.

A podium was set in the women's section and Amy was to start with a responsive reading. Several years before, Amy's older brother Allen was informed in this very *shul* on the morning of his Bar Mitzvah that he had learned the "wrong" *parsha*. He was given the choice of chanting the one he had learned or reciting the "right" one, with twenty minutes to prepare. He chose to become a man with a very adult-like decision and chanted the "right" *parsha*. Amy prepared for the responsive reading—she would read two lines, the congregation would follow with two lines, and so on. In an effort to be helpful, in his loud voice the rabbi decided to "start her off." Overpowering her 12-year-old voice, the rabbi read one line and waited for the congregation to respond with the next one. Once the rhythm was set, there was no going back. Could this be happening again? Two siblings, innocents, foiled during their rite of passage. Like her brother, Amy, too, rose to the occasion and just did what she had to do. She read one line, followed by the congregational response of one line. When the prayer was completed, the rabbi having caught his error too late, alerted the congregation that the mix-up in the timing was his and not the Bat Mitzvah girl's.

Following the reading, Amy delivered a speech that was tied into the weekly *parsha*. She talked about coming from a Jewish home. And now that she was an adult, keeping a Jewish home. Unbeknown to Amy, the Broome County Pops was having a concert on the river. The good folks of Binghamton, New York, had brought lawn chairs and sat on the bank listening to the live music. The concert concluded at just the same time that Amy ended her speech. As if on cue, with impeccable timing, a magnificent fireworks display was set off. With the great visibility afforded by the windows on both sides, Amy's guests

were treated to the beauty and splendor of the lights and colors. Waiting until the conclusion of the fireworks, Amy ad libbed and told the crowd that she would like to thank Broome County for helping her celebrate her Bat Mitzvah.

Her parents and Allen joined her, and they all converged at the *bimah.* The twilight turned to darkness, and they led the *Havdalah* service. They sang the blessing over the wine in a cup that was filled to overflowing. That custom of an overflowing cup is an expression of hope. Then, the blessing over the spices was sung. Saddened by the impending loss of *Shabbos*, we assuage ourselves with the lovely aroma. And finally, they sang the blessing over the braided candle with the two wicks. They held "their hands up and watched the reflection of the flame in their nails. The remainder of the wine was poured into the tray and the candle was extinguished. *Shabbos* was over, but the joy and celebration of Amy's Bat Mitzvah was just beginning.

Amy went on to graduate from the Hillel Academy, a Hebrew day school, and to this day she is grateful for the education that she received there. When she went on to high school, she was surprised at the distinction between her work and that of her classmates. While excellence was the norm at Hillel, many of her peers in high school were accustomed to mediocrity, at best. The education at Hillel served her well, as she continued on to major in biology at the University of Rochester and graduate from the SUNY Manhattan College of Optometry. She runs two practices in Brooklyn, New York, with her husband, who is an optician. And just as she promised in her speech at her Bat Mitzvah, she runs a kosher Jewish home. In her busy, hectic life, her home keeps her grounded so that she doesn't lose sight of what is important. Her Bat Mitzvah was ushered in with lights and music times two—the concert and the fireworks, plus the music and the flames from the Havdalah service. And the promise of the overflowing wine cup has been fulfilled, bringing her joy and spiritual abundance.

46

THE GARDEN OF EDEN: PLANTING NEW SEEDS

Eliza Halle Ruder—October 9, 1999
(by Abby Ruder)

Eliza Ruder is a high school student in Philadelphia. She plays varsity volleyball and is able to enjoy her passion of riding horses. She is a loyal friend and continues to focus on issues of culture, race, and diversity.

Eliza's Bat Mitzvah story began almost fifteen years ago. She was born on September 24, 1986, in Atlanta, Georgia, and arrived home in Philadelphia to her loving parents, Abby and Ellen, and older brothers, Dylan and Aaron, seventeen days later. She brings the blessings and complexities of having a dual heritage into our family. Born to Irish Catholic and African-American parents and raised by Eastern European Jewish parents, Eliza identifies herself as

biracial, African-American, and Jewish. Her experience is built on the strength of both her legacies, by birth and adoption. Eliza proudly claims her racial identity as a person of color, while having a strong sense of her own Jewishness. She embraces her African-American, Irish, and Jewish heritages, and so do we, her family. Our identity as a family is expansive. It has grown to include all of our experience. We are an interracial and Jewish family formed by birth and adoption, with two women at the helm. Together, we have a shared history and continue to discover our unique shared destiny.

Welcoming Eliza into our family was joyous. She arrived just before the High Holy Days. We were called up to the Torah for an *aliyah* and special prayer of thanksgiving for the gift of Eliza coming into our lives and our becoming her parents. A year later, we made a beautiful Ceremony of Welcome. On a gorgeous, sun-filled fall day Eliza was surrounded by the warmth of those dearest to her. She crawled from one set of arms to the next as we all gathered with blessings and songs for her. We expressed our hopes and prayers for her future and our tremendous gratitude for her birth parents, who had brought Eliza into this world and our lives. Amidst the love of family and good friends, we gave Eliza her Hebrew name, Elianna, which means "God has answered my prayer."

It was a rude awakening to discover a year later that Eliza was not considered Jewish by *halachah* because she was not my daughter by birth, but by adoption. I mistakenly had thought that Jewish law honored civil law, which is not true when it comes to defining who is a Jew. This was a painful revelation. As my child's legal parent and being spiritually, emotionally and materially responsible for her well-being in every way, I could not fully confer Jewish identity on her, according to Jewish law. I was angry with the narrowness of *halachah* (Jewish law) and initially felt diminished by it. But I did not choose the way of halachic conversion. Instead, I decided that my role was to raise Eliza with the gift of our Jewish heritage, now hers, in the best way I knew how to convey it. I also wanted Eliza, at the time of her Bat Mitzvah, to have a say in choosing Judaism for herself. Ellen and I hoped that Eliza would grow up able to claim and bridge all the worlds that are a part of her. We believed she would find her way there.

As Eliza's parents, we have always focused on the priority of her developing a strong, healthy racial identity as a person of color. As a

multiracial family, we value living a racially conscious and diverse life on a daily basis. Our commitment to create and nurture meaningful connections with Eliza's racial heritage of origin is reflected in our family of choice, community involvements, and Eliza's daily activities. The guidance of dear friends has been invaluable in the formation of Eliza's racial identity. Eliza's godparents, who are African-American, are tremendous mentors for her and for us, in understanding how people of color survive and strive to flourish in a highly racialized society.

In looking for a spiritual home, we wanted to be in a congregation that was willing to explore issues of race and social justice and to become self-aware as a multiracial Jewish community. In the same way that families with members of color may be racially different from one another yet may share the experience of developing an interracial family identity, so, too, the American-Jewish community, which includes Jews of color and multiracial families, is both challenged and blessed to become more conscious of our multiracial identity. We have been involved in forming a wonderful progressive Jewish community, Mishkan Shalom, since its inception twelve years ago. Mishkan Shalom is a community committed to the integration of three primary areas of Jewish life, prayer (*avodah*), study (Torah and other scriptures), and action to repair this broken world and acts of caring (*tikkun olam/g'milut hasadim*). These values have been at the heart of Eliza's Jewish education and our family's evolving Jewish identity. Ours is a community founded on prayer-in-action, neither having the power alone that they have together. It is a community that supports diversity, strives for social justice, welcomes interfaith and interracial families, and encourages skeptics. It is a community that deeply honors many facets of Jewish civilization, preserving revered traditions and shaping new ones. Eliza is blessed, as are we, with several communities to which she belongs. Mishkan Shalom has welcomed our family, along with many others, as partners in creating a very special community that has made a home for us.

Eliza's preparation for her Bat Mitzvah was a right-of-passage in itself! She had an enormously significant and joyous year of study. We watched as her journey took shape and her belief in her own capacity to become a Bat Mitzvah was kindled. It was a great joy to see Eliza and her tutor, Rachel Gartner, engage so thoughtfully and with such fun and enthusiasm in Torah study and prayer. We were fortunate to

encounter Rachel's creative and loving spirit and to see Eliza's blossom under her guidance.

A week before her Bat Mitzvah, Eliza dipped into the chilly water of an outdoor *mikveh*. Our loving neighbor spent hours pouring pots of boiling water into a small, deep pool, raising the temperature just enough for Eliza to get in. On this cold, overcast October afternoon, in the presence of her parents and teachers, I watched this beautiful child participate in an ancient ritual she made her own. While affirming her Jewishness, Eliza was also celebrating her many legacies, which make up all of who she is. As she immersed herself several times, floating under the water's surface, she seemed to me all at once alone, at one with the mystery of creation, connected, and wrapped in the wings of the *Shechinah* (female aspect of God). We all blessed her when she emerged and embraced her in layers of warm towels. This transformation ceremony marked the culmination of more than a wonderful, spirited year of study and Jewish experience. In her process of continual growth, we were honoring Eliza becoming more of who she is.

Eliza's Bat Mitzvah service wove together traditional Jewish liturgy with poems and readings reflective of Eliza's African-American heritage and our multicultural family experience. Eliza led us in prayer during many parts of the *Shabbat* service, chanted her Torah portion masterfully, and discussed the meaning she derived from these ancient words in her *D'var Torah.* In the spirit of this congregation, Eliza shared actions she has taken to manifest compassion and justice in the world through both a personal *tikkun olam* (repair of the world) project and her ongoing participation in a community service program.

The service opened with poems by Maya Angelou, Langston Hughes, and Zarinah James, read by Eliza; one of her dear mentors, Ricky Sanders; and her Vietnamese godbrother, Hieu Ho. These passages created a spirit of honoring new beginnings, the infinite beauty of the souls and physical attributes of Black people, the great civilizations of Africa and China, and Latino and Native American culture as they are reflected in the strength and potential of all young people of color.

Eliza's *parshah* (Torah portion) was the beginning of the Book of Genesis. In thinking about the creation of the world and every living thing on earth, Eliza became fascinated with the stories about the creation of humankind. In them, she discovered seeds of making human connection and building community. Eliza's *D'var Torah* became her vehicle for expressing many of her own ideas, including her notions of fairness, conflict, gender roles, appreciation of difference and uniqueness, the importance of personal responsibility, and equal rights for all humanity.

D'VAR TORAH
by Eliza Ruder

This morning I'm going to present to you a *midrash*. A *midrash* is a story based on the Bible, but not written in the Bible. The ancient rabbis were the first to invent *midrashim*. Very often, the rabbis based their *midrashim* on stories in the Bible that were confusing, that did not make sense in some way, or that had problems. My *midrash* is based on a problem in my Torah portion that does not make sense.

My Torah portion is about the creation of the world and the creation of humanity. The problem in it is that woman is created twice. First it says, And God created from the earth, human, Male and female, God created them. To me, this means that man and woman were created at the same time and were equal. It might also mean that there was one human being that was both male and female.

Next comes the story where woman was created a second time from Adam's rib. How could there be two different stories that explain the creation of woman? To solve this problem, the rabbis wrote a *midrash*. In their *midrash*, they say there must be two different women. They called the first one Lilith, whom they didn't like very much, and the second one Eve, who was their perfect woman.

The rabbis wrote their *midrashim* to teach people lessons. In the one about Lilith and Eve, they wanted to teach people how women should act compared to men. Lilith was trying to be equal to Adam. According to the rabbis, that was bad. So they kicked her out of the garden. The rabbis said that Eve was not trying to be equal. According to them, the women should serve the men.

I disagree with the rabbis on how women should behave. I think women are equal to men and should not have to be their servants. I also disagree that there should be only one woman in the garden. If there were two women in the garden, they would learn how to get along and they could also have more votes than one man.

So my *midrash* teaches some different lessons. It is in the form of a play, and I've asked my two best friends and my brothers to take some of the parts.

THE PLAY

Lilith: Caroline
Adam: Aaron
Eve: Nora
Narrator: Dylan
God: Eliza

Lilith and Adam's First Conversation

Lilith: Hi. My name is Lilith. What's yours?

Adam: My name is Adam!

Lilith: So, Adam, I have a question for you. Why are women not equal to men? I don't get that.

Adam: Well, men are just better than women because we have more rights than women do.

Lilith: But that's not fair. Women should have the same rights as men.

Adam: Well, you don't! So deal with it, OK?

Lilith: I'm glad I'm not a boy. One reason is they can be so rude, and second, because I want to be a girl. But I still want to be equal. If I can't get any respect around here, then I'll just have to leave and make my own choices, find my own way in the world. Not very nice meeting you, Adam!

A Conversation between God and Adam

Narrator: A long time has passed since Lilith left the garden.

Adam: Lord, I'm not feeling so good these days.

God: What was that thing between you and Lilith?
Adam: Oh. nothing . . . OK, so it was a fight.

God: Adam, when you are in My garden, you do not fight. I want it to be peaceful here. Is that understood?

Adam: Well . . . I guess I can try not to fight.

God: Good! So will you please go and get Lilith and work this out?

Adam: Um . . . But God. Lilith left, remember?

God: Oh, darn it! I wanted you to work it out and make up.

Adam: Make up with her? No way, after how she treated me! She walked out!

God: Don't be silly. You will have to make up with her if you want to stay in My garden because in My garden everyone is friendly.

Adam: I bet she does not want to make up with me. I mean . . . I said a lot of mean things to her. I admit I was pretty mean to her.

God: What did you say?

Adam: I said that she could not be equal, that she wasn't as good as me.

God: Why did you say that? Do you think you're God or something?

Adam: Well, I don't know. Maybe . . . I think I thought she was going to have power over me and I wanted to get power before she did. Or she would get the best fruits and not leave any for me. Or maybe I thought You would like her better than me. She would be Your favorite.

God: You know I don't have favorites, Adam. I love both of you the same. I even created you together!

Adam: I see that now. I kind of miss Lilith. She was my really good friend. I wish she would come back to the garden

God: I know you do, Adam, but I can't bring her back. In my garden, people make their own choices and other people can't make choices for them. Even though I'm God and I created the world, I can't bring someone back who chooses to leave. Lilith needs to decide on her own, without my help.

Adam: But I'll be so lonesome.

God: All right, I'll create another woman to be with you, but don't blow it this time! (Adam shakes his head "Oh no.") Just relax and go to sleep and I'll go to work.

Narrator: So while Adam went out like a light. God created Eve. Adam had learned a lot from Lilith, so when he and Eve woke up, Adam was a lot kinder and didn't try to be the BIG BOSS. He and Eve talked and got to know each other. And they decided to stay together and make their life in the garden. Then one day, someone unexpected came to visit. . . .

. . . .

Lilith (to Eve): Hey! Who're you?

Eve: I'm Eve. I'm Adam's partner.

Lilith: Partner . . . is that like a servant? You know, I tried that once, and it didn't work for me at all.

Eve: No, I'm not a servant. Adam and I help each other. I like the garden very much. It's peaceful here.

Lilith: Well, it was peaceful until Adam broke the silence by yelling at me.

Eve: What do you mean?

Lilith: You know, Eve, I just realized I need to talk to Adam about this!

. . . .

Lilith (to Adam who enters): Look, Adam, about the fight we had before I left. Well, I know that I was mean to you. Your idea that women were not equal to men just made me very upset and angry. But I did not mean for it to come out by being nasty. And I know I was a little hard on you and I'm sorry.

Adam: I feel the same way. I was scared you were going to be God's favorite or get the best fruit or take over the garden. But what came out of my mouth was you're not as good as me. So what I want to say is that I'm sorry.

Eve: I'm so glad you two are making up. Why don't we all try living in the garden together? Then we can all share the best fruit and be God's favorites.

Adam: Great idea, Eve! And I want you both to be equal with me.

Lilith: I think I'll pass on being God's favorite, but sharing the fruit and being equal with both of you sounds cool to me.

Lilith (looking toward heaven): Hi, God! I'm back! What's new with you?

God: Oh, nothing. Just being my old spirity self, having a good time resting in my big comfy clouds. It's good to see you back in the garden.

Lilith: It sure is good being back here. I really missed the company of people. Adam and I have worked things out and I think I could be good friends with him and Eve.

Narrator: Although Lilith, Adam, and Eve could not really see God, they could tell she was smiling because the sun was shining brightly.

THE END

Besides the fact that we are all equal and need to treat each other that way, I wanted to teach some other lessons in my midrash. One of the lessons is that people make their own choices; God doesn't make them for us. This means to me that we each have to take responsibili-

ty for how we act and how we live, instead of blaming others for our own mistakes.

The second lesson is that God has no favorites. To me, this means that every person is created in God's image, not just White people or Black people, Jewish or Moslem or Christian people, or poor people or wealthy people, or women or men. In God's universe, we are all special.

Some of the most special people I know are the people with physical and mental disabilities whom I met at Thorncroft, which is a place where handicapped people do therapeutic horseback riding. I worked there this past school year as part of my *tikkun olam* project. My friend, Bob, whom I met there, is mentally impaired. My teacher said that he was the smartest person about horses that she ever knew. I learned to be a better rider just by watching Bob. Little Andrew, who is 5, has cerebral palsy and has worked hard his whole life to be able to crawl and pull himself up. Andrew taught me about keeping up my spirit and to keep on trying. There are also people at Thorncroft who became disabled after an accident or an illness. Sometimes people there get frustrated, angry or sad because their body doesn't work the way they want it to. But it made me happy to see how horses could help people move their bodies and enjoy riding.

I've been going to St. Vincent's dining room in Germantown with my parents and Hebrew school class for four years. The people who come to St. Vincent's are poor. Some have jobs and are still poor. Some are children. Some adults take drugs. A lot of people who come there don't feel well. We make people feel welcome by putting flowers on the tables, smiling, and being friendly. Sometimes this is hard for me because I feel shy. My favorite job is serving big portions of macaroni and cheese. It makes me feel hungry, and then I remember that the people coming to eat are a lot hungrier than I am. I'm lucky because I can eat when I'm hungry. They need to eat a lot when they're here because they can't always get food when they want it.

At St. Vincent's I've learned how much it matters to share the best food with everybody and not be greedy and keep it all to yourself.

The last lesson I want to teach is about not being afraid of someone who is different. Even though when they met, Eve and Lilith were suspicious of each other, they got to know each other and became good friends. We have to give new people a chance and not exclude them. This is how people learn to live together. In my *midrash,* we have a lot to thank Lilith, Adam, and Eve for.

In our congregation it is customary to give parental blessings at certain times during the Bat Mitzvah service. Abby made this blessing on giving Eliza her *tallit*

> I have wanted to weave this *tallit* for you for thirteen years, and I am so thrilled to give it to you today. Several months ago, when we started talking about colors and design, you told me you wanted a deep sky blue *tallit* with turquoise and purples, and I could not imagine it. When you chose the yarn, I still could not imagine it.
>
> Then I wound the warp and put it on the loom. And the colors began to sing to me. You chose colors that reflect your spirit: vibrant, rich, and deeply beautiful. Like you, these colors shine from the inside out.
>
> Whenever you wear your *tallit*, I hope you will remember how filled with happiness, strength, and love you feel today. May you always feel wrapped in light and the comfort of my love.

Later in the service, her parental blessing continues.

> In addition to today being your Bat Mitzvah, this weekend is also the anniversary of your coming home and our becoming a family. Thirteen years ago I met you for the first time. You were a tiny, beautiful bundle of a being, and when you were placed in my arms, I knew then that your soul and mine were meant to be together.
>
> Becoming one of your moms is my greatest joy. You teach me all the time about how to be your parent, and I hope you think you're doing a good job!
>
> One of the most profound things you have taught me is that you are not only my child. I can't think about how lucky I am to be your mother, along with Ellen, without also thinking about your birthparents. I know they are always in your heart, and they are also in mine. I also know that if they were here today, they would be as proud of you as I am.
>
> Before my eyes, I have watched you become even more beautiful, caring, and thoughtful. Today you are a wonderful, self-assured, strong young Black woman who deeply cherishes her Jewishness.

> After your last official practice for today, you came bounding downstairs and said, "I'm just gonna do this for the love of doing it." And that's exactly what you've done. Eliza, I delight in your exuberance, how much you love life, and how your life enriches mine.

Ellen's parental blessing begins:

> I have a song, Eliza. It's about you.
>
> It's about somebody who has worked so hard and diligently to get here today: by studying almost every day for more than a year, by thinking about BIG STUFF and writing about it and asking lots of questions, and then going off and thinking some more; by laughing about and playing with new ideas; and by putting old important ideas, into your own words and your own actions.
>
> This is a song about somebody who truly has faith and practices it. You have taught me so much as you prepared for today. Many times this past year I felt humbled by your open-hearted courage to do something new and difficult: like learning an incredibly long Torah portion, like showing up regularly and without complaint at St. Vincent's, like immersing yourself in the *mikveh*. Not because you knew how any of it would turn out, but because you trusted that if you chose to try something, even something that looked hard or even scary, you could master it and make it yours. And you did. That's what I mean by faith.
>
> Along the way you've helped me learn to be more open and trusting, too.
>
> And I have a song about the young woman you are becoming: open and brave, bursting with energy, somebody who knows who she is and celebrates every part of herself, someone with a fierce sense of justice and a heart as big as the sky. Someone the world needs.
>
> This song is about my love for you and my delight in you and my pride in you. And about my gratitude for all you bring to my life and my confidence in all you are and all you will be.
>
> This song is about you, Eliza, and it isn't finished.

As the keepers and teachers of the African tradition in Eliza's life and the life of our family, Eliza's godparents, Sunni and Rudi Green-

Tolbert, also joined in giving her blessings from the family. Sunni writes:

> God bless you, Eliza darlin'. Welcome to womanhood. Welcome also to the sisterhood of women of African descent! . . .. For the next stage of your life's journey, I commend to you the importance of KUJICHAKALIA, which means "self-determination." I pray that you will have the courage to hold onto your values, that you will define yourself and speak up for yourself and not be defined by others.
>
> . . . As your godparents, we promise we will be there for you—as long as there is breath, and beyond. May you be held gently, firmly, and lovingly in the palm of God's hand. We love you—always.

Rudy writes:

> Eliza, as you are called to the Torah, we recognize that you are the product of two cultures—with histories tied to two great rivers, the Nile and the Congo. Each of these two cultures has been subject to some of the worst evil that humans can wreak upon each other. Each has made lasting contributions to our world, and both have had to struggle for self-determination. Please learn from these experiences, learn courage, learn faith, learn endurance—the strength to stay until the end.
>
> Children are in a constant struggle for self-determination and soon, as a teenager, your struggle will enter a new phase. For soon, if not already, you will feel the currents of a new river: "Be like us, go with the flow." . . . They will invite you into strong currents filled with rocks, shoals, whirlpools. "Everybody is doing it," they will say.
>
> They will tempt you, they will sweep you along, the currents will seem too strong to resist and you will tire. Going with the flow may seem the easiest course to take because you will be tired and weary of the struggle and you will want to be popular.
>
> But there is a way! When you tire, use your remaining strength to head for the firm banks of the river. Swim, swim hard for those banks! Go there to be renewed! Swim for the firm banks of proven friends, the firm banks of family, the firm banks of God! Rest, rest until your strength returns.

We will talk again, Eliza, . . . for there are life lessons to be learned everywhere.

Eliza's beloved. grandmother Ethel Wertheim read a passage by Rainer Maria Rilke about having patience to love life's questions, living fully each moment, and trusting each day to unfold teaching Eliza what she'll most need to know. This message is especially poignant as Ethel died six months later. At the end of the service, in an impromptu blessing, Eliza's grandfather Bill Ruder acknowledged the gifts of her ancestors as they were celebrated in Eliza's presence today. He thanked his granddaughter for her Bat Mitzvah service, which made him feel "wrapped in a warm cloak of family and community and has cradled me in an ocean of love."

Postscript from Mom:

> My dear Eliza, this Jewish rite of passage, made up of the strong threads and rich hues of your experience, is now woven into the growing tapestry of your life. You stand at the threshold of becoming a young woman, poised to leap wholeheartedly with all aspects of yourself. Always remember these gifts. You came into the world full of potential, your life is filled with possibilities, and you care deeply about others. In you are the seeds planted long ago in Gan Eden. Grow them well.

47

MY ROCK

Alexandra Weiss—October 24, 1998

When Allie applied to high school, she had to write an entrance essay about what made her different. She wrote about her experience in recognizing that she was not free to be herself at her first school, and she was the driving force behind the switch to a new school. She recognized the need for honest expression and knew that the only way she would have that was in a place that was not judgmental and that fostered individual differences. She admires many people, but she has no role models. She likes to say that "she is made from scratch." She likes being different and tries not to follow the trend.

As for her skating skills, she mastered both roller skates and roller blades. Her interests, however, lie elsewhere. She turned the wheels in for silver blades and devotes her extra time to ice-skating. At first it was just for fun, but more recently, she has taken to competing on the ice. She went into her first competition just being grateful that she was there. When she took home two gold medals, her feet didn't touch the ground for a week, as she flashed both the medals and her beautiful smile. But, then again, knowing my daughter's determination, anything is possible.

When my daughter Allie was 3 years old, she showed me what she was made of. She had been invited to a roller skating party. Having never skated before was not a deterrent for her. She waited patiently while I strapped the little plastic wheels onto her light-up sneakers and set out for the rink. She wasn't out there thirty seconds when—down she went. I watched with a sense of horror as the older, more experienced skaters dodged the puddled mass that was my daughter. In spite of the traffic whizzing by her, she pulled herself upright. Anticipating her coming back to me, expecting hugs and words of comfort, I stood near the entrance of the rink. Instead, she righted herself and headed in the other direction. And boom! Down she went again, without going thirty feet. Once more, she got up and kept going. She fell so many times that day that a big red mark formed on the side of her face, where her cheek repeatedly met the hard wood floor. And yet she made no attempt to quit or give up. She demonstrated, as early as age 3, a dogged determination that has extended itself far beyond just skating around the rink.

In larger metropolitan areas, parents are presented with many options regarding their child's education. In our small town, if we wanted our children to get a Hebrew education, we had only one option: the local Hebrew day school. Although a nurturing environment is provided, the emphasis on strict religious practice made the school somewhat uncomfortable to some students other than the most observant. Allie just didn't want to "fit in." With her short skirts and worldly ideas, she found the cloistered environment oppressive. She didn't feel safe and free to express herself. At first, she asked tentatively if we would consider transferring her to another Hebrew school twenty miles away. In a town where everything is a five-minute drive, her request seemed out of the question. Why would we risk an hour-long bus ride in potentially bad weather when a perfectly good school was within walking distance?

Allie's insistence on transferring schools began to escalate at the same time she started attending Camp Ramah in the Poconos. While being strictly observant, the camp practices Judaism with joy, camaraderie, enthusiasm, music, and egalitarianism. My daughter came home from camp calling me "Imah" and answering questions with "*lo*" (no) and "*cain*" (yes).

She entered the sixth grade. And only when the school had hired its third English teacher (by October) did we seriously start to consider a transfer. We went to talk to the principal of the United Hebrew Institute, an Orthodox day school twenty miles from our home. The principal suggested that Allie come and spend the day, and we could make up our minds after that. She came home thrilled! Regardless of the "honeymoon period," the kids were great and she was excited about what they were learning. The school's philosophy is to instill pride in the students about their Judaism, while at the same time fostering individual expression. We made the switch and from the very first day we realized what a good move this was (and that we should have done it a lot sooner).

As Allie approached Bat Mitzvah age, I recognized that my daughter was living with one foot in each of two different worlds. While attending an Orthodox day school and *shul*, she was exposed every summer to an intense camping experience where women are afforded the same privileges and responsibilities as men. We had to make some decisions about how and when Allie would face her rite of passage.

First off, she decided that she wanted everything to take place when she was 12 years old. Although, in our *shul*, women do not approach the *bimah*, let alone *layn* from there, Allie spent every summer with women who were excellent *Ba'al Korei* (readers of the Torah). She had to decide whether she would follow other young women in our community and make a speech in the social hall or create a new environment where she, too, could read from the Torah. After a great deal of discussion, she decided to go for the more traditional approach. The reason being that if we create our own "*shul* for the day," the rabbi wouldn't come, her teachers wouldn't come, and taking the good along with the bad, this was the *shul* that she grew up in, and she wanted to celebrate there.

So, she threw her efforts into studying her Torah portions with her teacher, Mrs. Sharon Polatoff. Although she wasn't reading from the Torah, she took her studying very seriously. We picked a date that was after the Jewish holidays to make it less hectic. Allie decided to incorporate not only the *parsha* of that week, but the one that would have coincided with her birthday. She then had another decision to make. Should she choose a huge celebration like her brother had the year before, or should she have a kid's-only party and celebrate with a family trip to Paris? The lure of France won out, and a smaller gathering was planned.

The night before the Bat Mitzvah, the house was alive with the chatter of camp friends who had come from all over for this event. Extra tables were set up with pretty tablecloths and special food for *Shabbos* dinner. The next morning in the synagogue the service felt special, even though it was run like every other week. Upon completion of the service, the guests quietly moved from the sanctuary into the social hall and anticipated the guest of honor's speech. Allie climbed the stairs of the stage and projected her voice around the auditorium. She was poised and confident (and didn't giggle once) as she shared her insight into both *parshas*. My daughter has a smile that lights up a room. Not only does she have a "face-splitting" grin, but two huge dimples frame her mouth like parentheses. When she smiles, it's infectious. She stood on the stage, tall for her age and dressed in a purple suit, and had the crowd awaiting her every word. I was so proud to see her handle her first public appearance so full of grace and ease. There was thunderous applause when she finished.

On Sunday night, when the last guest had gone, the clean-up was completed, and the gifts put away, Allie and I sat down for a re-cap and what we had instead were tears, lots of them. "It's over," she wailed. "I'll never have another weekend like this again, ever." She told me she had waited her whole life for this, her Bat Mitzvah, her special day, and now it was over. I tried to reassure her that there would be other special days to look forward to, other celebrations, but that night she was inconsolable. It broke my heart to think that at the age of 12, she thought that this was "as good as it gets."

As it happened, that year was the Bar and Bat year of many of her classmates. Two of the other young women in the class belonged to Conservative synagogues, and they were going to read from the Torah for their celebrations. They asked Allie if she would learn an *aliyah* and chant from the Torah as part of their services. She gladly agreed and was given a tape of her part by the cantor. She memorized it. Not long after her own Bat Mitzvah, she was actually called to the Torah and sang the holy words for the first time. Even though this was not her ceremony and her family was not even there (we weren't invited), this was so special to my daughter because it was just about her and reading from the Torah. It didn't hurt that the cantor told her that she was a "natural" and was welcome to come back at any time.

She has been honored with *aliyot* now several times. The first time I saw my daughter recite the blessing over the Torah, I was overwhelmed to the point of joyful tears. Even though I have attended many Bat Mitzvahs, this was *my* daughter sharing in the privilege previously afforded only to men. My tears were also those of conflict and some remorse. Had we done enough for her? In any family, parents try to share their time, energy, affection, and resources equally between their children. When the family dynamic includes a sick child who requires constant care, there is a tendency to later play "make-up" to the other children, who may have missed out on things while their parents were otherwise preoccupied. When our oldest son was diagnosed at the age of 6 with leukemia, we whisked him away to Children's Hospital, leaving behind a confused 4-year-old, Allie, and a 3-month-old baby, Ben. Regretting the school plays and activities that went unattended, we have tried to make it up to the kids in other ways. We hand-designed and printed Allie's Bat Mitzvah invitations, trying to incorporate a more personal touch. Should we have tried to convince her to have her own special ceremony where she, too, was called to the Torah?

Now two years later, she looks back with the maturity of a seasoned 14-year-old. She told me:

> I'm happy that I went to Paris, I always wanted to go. I had to choose between a big Bat Mitzvah celebration and Paris. Making such a big decision was a new experience for me and part of getting older and learning new things. I was not sorry then that I did not read from the Torah at mine, but I was the first to read at my friend's Bat Mitzvah. And yes, I was both excited and nervous. I feel that I have become a Bat Mitzvah, because I still had to focus on learning and prepare. Before I gave my speech, I got up and looked at the people's faces and I knew that I could talk to everyone. I got into it. I didn't laugh once, and I was very proud of myself. It was a nice service and a nice *Kiddish*. I feel like I got older and took on new privileges. Like fasting, I started doing that when I was only 11. I didn't have to, but I wanted the obligation. The first time I read from the Torah was the June after my Bat Mitzvah and it was really exceptional. I have read, all total three times, but the first time was the most special.

When Allie applied to high school, she had to write an entrance essay about what made her different. She wrote about her experience

in recognizing that she was not free to be herself at her first school, and she was the driving force behind the switch to a new school. She recognized the need for honest expression and knew that the only way she would have that was in a place that was not judgmental and that fostered individual differences. She admires many people, but she has no role models. She likes to say that "she is made from scratch." She likes being different and tries not to follow the trend.

As for her skating skills, she mastered both roller skates and roller blades. Her interests, however, lie elsewhere. She turned the wheels in for silver blades and devotes her extra time to ice-skating. At first it was just for fun, but more recently, she has taken to competing on the ice. She went into her first competition just being grateful that she was there. When she took home two gold medals, her feet didn't touch the ground for a week, as she flashed both the medals and her beautiful smile. But, then again, knowing my daughter's determination, anything is possible.

GLOSSARY

Aliyah — Literally means "going up" and is used when one goes up to the *bimah* in the synagogue to honor the Torah.

Aliyot — Plural of *aliyah.*

Am Yisrael Chai — "The Jewish people live."

Baracha — Blessing.

Bashert — Meant or fated to happen.

Bimah — Platform either in the front or center of the synagogue from which the Torah is read.

Bris Milah, Bris Milot — Ritual circumcision.

Bubbe — Grandmother.

Chazan — The person in the synagogue responsible for singing and chanting much of the Service.

Chumash — The text containing the Five Books of Moses.

Chupah — A canopy under which a couple is married.

D'var Torah — Speech about the Torah portion.

Davening — Praying.

Dayenu — Translated as "enough"; usually associated with the song during the Passover seder.

Erev Shabbas — Friday night.

Frum — Religious.

Haftorah — The complementary reading from the Prophets chanted by the Bar or Bat Mitzvah.

Haganah — The underground armed forces of pre-state Israel.

Haggadah — The book used on Passover that recounts the story of the Exodus from Egypt.

Hamentaschen — Three-cornered cookies made during the holiday of Purim.

Hashem — God.

Havdalah — The closing services of the Sabbath, in which blessings are made on wine, spices, and a braided candle.

Kaddish — A doxology that is used both to mourn for the dead and to close parts of the service..

Kichel — Crispy pastry, often shaped like a bow tie and covered with sugar.

Kiddush — Refreshments served after a *Shabbat* morning service.

Kipot — Plural of kipah (yarmulke).

Knish — Pastry dough that is filled with some stuffing, most traditionally potatoes.

Kol Nidre — The prayer that is recited on the eve of Yom Kippur.

Kotel — The Western Wall, the last remaining wall of the destroyed Second Temple, located in Jerusalem.

Kvell — To "swell with pride."

Kvetches — Complaining.

Latkes — Potato pancakes.

Layning — Reading from the Torah.

Maftir — Literally, the last few lines of the Torah portion that are repeated and are traditionally read for either the Bar or Bat Mitzvah.

Mamaloshen — Translated as "mother tongue" and refers to Yiddish.

Matzoh balls — Fluffy (they are supposed to be) round balls or dumplings made of matzoh meal and whipped eggs that are served in chicken soup.

Mazel Tov — Congratulations or good luck.

Mechitzah — Some kind of partition separating the men's and women's sections of an Orthodox synagogue.

Megillah of Esther — The scroll that holds the story of Queen Esther.

Mensch — A kind and gentle person who knows the "right thing to do."

Mikveh — A ritual bath.

Mincha — Afternoon prayers.

Mishpacha — Family.

Mitzvot — The plural of mitzvah, usually translated as a good deed or a commandment.

Nachis — Pride.

Parsha — A portion or chapter in the Torah.

Schnapps — Liquor.

Shacharit — Morning services.

Shalom Aleichem — Literally translated as "peace be with you"; used as a greeting and is the prayer sung upon returning home from *shul* on Friday evening.

Shechinah — God's Holy Spirit.

Shema — The central prayer of Judaism, proclaiming our monotheistic beliefs.

Shlepping — To carry or drag.

Shofar — A ram's horn that is blown to usher in the new year.

Shteble — Small ghetto *shul*.

Shul — Synagogue.

Siddur — Prayer book.

Simcha — Joyous occasion.

Tallis — A four-cornered prayer shawl with fringes.

Talmud — The compilation of Jewish law containing the six divisions of the Mishnah (oral law) and the Gemarrah.

Talmudic Scholar — A person who is an expert on the content of the Talmud.

Tefilah — Prayer.

Tefillin — Phylacteries; two small boxes that contain a prayer inside written in parchment; one is affixed with leather straps to the head and one on the upper arm. They are worn during weekday morning davening.
Tikkun Olam — Repair the world.
Tisha B'Av — The ninth day of the Hebrew month of Av. It is a day of mourning, for the Holy Temple was destroyed on this day.
Torah — The Five Books of Moses, hand-lettered on parchment.
Trup — Traditional tune for chanting the Torah and the Haftorah.
Tzedekah — Charity.
Tzitsit — The fringes on the four corners of a garment worn by religious men.
USY — United Synagogue Youth, a national youth organization.
Va'ad — Committee permission.
Vimalay — A prayer that is sung at weddings.
Yarmulke or Kipah — Skullcap.
Yasher Koach — Literally translated as "May your strength be firm"; used as an expression of congratulations for fulfilling a religious duty.
Yeshiva — A school with a dual curriculum where both secular and religious subjects are taught.
Yeshiva Bocher — A boy who attends a yeshiva.
Zeide — Grandfather.

Author's note: The definitions in the previous glossary are my everyday explanations. I make no claim to scholarly interpretations. They are presented here only to clarify the meaning in the story. The reader will notice that the spelling of several words like *Shabbat/Shabbos* and mitzvot/mitzvos varies from story to story. The reason for this seeming inconsistency lies in the orientation of the school or synagogue. Orthodox *shuls* tend to use the Ashkenazi (eastern European origin) pronunciation that leaves the words pronounced with an "s" (*Shabbos*) sound at the end. In *shuls* that pronounce the Hebrew with the more modern or Sephardic (of Mediterranean origin) endings, you will note the "t" (*Shabbat*) sound. While every effort has been made to keep the Hebrew words and spellings consistent throughout the book, some variations are kept out of respect to the user and to remain faithful to their story.

ABOUT THE AUTHOR

Arnine Cumsky Weiss is a nationally certified sign language interpreter. As the subject of a documentary entitled "Between Two Worlds" that aired on PBS, she became fascinated with video production. After an internship at a local CBS affiliate, she wrote and produced "Across America," a short documentary about two deaf college students who biked across the country. "Across America" aired on PBS. Weiss also wrote and produced several fundraising, promotional, and informational videos. She is married to Dr. Jeffrey Weiss; they live in Scranton, Pennsylvania with their three children, Matt, Allie, and Ben.